IMMACULATE
HEART of
MARY
TRUE DEVOTION

Also by Father Fox:

The Catholic Faith
A Catholic Prayer Book
A Prayer Book for Young Catholics
Rediscovering Fatima
A World at Prayer

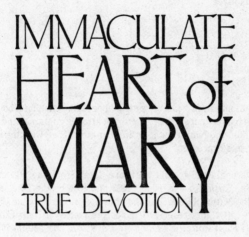

IMMACULATE HEART of MARY

TRUE DEVOTION

Rev. Robert J. Fox

Our Sunday Visitor Publishing Division
Our Sunday Visitor, Inc.
Huntington, Indiana 46750

Nihil Obstat:
Rev. James M. Joyce
Censor Librorum

Imprimatur:
✝Paul V. Dudley, D.D.
Bishop of Sioux Falls
December 8, 1985

The Nihil Obstat and Imprimatur are official declarations that a book or pamphlet is free of doctrinal or moral error. No implication is contained therein that those who have granted the Nihil Obstat or Imprimatur agree with the contents, opinions or statements expressed.

I Am All Yours, My Queen, My Mother, And All That I Have Is Yours

In The Spirit Of Total Consecration
To The Immaculate Heart Of Mary, The Mother Of God,
I Consecrate This Book Totally To Her.
— Father Robert J. Fox

† Contents †

✝ Introduction ✝

THE MIND of the Catholic Church is that true devotion to Mary should express the Trinitarian and Christological emphasis that is essential if it is to be authentically Christian. Such devotion to Mary has its roots revealed in the Sacred Scriptures and is expressed in the official teachings of the Church. The divine reality of such truths needs to come alive in human souls in our times. The role of Mary for the third millennium of Christianity is only beginning to be realized by many Christians. It will gradually become more fully appreciated by religious people of all persuasions.

The purpose of this book is to present the Immaculate Heart of Mary in the Trinitarian and Christological light that illumines the authentic Christian life. At times the reader will find the message simple, pleasant, and heartwarming, a discovery that comes easily to one with faith. At other times in this book, dedicated as it is to developing a true devotion, the message will require close reading, careful meditation. The heart of Mary is so penetrated by union with the Blessed Trinity, and divine Wisdom expressed in the Word made flesh is so deep and breathtaking, that more is required than easy reading for effortless piety. At all times, for those who dip into the waters of the Divine, there will appear ever more fully a creation of God, a kind of new substance, that the human mind could not conceive by its own power, unaided by divine revelation.

The message, whether expressed in lighter or darker tones, in easier or heavier passages, is always meant to elicit a response of faith and love from the heart of each one of us. Mary is more than a beautiful woman physically. Mary is the Mother of God, whose Immaculate Heart speaks of the Word incarnate, of the love she has for her Son and for each of us. Her Immaculate Heart speaks also of her total person and challenges all to a faith more vibrant than many have imagined possible, and to a love much stronger than most Christians have been willing to let grow within them.

These pages will demonstrate Mary's relationship to the Blessed Trinity, which few Christians understand, and open hearts to possibilities for every Christian of entering into the life of the thrice-holy God. Such can be the fruit of getting to know the heart of God's Mother more intimately. She reveals the secrets of the King's Heart to those of great faith and to those who surrender in total love. Having shown the greatest faith first, having surrendered in total love as no one before her or since, the Mother of God is best suited, as Mother of the Church, to perform this favor for all her spiritual children.

Many have mistakenly thought that God has given Mary only a minor role in the economy of salvation, because there seem to be few biblical references to Mary. This fallacy is a tragic one, for it robs them of a vital link in salvation history. It deprives them of the richness in the full story of God's becoming man through Mary and giving her to all as Mother.

If devotion to Mary were contrary to the Gospels, Christians of the very early Church would never have given such prominence to Mary in both the East and the West. Prayers had developed by the end of the third century, rich in theological content and in harmony with Scripture. By the fifth century, feast days and churches were dedicated to our Lady. Early Church Fathers proclaimed Mary the "new Eve" and associated her with the redeeming work of the "new Adam."

If the importance of Mary depends on how many verses in Scripture explicitly deal with her, what are we to say of the central events of the life of Jesus Christ? The institution of the Holy Eucharist, Good Friday, the Resurrection — all are treated rather sparsely in the Bible. What authentic Christian doubts the centrality of these Christian mysteries? The early Christians called themselves "children of the Resurrection" as they soon called themselves "children of Mary." From brief messages of the Scriptures, Christians soon realized the central importance of the Holy Eucharist, the day Christ died, the day He rose from the dead. From other brief texts emerged the "Woman" who shines out in glory over all history.

We are living in times when what has been secret to many is being discovered about Mary in the very pages of the inspired word of God, the Sacred Scriptures. Mary is emerging as the great Woman of the Bible, a woman of love and faith. While spiritual writers loyal to Catholicism have hesitated in the past to see Mary as teacher, she is emerging today as a teacher of true faith.

The role of the Holy Spirit is becoming appreciated more in modern times. It is all part of a new Pentecost gradually coming upon the world, a deeper presence and action of the Holy Spirit among God's people, for which Pope John XXIII prayed when he convoked the Second Vatican Council. The Holy Spirit reveals Jesus Christ in us and among us, who Jesus is, and who we are in relation to the Father. The Mother of God is now seen more clearly as the spouse of the Holy Spirit and close collaborator of the Holy Spirit in making Jesus, the risen Lord and Savior, present in us and among us. True devotion to Mary brings Jesus Christ, in fact the entire Blessed Trinity, into our lives.

In these pages is to be found the manifestation of the Immaculate Heart of our Mother.

CHAPTER 1

† The Beautiful Heart of Our Mother †

IN ALL THE world there has been only one human person who ever lived the Christ-life without flaw or fault. There has been only one woman upon this earth who, from the first moment of her existence until the last breath of her mortal body, was found to fulfill the will of God perfectly in every respect. At each moment she was "favored, full of grace," and each moment she grew in grace still more. The perfect correspondence of her will to the will of God has given the world a heart most pleasing to God and therefore a model for every Christian. That same unsullied heart, ever indwelt by the Holy Spirit, ever ablaze with the fires of divine love fed from the Eternal Flame of God, has given Him greater glory than all His creation except the Heart of her Son, substantially united to the Word of God because she willed it.

This heart, made immaculate by God because He willed it, was the heart of a woman, fully human in her person, the like of which the world had never seen before and would never see again. This heart had to be so pure, so holy, so loving and tender, so full of mercy, excelling in every virtue — humility, purity, faith, hope, love — that it would be worthy to be the heart of the Mother of God. Only the mind and infinite powers of God would be capable of creating a heart so full of virtuous beauty that it would proclaim forever the greatness of the Lord, be called blessed for all ages, and be worthy to give flesh to the eternal Word of God.

That Immaculate Heart would be a heart for all. It would be a model and inspiration for all. If all other created hearts failed and disappointed God throughout their earthly lives and even into eternity, the Immaculate Heart of this woman, chosen from all eternity to be Mother of the Word incarnate, would forever give joy to God her Savior, in whom she in turn found joy.

So devoted himself to this Immaculate Heart, God willed that all mankind have devotion to the Immaculate Heart of His Mother. It must follow: as all of us, mere creatures, would expect reverence for our mothers from those we call friends, so too God must will that all who are created in His own image and likeness will be devoted to the heart of His Mother, whom He will designate as our Mother too by grace, because He wills our salvation.

All human hearts but one have been in sin. Most have repeatedly offended the divine Majesty, the holiness of God. In this one heart God has always found a pleasant resting place, a tabernacle of delight, a place on earth where His will is done as it is in heaven. There is also the Heart of God's Son made man, it is true, where God has found a human nature with a love, a power, a plentitude of grace that makes even the heart of His Mother seem dim by comparison, but such a Heart is of a divine Person, such a Heart is the Heart of God. Here we speak of a heart wholly human, entirely created in her person. This Immaculate Heart is brighter, more glorious than all other hearts combined.

To this Immaculate Heart of Mary, God looks with radiant delight because here is a heart that reflects what great holiness and participation in His own divine nature He has willed for the human race. Only in Mary does God find one whose heartstrings vibrate in perfect harmony with the divine will. For all other hearts to become pleasing to God, somehow they must sing in harmony with the heart of our Mother, so that Christ may be formed in them as the Word was first formed in her heart. Mary is the perfect mode for Jesus to become man so that we may become the children of God and the children of Mary.

While it is true that this woman first conceived the Word of God in her Immaculate Heart before she did in her womb, it is also true that almighty God first conceived this woman in His eternal mind, loving her with an everlasting love before He created her soul immaculate and her body all pure, holy, and beautiful.

In every child one can see resemblances to the parents. This is true of physical characteristics and of other marks, such as attitudes of mind and will, patterns of speech and human behavior, which come from the spiritual qualities — that part of human nature which is immortal, the soul. God knew this, for He had created human nature. He knew this when, in the eternal counsels of the Blessed Trinity, He conceived the idea of the woman who would mother the Son of God.

The woman who would become the Mother of the Second Person of the Blessed Trinity made man must have a dignity worthy of such an exalted position. No creature could have a higher and holier state unless the creature could become God himself. So it was of Jesus Christ. Such is the Hypostatic Union, the joining of the human and divine nature in the one divine Person of Jesus Christ. Here in this man we have the Hypostatic Order, the union of God and man in Jesus Christ, the Word made flesh who dwells among us.

So that the Word of God might dwell among us in human form, God determined from eternity that greater than all the rest of His creation, He must create a masterpiece to outshine all those billions of galaxies hurtling through space obeying laws implanted in their very nature — laws of motion, laws of gravity, laws of precision and perfection according to the divine will — because they can do no other. This masterpiece of His loving creation would have a human will, a human intellect — the highest faculties of her immaculate being. Thus *freely* would she love and consciously would she know her God.

This masterpiece in the order of nature and grace would bear an immediate relationship to the Hypostatic Order, constituted by the mystery of the Incarnation of the Word. And what would that relationship be? To be MOTHER OF GOD. What a heart must God create for His Mother, who will in a human way become the Mother of the Way, the Truth, and the Life, without a human father. Whatever the Word made flesh will bear of human characteristics will come from one human parent, not two, while His divine qualities will depend entirely on the eternal Word, sent now by the Father.

Upon this woman, the masterpiece of God's creation, would be bestowed many titles, each vying with the other to reflect in some manner her beauty, her dignity, her uniqueness, the qualities of her love. She will be called "Mother of Divine Grace . . . Seat of Wisdom . . . Cause of our Joy . . . Spiritual Vessel . . . Mystical Rose . . . House of Gold . . . Ark of the Covenant . . . Gate of Heaven . . . Queen of Angels, Prophets and

Apostles. . . ." But no title will be greater than "Mother of God." And when mention is made of her Immaculate Heart, it will contain all she is, all God made her, and all she freely became.

If God would have us freely praise all His creation — as testified in the Psalms of Sacred Scripture, those divinely inspired hymns of praise — how much more will God have us sing of the glories of His Mother and have devotion to her Immaculate Heart! God expressed desire that henceforth all sing her praises when, moved by the Holy Spirit whose spouse she is, at the beginning of her motherhood she sang: "Behold, henceforth all generations will call me blessed; for he who is mighty has done great things for me, and holy is his name" (Lk 1:48-49).

God created the earth, and on it He placed man and woman made in His own image and likeness. Created in grace, our first parents soon marred the beauty of their souls and disturbed the perfect balance of nature in their bodies. God was not well pleased when that first man and first woman sinned. God would have another man and another woman, the beauty of whose souls would surpass even that of His first creation of human nature. Oh! happy fault, for which God found a remedy in becoming man himself through a woman whose heart would forever be immaculate and whose very nature would be at enmity with the wicked foe (see Gen 3:15). The dawn of creation already hailed this magnificent creature, whom God would use in crushing the head of the serpent and whose Seed would be the Lord himself.

God's first created man and woman incorporated all aspects of His creation, spiritual and material. They should have given more glory to God because He created them free. They looked instead to their own glory. God would create yet another man and woman, also free. This time their beauty would surpass the first, and the glory given the Creator would outweigh every song of praise given by angels or men until the end of time. While no other created man or woman could ever match the greatness and beauty of the new Adam and the new Eve, they would still belong to all and be models for all. All humankind could look to the Christ as Savior and to Mary as Mother.

This masterpiece of God who mothered the Word of God had in her Immaculate Heart the one place in His creation entirely, intelligently, freely, and knowingly receptive, without the slightest hindrance, so that the Word might have fullest effect and blossom into greatest beauty. In the garden of this heart, God would find no movement that was not pure, no desire that was not united to His own will.

The eternal Word was forever spoken as one Word by the Father. "He is the image of the invisible God, the first-born of all creation" (Col 1:15). Once become flesh so as to dwell among us as men, He — who has "glory as of the only Son from the Father" (Jn 1:14) — will speak many words and do "many other things" (Jn 21:25). And Mary as Mother and model will give us the example of how to react.

> But Mary kept all these things, pondering them in her heart. (Lk 2:19)
> . . . and a sword will pierce through your own soul also), that thoughts out of many hearts may be revealed. (Lk 2:35)
> . . . and his mother kept all these things in her heart. (Lk 2:51)

To establish the soundness of devotion to the Immaculate Heart of God's Mother, we need not establish the authenticity of reported apparitions from heaven which call for devotion to the Immaculate Heart. Other books have dealt with those subjects well and thoroughly. It still must be said that, essentially, the soundness of devotion to the Immaculate Heart rests on public revelation contained in the Sacred Scriptures and the official teachings of Holy Mother Church. It remains for future chapters of this book to explore the meaning of devotion to the Immaculate Heart of Mary and how to implement it in our lives.

The teachings of the Church concerning the Mother of God are not dry, abstract doctrines. Devotion to her Immaculate Heart is a means of salvation. This is why God desires devotion established in the world, in order to save it. The salvation does not come from Mary but from her Son, as her heart teaches us to "do whatever He tells you" (Jn 2:5). The heart of Mary teaches us how to live the Christ-life and be saved.

The Church teaches us to interpret the texts of Sacred Scripture, not in isolation but as part of the whole of public divine revelation. It is in this context that we place devotion to Mary's Immaculate Heart. Always to be kept in mind is the dogma that Jesus is our sole Savior and Way to the Father. Mary's role is one of intercession and inspiration for us, in, with, and through her divine and incarnate Son. In begging her intercession, we ask at the same time, and together with her, the intercession of Jesus Christ and the effective application of His divine merits.

Pope Paul VI issued an Apostolic Exhortation to the whole world on Devotion to the Blessed Virgin Mary. He wrote:

"Christ is the only way to the Father (cf. Jn 14:4-11), and the ultimate example of whom the disciple must conform his own conduct (cf. Jn 13:15), to the extent of sharing Christ's sentiments (cf. Phil 2:5), living his life and possessing his Spirit (cf. Gal 2:20; Rom 8:10-11). The Church has always taught this, and nothing in pastoral activity should obscure this doctrine. But the Church, taught by the Holy Spirit and benefiting from centuries of experience, recognizes that devotion to the Blessed Virgin, subordinated to worship of the divine Savior and in connection with it, also has a great pastoral effectiveness and constitutes a force for renewing Christian living. It is easy to see the reason for this effectiveness. Mary's many-sided mission to the people of God is a supernatural reality which operates and bears fruit within the body of the Church. One finds cause for joy in considering the different aspects of this mission, and seeing how each of these aspects with its individual effectiveness is directed towards the same end, namely, producing in the children the spiritual characteristics of the firstborn Son. The Virgin's maternal intercession, her exemplary holiness and the divine grace which is in her become for the human race a reason for divine hope" (57, *Marialis Cultus*, Feb. 2, 1974).

St. John Eudes (1608-1680) said that he heard these words of our Lord: "I have given you this admirable Heart of my dearest Mother which is but one with Mine to be truly your heart also in order that the children may have but one heart with their Mother and the members have no other Heart but that of their Head so that you may adore, love, and serve God with a Heart worthy of His infinite greatness."

Why has heaven intervened at times to manifest devotion to the Immaculate Heart of Mary if such is already contained within the doctrines of the Church and at least implicit in Sacred Scripture itself? Can it be that many members of the Church have ignored this aspect of our faith and the important role Mary has next to Christ?

It is up to each faithful Christian to place his or her own heart between the Hearts of Jesus and Mary. From the Sacred Heart of Jesus flow all graces as from the source of our redemption. From the Immaculate Heart of Mary flows the power of her intercession, and in it is seen the perfect manner of living His life and availing oneself of His infinite merits earned for us on the cross. It is the love of God that unites three hearts — our own with those of Jesus and Mary.

From Mary, each can learn the marvels of Jesus' love and the inexplicable secrets of His Sacred Heart. The Heart of Jesus is discovered by the soul with Mary's help to be full of love for each one of us, full of flames of burning charity. This Heart of Jesus is found and contained in the Holy Eucharist, and it is there that the heart of Mary will lead us. Jesus, the King, has priceless treasures and desires to enrich us with them.

Graces through the mediation of Mary are the fruit of devotion to her Immaculate Heart. God desires that we ask special graces through the intercession of His Mother. The King has shared much power with the Queen of heaven. How He loves to grant us graces we ask of Him through the heart of His Mother. How pleasing it is to God and to Mary herself when we ask special graces of God through her motherly intercession.

God desires that we come to the heavenly throne, asking for graces of conversion, and do so with confidence. And what confidence we can have when we approach the throne of grace in the company of God's Mother. "My Mother. My Confidence."

While our heavenly Mother was still upon earth, as soon as she knew the will of God she accepted it. Thus it was when the Angel Gabriel announced to her the vocation to which God had called her. She asked a question only to be fully informed of the will of God: "How can this be, since I have no husband?" (Lk 1:34). When she accepted the will of God as her own will, the Holy Spirit came upon her and the power of the Most High overshadowed her. This was to happen repeatedly throughout her life, a continuous process as the Mother resembled the Son and the Son resembled the Mother.

As Mary conceived the Christ Child by the Holy Spirit, she also learned from the Angel Gabriel that Elizabeth her kinswoman had conceived a son in her old age. As the woman of charity, Mary knew her cousin would need assistance in the last months before delivery. She went in haste through the hill country. Mary always accepted the will of God with haste. She greeted Elizabeth.

"And when Elizabeth heard the greeting of Mary, the babe leaped in her womb; and Elizabeth was filled with the Holy Spirit and she exclaimed with a loud cry, 'Blessed are you among women, and blessed is the fruit of your womb! And why is this granted me, that the mother of my Lord should come to me? For behold, when the voice of your greeting came to my ears, the babe in my womb leaped for joy. And blessed is she who believed that there would be a fulfillment of what was spoken to her from the Lord.' And Mary said,

" 'My soul magnifies the Lord, and my spirit rejoices in God my Savior. . . ' " (Lk 1:41-47).

It is she whose "soul magnifies the Lord" to whom God wishes us all to have devotion. Authentic devotion to the Immaculate Heart of Mary will reveal within each of us the greatness of the Lord.

As the moon reflects the light of the sun to all God's creatures upon the earth, so Mary, "full of grace" (Lk 1:28), in all her beauty and magnificence, shows herself to us not for her own sake but God's, "for he has regarded the low estate of his handmaiden" (Luke 1:48). It is Jesus, her Son, she would have us proclaim so that we might accept God as our Father in faith and love.

Mary's coming to us, as to Elizabeth, brings with it a coming of the Lord. Her coming sheds a light that will penetrate to our inmost hearts, make us see ourselves in God and behold the true Light of the world. Approaching Mary, we repeat, will be at the same time a meeting with the Lord and an encounter with God in love — like our meeting the entire Blessed Trinity in the Most Blessed Sacrament.

Do you want this devotion to the Immaculate Heart of Mary that God desires of us? Then ask it of God. He will shed a light upon you, a light to penetrate your soul so as to appreciate the meaning of the Immaculate Heart in a depth human words cannot describe.

Certain souls have been touched by God with a light proclaiming the greatness of the Lord. Souls have been set on fire in the light that is God. Attempting to put their experience into words, they never could — something to be experienced but not explained. But such is for the chosen few, you may protest. Why are you fearful, O soul? Why do you fear to ask Him? If you fear to ask Him, then ask her.

God has destined each one of us for the beatific vision. We are all called to salvation. That means eternally to see God face to face, the eternal Light even as He is: ". . . this will be made manifest at the proper time by the blessed and only Sovereign, the King of kings and Lord of lords, who alone has immortality and dwells in unapproachable light, whom no man has ever seen or can see" (1 Tim 6:15-16).

While it is impossible to see God in this life and live, we can catch glimpses of Him: ". . . now we see in a mirror dimly, but then face to face. Now I know in part; then I shall understand fully, even as I have been fully understood. So faith, hope, love abide, these three; but the greatest of these is love" (1 Cor 13:12-13).

And what a beautiful glimpse we catch of the likeness of God when we see the beauty of His Mother. We can gaze upon the moon easily. The sun is too bright; it hurts the eyes and would destroy them if we dared more than a brief glimpse now and then. The light from Mary is the same light of God, but by reflection. It is in the same manner as the moon is related to the sun in bestowing light.

How often we hear people speak of the beauty of the moon. "Isn't the moon beautiful tonight?" People praise the sunlight. They love a sunny day. How seldom anyone stares at the sun and says, "Isn't the sun beautiful today?" Often people will remark that the sun is too bright to see, that the day is too hot as the sun beats down directly. The sun is no less beautiful for all that. The moon would show no beauty if it weren't for the sun. Mary would have no beauty without her Son and the God who created her.

Let us look at the moon, then, to appreciate the sun. Let us discover the Light, in Mary, the Eternal Light that we all want to have shine upon us in the end, which will mark the beginning. In her Immaculate Heart we will find a refuge and a way that will lead us to God.

Our devotion to our heavenly Mother, while including study

and meditation on the historical Mary and the biblical Mary as woman of faith, must not stop there. Mary's role did not end with her assumption into heaven. Her life on earth and her marvelous cooperation with God in giving us the Redeemer were only the beginning of fulfilling the call she had answered so well: "I am the handmaid of the Lord; let it be to me according to your word" (Lk 1:38).

Our devotion to Mary must include Mary as "Mother of love . . . Mother of grace." At this moment in heaven, where she knows and loves us and is concerned about each one of us, Mary is still Mother of love . . . Mother of grace. God's Mother, who is Mother of the Church and therefore Mother of us all, still has an active role on behalf of all her children.

It has been said that if any of us had had the privilege of choosing our own mother, we would have chosen the most beautiful woman we could possibly find. While the thought is somewhat frivolous, not so with God. Almighty God not only chose His own Mother, He made her. He made her fitting for the dignity to which she would be called and with which she would respond. He gave her a Heart Immaculate. He made her the most beautiful woman the world will ever see.

Mary's Immaculate Heart is the most beautiful heart of any human person in heaven. It is more beautiful than all the angels and saints.

The wonder is this: not only is she God's Mother; she is our Mother too.

CHAPTER 2

† The Meaning of Devotion to the Immaculate Heart †

WHATEVER IS said of the Immaculate Heart of Mary must always be interpreted in terms of her heart being inseparable from the Heart of her divine Son, to whom she points and draws us.

St. John the Apostle is described by the recorded word of God as "the disciple whom Jesus loved." Jesus loves everyone. He obviously had a special love for His Mother, and among the apostles He had a special love for the youngest of them, John. St. John the Apostle was apparently especially dear to Jesus because of his great purity of heart. It was this apostle in particular who penetrated deeply into the love of Jesus' Heart.

On the evening of the first Holy Sacrifice of the Mass, the beloved disciple John reclined on the breast of Jesus. John stayed with Jesus and Mary to the end and witnessed the Savior's death on the cross for the redemption of the world. ". . . one of the soldiers pierced his side with a spear, and at once there came out blood and water" (Jn 19:34). It was to this same apostle that the Sacred Heart of Jesus from the cross confided the loving care of His Mother. Jesus' words, "Behold, your mother!" were directed to men of the whole world for all time. John, burning with love, was taught to love even more intensely by the perfect Christian and Mother of the Church whom he took into his own home from that day on. One day, in a burst of love and fervor, he would be able to sum up his teaching in three words: "GOD IS LOVE."

Through the centuries, other souls have also contemplated the pierced side of our Lord Jesus. Their thoughts have gone beyond the wounded side to the wound of love in His Sacred Heart. During the thirteenth century, St. Gertrude was led by St. John to "the opening of the divine Heart" whose beating filled her with ineffable joy. She asked St. John why he had not written of

23

this directly in the Scriptures. She received the answer that this language of love of the Sacred Heart was reserved for later times when the world would have grown cold to God's love.

More than three centuries after the mystical experiences of St. Gertrude, God revealed His Sacred Heart at another place, Paray-le-Monial in France. Again, almost two hundred fifty years later at Fatima, heaven reveals the Sacred Heart of Jesus and the Immaculate Heart of Mary as inseparable. The Immaculate Heart of His Mother is presented to us at Fatima through the medium of three small children to teach us love.

Devotion to the Sacred Heart of Jesus is inseparable from devotion to Jesus in the Most Blessed Sacrament of the altar. The Eucharistic Heart of Jesus is present substantially, living in our tabernacles and in the Sacrament we receive in Holy Communion. Since the love of the Immaculate Heart of Mary desires to draw each one of her children to her Son, Jesus Christ, we shall discover, as we meditate on the real meaning of true devotion to the Immaculate Heart of Mary throughout this book, that it is primarily to the Eucharistic Heart of Jesus that Mary is drawing us. We shall see that the effects of union with Jesus in the Sacrifice of the Mass and in Holy Communion are a deepening of our bond with Christ and thereby an opening of the soul more profoundly to the life of the Most Blessed Trinity dwelling within us.

The heart of a mother loves all her children, whether they be good or bad. The heart of any good mother goes out especially to the child who is sick or most in need. Our Lady knows what is needed for the present crisis — the loss of innumerable souls — through which her family is passing. Her Immaculate Heart is asking us from heaven to live in faith, hope, and love, in adoration and reparation with respect to her Son. Mary knows that the sacraments are indispensable in the life of the Church of which she is Mother. There must be a reverent and frequent use of the sacrament of reconciliation, confession. There must be a devout and holy union with her Son, Jesus Christ, in the Sacrament of Love, the Holy Eucharist. As the meaning of the Sacred Heart and Immaculate Heart can be summed up in one word, "Love," so devotion to these two hearts must lead us to the Sacrament of Love.

The devotion God desires for the Immaculate Heart of Mary is not simply to the material, physical heart of Mary. In the biblical understanding of heart, there is the expressed aspect of the *total person* considered. The Immaculate Heart of Mary, like the Sacred Heart of Jesus, is a natural symbol manifesting love. The heart is the universal symbol of love.

Jesus was most intent on teaching His love for each one of us when He was upon earth. Didn't the Father send His Son to this earth to reveal His love for us? "God so loved the world that he gave his only Son, that whoever believes in him should not perish but have eternal life" (Jn 3:16). God does not love us because we love Him. He loved us first, when we were deep in sin. "In this is love, not that we loved God, but that he loved us and sent his Son to be the expiation for our sins" (1 Jn 4:10).

John, the apostle of love, tells us about Jesus as the Good Shepherd in Sacred Scripture. The biblical image of Jesus as the Good Shepherd is the same message of the love of God for us as was revealed to St. Margaret Mary Alacoque in the message of the Sacred Heart of Jesus. "I am the good shepherd; the good shepherd lays down his life for the sheep . . ." (Jn 10:11).

The good shepherd will leave the ninety-nine and go in search of the one sheep that is lost. Jesus loves us not as a vast flock of people. Jesus loves each one of us individually for what we are. So does His Mother. That is the image of the Immaculate Heart of Mary, as it is in the Sacred Heart of Jesus. This message of Jesus is revealed in his parable of the Prodigal Son (see Lk 15:11-32). Immediately before His more lengthy account of the Father's love for the son gone astray, Jesus gave two accounts of God's love for each individual soul. As the shepherd rejoices over finding the one lost sheep, so the woman who has lost one silver piece sweeps the house in a diligent search until she has found what she lost. She then calls in her friends to rejoice with her. "I tell you, there is joy before the angels of God over one sinner who repents" (Lk 15:10).

A tremendous change comes over individuals on the day they realize that God loves them. Many a person feels lost in the vast crowd of humanity. Jesus and His Mother do not see us that way. Their love for each individual is deep and personal. Jesus told St. Margaret Mary that He asks "love for love." The Son of God made man wants from each of us a deep personal relationship. Jesus wants us to know Him and love Him as a personal Friend, the best there is possible. It is the purpose of the Immaculate Heart of Mary to lead us to the love of her Son.

As the Mother of the Head of the Mystical Body of Christ, the Church, Mary loves each one of her children. She is the Mother of Christ, the Mother of the Church, and her knowledge and love extend with Jesus to each individual soul. In loving the Vine, she loves its branches. As the perfect Christian, as the model of everything the Church is and hopes to become, Mary teaches us by the example of the life of perfect faith, trust, and love.

The meaning of the Immaculate Heart of Mary, calling us to love and reparation, can be grasped by children, or it can be explained and understood in scientific terms to please the theologian. Always, what Mary is calling for is that we seek refuge within her immaculate heart so that she may show us Jesus. It is impossible to appreciate the Incarnation, "the Word made flesh" in order to save us, without considering the human means, the heart of Mary, which God used to break into our world in human form. St. Augustine made this claim: "Blessed Mother, you are worthy to be called the Mold of God." Cardinal Leo J. Suenens said, "Christianity without a Mother would be an abstraction."

Mary's great faith and love for Jesus Christ while upon earth is verified in Sacred Scripture. Conceived in grace, perfectly attuned to the inspirations of the Holy Spirit, who is the primary Author of both the Old and New Testaments, Mary gained fruitful insights into God's Word more perfectly than any other Christian. She is the perfect model for Christian faith and response to God's Word. As Abraham was the man of faith under the old covenant, Mary is the woman of faith as mankind passes into its new covenant with God.

Being God in His very Person, Jesus Christ, according to St. Thomas Aquinas, had no need for faith. He is the very object of our faith and source of our salvation. He knew and understood the divine mysteries directly. Pope Pius XII said Jesus had the beatific vision from His Mother's womb (*Mystici Corporis*). The Person of Jesus is divine, not human, although He possesses a human nature which He received through the will of His Mother's heart. It is precisely that Person of Jesus — who assumed a human nature, a body and soul, and became thus one with men — in whom we place our faith. Mary shows us the Way.

For "if you confess with your lips that Jesus is Lord and believe in your heart that God raised him from the dead, you will be saved. For man believes with his heart and so is justified, and he confesses with his lips and so is saved. The scripture says, 'No one who believes in him will be put to shame' " (Rom 10:9-11).

Who has ever manifested a greater faith than Mary? There is none in recorded history. Mary believed that without knowing man she would conceive a Child who would be the Son of the Most High. Why does St. Elizabeth, speaking under the influence of the Holy Spirit, praise Mary so greatly? It is because of her great trust and faith: ". . . blessed is she who believed that there would be a fulfillment of what was spoken to her from the Lord" (Lk 1:45). Mary's greatness is in her faith and love, more than in being the physical instrument to conceive the Christ Child.

What faith did Mary have at the wedding feast of Cana when she noticed the wine had given out and called it to the attention of Jesus? Can't we discern that Mary knew Jesus had the power to do something about it? "O woman, what have you to do with me? My hour has not yet come" (Jn 2:4). But then Jesus does make the woman's concern His own. He performs His first public miracle. That miracle has eucharistic overtones. If Jesus can change rainwater drawn from a cistern into the finest wine, can't He change wine into His own precious blood? This first miracle was due to the compassionate heart of the woman who would one day be called "Our Lady of the Holy Eucharist." In divine providence, Mary played a unique role.

The account of the miracle at the wedding feast concludes with: "This, the first of his signs, Jesus did at Cana in Galilee, and manifested his glory; and his disciples believed in him" (Jn 2:11). They came to believe in Him because Mary first believed in Him and interceded.

What faith was required of Mary when leaders among God's chosen people were rejecting Him! When Jesus went to His own town of Nazareth, "They took offense at him. But Jesus said to them, 'A prophet is not without honor except in his own country and in his own house.' And he did not do many mighty works there, because of their unbelief" (Mt 13:57-58). Even in His hometown, where Jesus spent time teaching in the synagogue, the people did not believe. The day would come when His own people would attempt to throw Him over the cliff at the edge of town. But Mary, His holy Mother, had the greatest faith in Him the world would ever see.

In the Hebrew Bible, the expression "daughter of Zion" referred to the entire people of God. God's people are often described as a woman, the bride of God. In Christian tradition, Mary of Nazareth is the individual daughter of Zion. In her the hopes of her people come to perfection. In Mary, salvation comes to fruition. "Blessed are you among women, and blessed is the fruit of your womb" (Lk 1:42).

St. Augustine looked to Mary as the daughter of Abraham in her faith. No one was ever a greater daughter in the faith of Abraham. The words of the Magnificat (Lk 1:46-55) show Mary's own consciousness of herself as a daughter of Abraham. Jews, Christians, and Muslims all honor Abraham as their father in faith. The Gospels present Mary as the woman of faith, as the mother of believers.

What should be kept in mind is this: Devotion to the Immaculate Heart of Mary means devotion to the total person of Mary. God wants to give us this perfect example of faith and love.

Mary in her great faith did not have it easy. She suffered. Her faith was tested. But she never faltered for an instant, and was never in the slightest sin even for a moment. Her heart, her person, was immaculate from the first instant of her creation. Immaculate means all-pure, all-holy.

The purity of Mary's heart means more than freedom from sensual sins connected with concupiscence of the eyes or flesh. The purity of Mary means that she was free from anything that weakens, impairs, or changes the nature of perfection. Her purity of faith means she was absent from error. Her purity of intention means the exclusion of self-will in her desire to do God's will perfectly. The Immaculate Heart means purity of conscience, the absence of any sense of guilt in the performance of moral actions.

Seeing Mary as pure in intention, pure in faith, pure in body and soul to a perfect degree — one whose very being was described by the angel as "full of grace" — one can understand better how this holy one suffered when, after she had conceived the Word of God, giving the Son of God human nature from her humanity through the power of the Holy Spirit, St. Joseph did not know the source of her pregnancy: ". . . her husband Joseph, being a just man and unwilling to put her to shame, resolved to send her away quietly. But as he considered this, behold, an angel of the Lord appeared to him in a dream, saying, 'Joseph, son of David, do not fear to take Mary as your wife, for that which is conceived in her is of the Holy Spirit . . .'" (Mt 1:19-20).

There was only one greater suffering in Mary's heart than during the days when her husband Joseph did not know the source of her pregnancy. It was when she stood beneath the cross and witnessed her Son's rejection and death by the sins of men. Then was completed the prophecy of Simeon that a sword would pierce her own heart (see Lk 2:35).

Bringing forth Jesus was "not of blood, nor of the will of the flesh, nor of the will of man, but of God" (Jn 1:13). Yet it was by Mary's consent. In saying "yes," her Immaculate Heart was one with the Heart of God. She was spokesman for the entire world in accepting its Savior.

Mary is the "daughter of Zion," as St. John obviously realized in writing his Gospel. Mary at Cana asks for wine, but not simply to save embarrassment at the wedding feast. There is profound symbolism in the Cana events. She is asking for the wine of the new covenant, which had been promised for messianic times. Man was about to enter into a new contract with God in Jesus Christ, as he had been living under the old contract of the Mosaic dispensation. Jesus would strike a new covenant (contract) between God and man, to be sealed with His precious blood on the cross, derived from blood He had received through the heart of Mary.

When Jesus answers, "My hour has not yet come" (Jn 2:4), He is looking forward to the time when His "hour" would come. When that hour came, Mary would be there, with a sword piercing her Immaculate Heart.

The Church is born from the pierced side of Christ, and He presents Mary as the Mother of the Church. At both Cana and Calvary, Jesus addresses Mary by the very respectful title of the times, "Woman." Both occasions signify mysteries of Christ and the Church.

The words of Jesus Christ, victorious as He hangs dying on the cross, ring out the promise made to the daughter of Zion: that she would have a progeny that would include all nations. The Messiah will be the "hope of the nations." Mary, standing at the foot of the cross, symbolizes mother Church, the new Israel, the mother of all humans. As the side of Christ is pierced and blood and water flow forth (see Jn 19:34), the sweet heart of Mary is transfixed.

At the Last Supper, the first Sacrifice of the Mass ever offered, Jesus gave us the means to strike anew, again and again, the new covenant of His blood shed on the cross. It was then He said: "When a woman is in travail she has sorrow, because her hour has come; but when she is delivered of the child, she no longer remembers the anguish for joy that a child is born into the world" (Jn 16:21).

Mary, the "Daughter of Zion," the "Mother of Faith," the "Mother of the Church," is in sorrow as she suffers in heart with her Son, Jesus Christ, on Calvary. There is no need to describe the love of Mary's heart involved here, nor could we adequately attempt it. But faith was present too. Mary had faith that Jesus would keep His promise: after being lifted up on the cross, He would rise again in three days.

There are Gospel accounts indicating that the faith of the disciples of Jesus, even His chosen few, weakened after His death on the cross and His burial. There is no indication that Mary's faith weakened. She "believed that there would be a fulfillment of what was spoken to her from the Lord" (Lk 1:45). Mary believed and trusted to perfection that her Son would rise again, even as she suffered on Calvary. No mother has ever suffered and no son endured so intensely the pains of spirit and body as Mary and Jesus did. One so perfect in nature will suffer more intensely.

Faced with a faith so perfect, a love so pure, we can better understand why God desires that devotion be established in the world to the Immaculate Heart of His Mother alongside devotion to the Sacred Heart of His Son. It is a call to faith and love modeled after Mary.

We live in a time when faith is weak, when love is mocked and selfishness dominates the world. Can anyone deny the weakening of faith among Christian people throughout the world?

How many ignore the commandments to purity, or the right to life of the unborn? Millions are killed by abortion. Millions die from starvation and wars. Attacks are made against the person of our Holy Father, the Pope, not only by bullets but by denials of dogmas of the faith. The respect, the love, the adoration due Jesus in the Most Blessed Sacrament; adoration of God on Sunday through regular and fervent participation in the Sacrifice of the Mass, perpetuating the Sacrifice of Calvary — these are too often ignored.

Immorality among youth, premarital sex, pornography, infidelity among married people, the breakdown of family life — all the failures that have intensified as faith has weakened and authentic love grown cold — are common knowledge. Often these evils are not considered sinful. In asking that devotion be established in the world to the Immaculate Heart of His Mother, God is requesting an end to disbelief and crimes flowing from the lack of love for God and neighbor. God asks that we accept salvation, showing us the perfect example: His Mother, who represented the whole human race in saying, once she knew the will of God, "I am the handmaid of the Lord; let it be to me according to your word" (Lk 1:38).

We are called to ponder the Word of God in our hearts as did Mary. We are called to respond to the Word of God with love, as did Mary.

The world has forgotten the meaning of the word *love*. In modern vocabulary, frequently "love" means only concupiscence or self-interest. It is love of self, a desire for self-fulfillment with selfish pleasures. Authentic Christian love, however, is concern for other persons. True love wills good to another. It means sharing what one possesses with the other and doing what that other desires. Ultimately, love wills the eternal salvation of the person loved.

In the case of the Sacred Heart of Jesus and the Immaculate Heart of Mary, it is always the glory of God and the salvation of souls they desire. There awaits us in heaven a happiness we cannot imagine. It will be ours in the light of glory, where each of us is called to be a "praise of glory": "What no eye has seen, nor ear heard, nor the heart of man conceived, what God has prepared for those who love him . . ." (1 Cor 2:9).

God has infinite life, infinite happiness, infinite love. It is His life, happiness, love that He wishes to share with us in giving us the Immaculate Heart of His sweet Mother. Jesus is the Way to the Father. He was the Way for Mary as well. Jesus redeemed His own Mother so perfectly that the moment of her creation in the womb of St. Ann was also the moment of her redemption, in what is known as the Immaculate Conception. It is she, then, who responds perfectly in faith and love to the Way of the Father, to her own Son.

Our Blessed Mother Mary did not live in glory when she was upon earth. She lived by faith. Her immaculate body did not then share in the glory of heaven. It was not yet glorified, as all bodies of men will be when resurrected from the grave and assumed into heaven.

Mary is no longer the Woman of Faith. One does not possess faith in heaven. She is, however, our Mother of Love, our Mother by Grace. It is in her intercessory power to obtain from her Son, Jesus Christ, the new wine of eternal glory for each one of us.

Mary knows our trials, every one of them. On earth she knew poverty. She knew the pain of misunderstanding — as when her husband, St. Joseph, perceived her to be with child and she was not able to tell him that her Child was of the Holy Spirit, for she had not been given that permission from heaven. She knew the pain of separation: first, when the Christ Child was missing for three days; then, when her husband Joseph died; again, when her Son died on the cross; and finally, when He ascended into heaven, leaving her behind with the infant Church. She knows what it is to be in exile. The Holy Family had to flee suddenly into Egypt and dwell at length in a foreign land. Mary experienced rejection in seeing her only begotten Son, who was her whole life and love, rejected.

No, Mary did not always live in glory. We Catholics may tend to forget that, recalling only the stories of supernatural happenings connected with reported apparitions that dazzle the mind. Mary lived in pain and suffering but kept faith. She grew in love for God and neighbor. So must we. It is the message of her heart.

Mary prayed with the disciples in the upper room (see Acts 1:14) and received for the Church the new wine of the Spirit. In heaven today, Mary still intercedes within the Communion of Saints as the Mother of the Church. The love of her Immaculate Heart continues for us now that she lives in glory. Earnestly praying for the salvation of each one of her children, Mary reveals the love of her Immaculate Heart. That love can only be grasped by one who has faith. Once possessed, that faith and love lead to salvation.

Devotion to the Immaculate Heart of Mary means to contemplate and embrace the maternal love that the Mother of God introduces into the mystery of the Redemption and into the life of the Church. Devotion to our Mother's heart is a recognition of the most significant and beautiful sign of the Father's love for us, next to the love of the Sacred Heart of Jesus. In fact, the hearts of Mary and Jesus are so intertwined that both reflect the love of the Father, the only difference being that the Person of Jesus is eternal and divine while the person of Mary is created in time.

True devotion to the Immaculate Heart of Mary means to entrust ourselves totally to the person of Mary, Mother of Christ, Mother of the Church. This entrusting to Mary's heart involves living the mystery of the Redemption in all its vivifying depth and fullness. And when the Christian life is lived so completely, we have entered into such a love that we are willingly at the service of our brothers and sisters, wherever they may be.

Devotion to Mary's heart, then, is coming to full Christian maturity. It is opening ourselves to the action of the Holy Spirit within us. While we all may have been validly baptized, yet the fruits of our baptism — of our confirmation, our participation in the Sacrifice of the Mass and the reception of the Lord's body, blood, soul, and divinity — may be limited because of the poor dispositions of our souls. By being devoted to the Immaculate Heart of Mary, we discover the magnanimous treasury of the regal and humble heart of Mary. In her riches, we see her as truly the "House of Gold."

Mary's heart is the symbol of the reality of her love, a love that freely, intelligently placed her total person entirely at the disposal of the salvific love of God, which wrought the redemption of the world. A person devoted to the Immaculate Heart of Mary will have his will and total life drawn to Jesus Christ and to all whom He came to save. If we grasp the full meaning, we can understand how devotion to Mary's Immaculate Heart is an efficacious sign of grace and salvation.

CHAPTER 3

† The Holy Spirit and the Immaculate Heart †

MANY CHRISTIANS think there is little in the Bible about Mary. There is much about Mary in the Sacred Scriptures. Many more are discovering Mary as they read the pages of the inspired word of God with their minds open to her, whom God used to break into our time and become one of us and one with us. Jesus became one with man so that we might become one with Him. God did this through Mary as she was overshadowed by the Holy Spirit.

The Sacred Scriptures give much evidence of the Holy Spirit's work in the life of the Blessed Virgin Mary. The Scriptures abundantly manifest Mary's role in God's plan for the redemption of the human race through Jesus Christ. More are admitting — when they read the Scriptures without prejudice to Mary and no longer ignore her presence — that not only are they meeting the person of Mary and experiencing her presence, but they are meeting the Person of Jesus Christ more profoundly as she introduces her Son to them. How can one encounter the humanity of Jesus while ignoring His Mother?

For too long, both Catholics and Protestants accepted the myth that the Scriptures were largely silent about Mary. Too often Catholics developed a devotion to Mary apart from the Scriptures, and Protestants rejected Mariology altogether.

Some who have opposed Mary are now discovering her as living and dynamic. Mary has entered into the lives of many through cooperation with grace, and only later they discovered the divine revelation of God's Mother to be found in the inspired texts of Sacred Scripture. Once open to such grace, one can be enlightened still further by the Holy Spirit.

Catholics who do not appreciate the scriptural orientation of the Rosary are turned off to it as a tedious thing. Christians who are not Catholic, who don't understand the soul of the Rosary rooted in the Scriptures, look at this beautiful prayer as "vain repetition." All this is changing. Mary is gently leading her children to Christian unity. A Methodist minister, J. Neville Ward, has written the book *Five for Sorrow, Ten for Joy* concerning the fifteen mysteries of the Rosary. Christians of other denominations, together with Catholics, are realizing that Mary is no barrier in going to Christ. She goes with them. She inspires them. They praise with her. She prays with them.

Cardinal Newman, whose cause for canonization is being promoted, was a great English convert to Catholicism. He had a strong devotion to the Mother of God. At the same time, this distinguished convert, whose love for Mary was so warm, was appalled at the excesses of some authors who sought to enhance devotion to Mary by exaggeration. Presenting Mary as the *sole* refuge of sinners, as *the* merciful one, and Jesus Christ as merely the God of Justice, is simple disloyalty to both Mary and Christ. "Sentiments such as these," wrote the Cardinal, ". . . seem to me like a bad dream. I could not have conceived them to be said. . . . I will have nothing to do with statements which can only be explained by being explained away."

The true teachings of the Catholic Church about Mary are so beautiful that exaggerations do not enhance her power, goodness, or holiness; they only distract and keep others from meeting and loving this most beautiful of humans next to Jesus Christ. Mary is certainly a refugee of sinners. She is the Mother of Mercy. She is all this and more in virtue of Jesus Christ, to whom she leads and whom she manifests.

Some, though baptized Catholics in infancy, have never developed a personal relationship with Jesus Christ. These have not made a personal act of faith in Jesus Christ as Lord, God, Savior. There may be a cold intellectual commitment. What is needed is an affair of the heart, a surrender of the will. This is where the Immaculate Heart of Mary comes in. While her heart properly has reference to the total person of Mary, the very expression speaks to our hearts. It invites us to have an affair of the heart and with her help to encounter Jesus Christ in a deeply personal way.

She is the spouse of the Holy Spirit, performing her work as a mother quite effectively, if we only permit her in and meet the real Mary.

Those who claim that Mary keeps one away from Jesus Christ have never met the real Mary. Those who know and love the real Mary find added power in their prayer as they go with her to the one Mediator between God and man, Jesus Christ. Even in their reception of Christ in Holy Communion, while Mary is not present, she does become present in some mystical way to one whose relationship with Jesus her Son is personal and deep. She is the spouse of the Holy Spirit. Acting together with the Spirit, whose power she implores, she brings Jesus to us. At no time is Jesus brought to us more effectively, substantially, and really than in the Holy Eucharist.

If we are in the state of grace, our very person — body and soul — is a temple of the Holy Spirit. "Do you not know that you are God's temple and that God's Spirit dwells in you?" (1 Cor 3:16). "Do you not know that your body is a temple of the Holy Spirit within you, which you have from God? You are not your own" (1 Cor 6:19). "For we are the temple of the living God; as God said, 'I will live in them and move among them, and I will be their God, and they shall be my people' " (2 Cor 6:16).

That is the promise to every sincere baptized Christian. What then of the Mother of the Church, the spouse of the Holy Spirit? The Spirit overshadowed Mary; "the Word became flesh and dwelt among us, full of grace and truth; we have beheld his glory, glory as of the only Son from the Father" (Jn 1:14).

To be in the state of sanctifying grace is to share in the life of God. Repeatedly the Scriptures speak of the person who is baptized and accepts Jesus Christ as one sharing in the life of God. Peter, the Prince of the Apostles, wrote that the divine power freely bestowed on us everything necessary that we might "become partakers of the divine nature" (2 Pet 1:4). In his first epistle, the Apostle John speaks of the "word of life — the life was made manifest, and we saw it, and testify to it, and proclaim to you the eternal life which was with the Father and was made manifest — that which we have seen and heard we proclaim also to you, so that you may have fellowship with us; and our fellowship is with the Father and with his Son Jesus Christ. And we are writing this that our joy may be complete. This is the message we have heard from him and proclaim to you, that God is light and in him is no darkness" (1 Jn 1:2-5).

"God is light."

"While pronouncing these last words [the grace of God . . .], Our Lady opened her hands for the first time, shedding on us a light so intense that it seemed as a reflex glancing from her hands and penetrating to the inmost recesses of our hearts, making us see ourselves in God, who was that Light, more clearly than we could see ourselves in a mirror. Then by an interior impulse, also communicated to us, we fell upon our knees, repeating in our hearts: 'Oh, most Holy Trinity, I adore You! My God, my God, I love You in the most Blessed Sacrament!' " (Sister Lucia writing on the first apparition of our Lady of Fatima, May 13, 1917).

Mary is Mother of the Word. She is Mother of Christ. Our Lady is Mother of the Church. Her great faith and openness to the Holy Spirit brought heaven to earth. It was the condition required by divine providence for the Word to be made flesh and dwell among us. Mary conceived the Word of God in her Immaculate Heart, and then by the overshadowing of the Holy Spirit the Word was conceived in her holy womb so that the Word of life might become visible to us. The light that comes from Mary is a reflection of the light that is God. The light we see coming from the moon is really light from the sun.

Mary is our perfect model in faith and openness to the action of the Holy Spirit within us. While we will never conceive Christ in the flesh, we can conceive Jesus Christ the Word in our hearts by faith and grace as did Mary. This is the vocation of every Christian, and to this Jesus Christ himself has called us.

"And his mother and his brethren came; and standing outside they sent to him and called him. And a crowd was sitting about him, and they said to him, 'Your mother and your brethren are outside, asking for you.' And he replied, 'Who are my mother and my brethren?' And looking around on those who sat about him, he said, 'Here are my mother and my brethren. Whoever does the will of God is my brother, and sister, and mother' " (Mk 3:31-35).

The evangelist who tells us so much about Mary in his Gospel recorded it this way: "Then his mother and his brethren came to him, but they could not reach him for the crowd. And he was told, 'Your mother and your brethren are standing outside, desiring to see you.' But he said to them, 'My mother and my brethren are those who hear the word of God and do it' '' (Lk 8:19-21).

In no way was Jesus discrediting His own Mother. Jesus is saying here what spiritual writers through the centuries have taught. The greatness of Mary is not merely because she physically conceived the Word of God but because of her great faith — because of her response to the word of God and the increase of grace in her whose will was so perfectly attuned to God that the angel could call her "full of grace."

Jesus presents His Mother as an example of one who hears the word of God in faith and responds in love — acts upon it. This is clearly seen further on in the account by the same Marian evangelist. Jesus had just cast a devil out of a man. He spoke of the necessity to be on guard when an evil spirit has been cast out, lest it return and enter with seven other spirits far worse than itself.

"As he said this, a woman in the crowd raised her voice and said to him, 'Blessed is the womb that bore you, and the breasts that you sucked!' But he said, 'Blessed rather are those who hear the word of God and keep it!' '' (Lk 11:27-28).

Many souls have been freed from sin through devotion to the Immaculate Heart of Mary. She has become a Mother to many and, as it were, even a girl friend to many a young man in his fight for purity. She is a model to young ladies in preserving their integrity. She is the Virgin Most Pure and Queen of Virgins. In going to Jesus in the company of Mary, we are welcomed in hearing the word of God and acting on it, for we are going to the Word made flesh with the perfect model of faith and love. We are called to be formed, each one of us, into the likeness of Jesus Christ. Each one of us is an extension of the Incarnation. No one had Jesus' likeness formed within her more perfectly than Mary.

Good Pope John Paul I — who was with us only thirty-three days when God called him to himself so that we might have Pope John Paul II, another great Marian Pope — once wrote that God had the qualities of a Mother as much as a Father. He had Sacred Scripture to back him up. " 'Can a woman forget her sucking child, that she should be without compassion for the son of her womb?' Even these may forget, yet I will not forget you. Behold, I have graven you upon the palms of my hands. . .'' (Is 49:15-16).

God has a tender, maternal love for us. In the passage above,

Isaiah compared Yahweh to a betrothed virgin who had inscribed the name of her beloved on the palm of her hand. It was the custom of the times. God lovingly writes our names in the palm of His hand as He does in His Heart.

God has manifested His great love for us in giving us Jesus as the Redeemer even unto death. But the Scriptures reveal that His love is also a maternal love. God's love for us is not manifested simply in justice but in mercy, compassion, mildness — feminine qualities we commonly see as special marks of motherhood.

In giving us Mary to be our spiritual Mother, God has made explicit the qualities of His maternal love for us which would not be visible in the man Jesus Christ. Again we see in this why God wants devotion to the Sacred Heart of Jesus alongside devotion to the Immaculate Heart of His Mother. We see why Mary plays such an important role in the Redemption.

No woman has ever discovered the power of the Holy Spirit in her life as did Mary. When one really takes Mary for his Mother he discovers a power in the spiritual life he never before experienced. Mother of the Church, she is the Mother of each Christian and spouse of the Holy Spirit, through whose intercession the Spirit descends into us so that Christ Jesus may be formed in us.

One who finds devotion to Mary threatening to his devotion to Jesus Christ should call on the Holy Spirit to grant knowledge and understanding of Mary. The conversion of souls testifies that acceptance of Mary as Mother is not achieved simply through the intellect. Being convinced intellectually is not enough. That is why it is necessary that each one of us have an "affair of the heart." Such souls are found open by the Holy Spirit. God is love. To the Holy Spirit is appropriated the love that exists between the Father and the Son. That Love which is God finds Its most pleasing Temple in Mary's Immaculate Heart.

Many individuals, formerly prejudiced against spirituality involving devotion to the Immaculate Heart of Mary, later came to experience Mary. They cannot explain it. They can only tell of their experience. The result has been a deeper identification with Jesus Christ in the unity of the Holy Spirit.

Of all God's people, Mary was the one who was most open to the coming of the Savior. While many of ". . . his own people received him not" (Jn 1:11), Mary as the daughter of Zion, representing all God's people, did accept the Savior most perfectly. As stated in the previous chapter, in the Old Testament "daughter of Zion" was a personal epitome of the people of Israel, the chosen people of God. Mary, as the spokesman for all of humanity in accepting its Savior, becomes known as the daughter of Zion. She is the personification of the Old Testament longing for the Messiah.

> Sing aloud, O daughter of Zion;
>   shout, O Israel!
> Rejoice and exult with all your heart,
>   O daughter of Jerusalem!
> The LORD has taken away the judgments against you,
>   he has cast out your enemies.
> The King of Israel, the LORD, is in your midst;
>   you shall fear evil no more.
> On that day, it shall be said to Jerusalem:
> "Do not fear, O Zion;
>   let not your hands grow weak.
> The LORD your God is in your midst,
>   a warrior who gives victory;
> he will rejoice over you with gladness,
>   he will renew you in his love. . . ."
>   (Zeph 3:14-18)

Literally, Zephaniah's expression "the LORD is in your midst" can be rendered "in your womb," as Luke does in seeing the comparison and making reference to Mary about to conceive: " 'Hail, full of grace [O favored one], the Lord is with you! Blessed are you among women!' But she was greatly troubled at the saying, and considered in her mind what sort of greeting this might be. And the angel said to her, 'Do not be afraid. Mary, for you have found favor with God. And behold, you will conceive in your womb and bear a son, and you shall call his name Jesus . . .' " (Lk 1:28-31).

Those accustomed to the translation "full of grace" should not be troubled, for "favored one" means that Mary is to be the recipient of special divine favor, the sanctifying power of God in view of her office of Mother of the Messiah. Being the special recipient of divine sanctifying power and the personification of God's people in waiting for the Savior, she is truly "full of grace." It is to bring grace that the Savior comes, and it is Mary He redeems most perfectly.

One who has an affair of the heart in experiencing the love of

Mary's Immaculate Heart may not be able to explain any scriptural basis for the experience. Biblical scholars, however, can explain the unique role of Mary and the prominent place she plays in the Scriptures. They show how the writers of the New Testament were aware of many incidences in the Old Testament where Mary was prefigured. A study of the Scriptures explains what many have experienced, not knowing how.

St. Luke frequently makes allusions to the unique place of Mary in the acts of redemption. St. Luke is obviously thinking of the mysterious cloud of glory which overshadowed the Holy of Holies, the repository for the Ark of the Covenant in the inner sanctuary of the temple, when he wrote of the Holy Spirit "overshadowing" Mary. Mary becomes the new temple for the divine dwelling. In Christian tradition, she has been called the Ark of the Covenant.

When the Ark of the Covenant was being brought to Jerusalem, David said, "How can the ark of the LORD come to me?" (2 Sam 6:9). Elizabeth cried out in a loud voice when Mary entered Zechariah's house, "And why is this granted me, that the mother of my Lord should come to me?" (Lk 1:43). As "Mary remained with her about three months, and returned to her home" (Lk 1:56), so David in the transfer of the Ark had it stay three months in the house of Obed-edom the Gittite (see 2 Sam 6:11).

It is remarkable how many Marian scriptural texts scholars are discovering. Since the Immaculate Heart of Mary represents the total person of this unique woman, as we keep insisting, we can discern the deeper and wider meaning of devotion to our Mother's heart. Through the centuries there has been an instinctive Catholic sense that called forth devotion to the Mother of God, who gave us our Savior through the action of the Holy Spirit. At the very time we are becoming more aware of God's desire that we have devotion to the Immaculate Heart, we are discovering more profoundly her unparalleled collaboration with the Holy Spirit, which overshadows her and dwells within her as a unique temple of God. All this is reflected in the meaning of the Immaculate Heart.

It is often said that the mother is the heart of the home. In presenting the heart of God's Mother, what we are beholding is the heart of God's family, the heart of the Mother of the Church.

The marriage and wedding feast at Cana are a symbol of the eternal marriage between God and the human race (see Rev 19:7-9; 21:2, 4). Things did not happen just by chance in the life of Jesus and His Mother, nor did the evangelists record things by chance. We are dealing with public divine revelation, the inspired word of God, with profound messages which the Church has meditated on for two thousand years. It will continue to explore them in meditation until the end of time to understand more deeply the meaning, often so obvious, often only slowly realized, but there all the time in the sacred deposit of faith. Call it "development of doctrine," but the faith has always been there, as has its deposit. In divine providence, it is now time to appreciate more deeply our Mother's Heart and her role as spouse of the Holy Spirit.

As the Mother of Jesus was so powerful in intercession at the wedding feast of Cana, so will she be in the eternal marriage between God and humanity in heaven — and for the Church which remains upon earth. Jesus and Mary appear at the love-feast of a wedding, which is also a symbol of the Agapē (love-feast), the Holy Eucharist, as well as the eternal heavenly banquet. The wine provided through Mary's intercession prefigures a new and better wine of the heavenly wedding feast.

The wine which spiritually inebriates souls was not present in the Mosaic dispensation. St. Paul explains that it is the Holy Spirit that should inebriate us. "Do not get drunk with wine, for that is debauchery; but be filled with the Spirit" (Eph 5:18). When the apostles were accused on the day of Pentecost of being "filled with new wine" (Acts 2:13), St. Peter stood up with the Eleven and said: "These men are not drunk, as you suppose, since it is only the third hour of the day, but this is what was spoken of by the prophet Joel: 'And in the last days it shall be, declares God, that I will pour out my spirit on all flesh . . .' " (Acts 2:4-16).

Mary's role as intercessor and Mediatrix of all grace is so profound that it is through her request that the Holy Spirit is poured out upon souls yet today, At Cana, Mary was asking for a future outpouring of the Holy Spirit.

Jesus was not a private person. All that He did was for the redemption of the world. This is especially true as He hung dying on the cross. In the supreme act of redeeming the world there was no place for private considerations such as "who will take care of my mother when I'm gone?'' Mary's role is also public, and in divine providence the Apostle John realizes all this in carefully selecting his texts for his Gospel.

> Standing by the cross of Jesus were his mother and his mother's sister, Mary the wife of Clopas, and Mary Magdalene. When Jesus saw his mother, and the disciple whom he loved standing near, he said to his mother, ''Woman, behold, your son!'' Then, he said to the disciple, ''Behold, your mother!'' And from that hour the disciple took her to his own home. (Jn 19:25-27)

The Apostle John is indicating here that Jesus, in the supreme act of the redemption of the world, is entrusting His Mother with a new and universal mission. Jesus first entrusts John to Mary. Only then is Mary entrusted to John. A further point often not realized is that John's own mother was standing next to Mary beneath the cross. John is revealing here the special role of Mary in the new covenant being struck on the cross. The respectful title ''Woman'' is used, the same word used in Genesis 3:15 and also at Cana.

Immediately after the human race fell in the Garden of Eden, God promised a Redeemer and mentioned a woman who would be at enmity with the serpent. John is pointing out that Mary is the New Eve, the new Mother of all the living. Her special role in the Church is also signified. There is no question here of equality between Jesus and Mary. The Person of Jesus is the second Person of the Blessed Trinity, the Son of God, and therefore uncreated and infinite. This Son of God is also the Son of Mary, making her the Mother of God. Yet Mary is a purely created human person, herself the perfect woman of faith and perfect disciple of Jesus.

John represented us all, the total believing community for all time, when he was given Mary as Mother and given to Mary as son. Since Mary is ever-Virgin, before, during, and after the birth of Jesus Christ, she is often seen as bringing forth her Firstborn without pain. The Christ-Child enters the world as sunlight passes through pure crystal. As Mary stood beneath the cross and was designated by Jesus to be Mother of the Church, there was great pain.

The prophecy of Simeon is beginning to be fulfilled: ''. . . (and a sword will pierce through your own soul also), that thoughts out of many hearts may be revealed'' (Lk 2:35). There would be great pain in her role as Mother of the Church, bringing forth her other children.

It would be the role of Mary to strengthen the faith of the infant Church and be the model for strength in faith for all ages to come, which would call her blessed (see Mary's Canticle, Lk 1:48). The early Fathers of the Church saw symbolically the Church being born from the side of Christ, as His sacred side was pierced and blood and water flowed out. Yet it is at Pentecost, sometimes called the Birthday of the Church, that the Church Jesus came to found comes to a fullness and is possessed of its Soul, the Holy Spirit. The faith community in Jerusalem found maturity in the Spirit.

Mary is seen in Acts 1 and 2 in the upper room with one hundred twenty people, awaiting the promise of Jesus made just before He ascended into heaven: "You will receive power when the Holy Spirit has come upon you; and you shall be my witnesses in Jerusalem, and in all Judea and Samaria and to the end of the earth" (Acts 1:8). Mary had already been overshadowed with the Holy Spirit at her conception of Jesus. No one was greater in faith, more open to the Holy Spirit, and better able to teach the disciples how to pray. Our Lord had worked at teaching the disciples to pray and had taught them the Lord's prayer. No fault on the part of our divine Lord that their prayers lacked perfection.

Even Abraham, the father of faith in the Old Testament, failed a test when told he would have a son. Abraham laughed and said to himself, "Shall a child be born to a man who is a hundred years old?" (Gen 17:17). A greater faith was required of Mary. She would give birth to a son without a human father. She believed perfectly. When Abraham, who was promised he would be the father of millions, was told to sacrifice his only son Isaac, he passed the test. An angel held the hand of Abraham, and the sacrifice of his only son was replaced with the sacrifice of an animal. When Mary stood beneath the cross on Calvary witnessing her only Son being crucified, no angel came at the last moment to save Him. Her faith and surrender were complete, and so she merits the title not only of "Woman of Faith" but "Mother of Sorrows." A devotion exists in the Church to her "Sorrowful and Immaculate Heart."

This is the woman of perfect faith, a faith tested and not

found wanting in the slightest, gathered with the disciples in the upper room praying for the coming of the Holy Spirit. There had been a weakening of faith on the part of the disciples after the death of Jesus on Good Friday and before He rose from the dead. Peter, who had been named to head the other bishops and all the Church, does manifest faith during the days in that upper room. Peter calls for a replacement of Judas saying, "One of the men who have accompanied us during all the time that the Lord Jesus went in and out among us, beginning from the baptism of John until the day when he was taken up from us — one of these men must become with us a witness to his resurrection" (Acts 1:21-22).

It is thrilling to consider that Mary was present upon the selection of a successor of the first apostles, the first bishops and priests who were appointed and ordained by Jesus himself. Matthias was selected in response to the prayer of those one hundred twenty: "Lord, who knowest the hearts of all men, show which of these two thou hast chosen to take the place in this ministry and apostleship from which Judas turned aside, to go to his own place" (Acts 1:24-25). Mary, queen of the apostles and clergy, prayed with the others. She whose "Fiat" gave us the first Priest, Jesus Christ, has a role in the selection of every priest, every man of faith who is to guide and inspire others to have faith in the resurrected Christ. Her Immaculate Heart is all-embracing. It embraces every one of her children, with a special love for her priests.

At the birthday of the Church, the Mother of the Church must be present in the plan of God. "And there appeared to them tongues as of fire, distributed and resting on each one of them. And they were all filled with the Holy Spirit and began to speak in other tongues as the Spirit gave them utterance. Now there were dwelling in Jerusalem Jews, devout men of every nation under heaven . . ." (Acts 2:3-5). The Christian faith with Mary as mother and model is for every nation under heaven. Mary becomes Mother of the new people of God redeemed by her Son. By divine providence, Jesus' redemption was accompanied by His Mother's cooperation in faith and love. On the part of Mary, maternal, sacrificial love and faith were perfected.

Mary is herself one of the redeemed, a member of the Church. She not only is the personification of the "daughter of

Zion" but now represents in her person what the entire Church hopes to be. Each one of us falls short as a member of the Church. Not so our Mother. She fulfills perfectly the description the Apostle Paul gives of the Church:

> . . .Christ loved the church and gave himself up for her, that he might sanctify her, having cleansed her by the washing of water with the word, that he might present the church to himself in splendor, without spot or wrinkle or any such thing, that she might be holy and without blemish. (Eph 5:25-27)

We can't but see in the Immaculate Heart of Mary the perfection of the Church, that glorious goal to which we are all called in heaven. What she is, we hope to become — in imitation and through her prayers. Her perfect love calls us to the perfect union with Jesus Christ that she has and would have us all possess.

On December 8, 1854, Pope Pius IX proclaimed the doctrine of the Immaculate Conception stating:

> The doctrine which holds that the Blessed Virgin Mary was at the first instant of her conception, by a singular privilege of God, preserved from all stain of original sin, has been revealed by God and is therefore to be believed by the faithful with firmness and constancy. (*Ineffabilis Deus*)

Four years later, in 1858, at Lourdes, France, Bernadette Soubirous astonished her parish priest, then all of France, and finally the world, by saying that the Lady who has been appearing to her gave her name in saying, "I AM THE IMMACULATE CONCEPTION."

Theologians were astonished at these words, "I am the Immaculate Conception." How could she say it? No one has thought more on these words and written more profoundly and boldly of them than St. Maximilian Kolbe, who was canonized a martyr-saint in 1982 by Pope John Paul II. St. Maximilian, who died in place of another prisoner at Poland's Auschwitz death camp on August 14, 1941, contemplated these words of Our Lady of Lourdes so much that his Marian spirituality involving the Holy Spirit is breathtakingly lovely to behold.

What caused Father Kolbe to meditate so much on the words spoken by the Blessed Virgin Mary to Bernadette was that "Immaculate Conception" is a divine Name, the Name of the third divine Person. Most properly, the Name "Immaculate Conception" could be applied only to the Holy Spirit who springs from the Father and the Son. Let us follow, in summary, Father Kolbe's thoughts below as he meditates on each divine Person:

THE FATHER

Our Lord is God, the unique God, infinite, infallible, thrice holy, all merciful. He, our Lord, our Father, our Creator, our End, is Intelligence, Power, Love, and all things. . . . Whatever is not God lacks all value apart from Him. So then, all love, without limits, for our Father, the best of Fathers. (Letter to his brother, April 21, 1919)

Ordinarily, everything comes from the Father through the Son and by the Holy Spirit; and everything returns by the Spirit through the Son to the Father. (Conference, June 20, 1937)

God the Father! What depths of meaning in our Lord's words: "Do not call anyone your father on earth" (Mt 23:9). Truly, no man can be a father in the full sense of that word; the primary principle of everything, the first Father of all that exists, is God the Father. Everywhere else we find only an echo of His father-hood. It is from the Father that all the divinity pours out, so to speak, from all eternity, on the Son; and from Father and Son on the Holy Spirit; and from the Blessed Trinity on the Virgin Mary, mother of Jesus, who is God. (Meditation, April 14, 1933)

THE SON

Who is the Son? The Begotton One, because from the beginning and for all eternity He is begotten by the Father.

From all eternity the Father begets the Son, without a mother. (Notes, 1939)

Before Christ, the mystery of the Blessed Trinity was scarcely known or hinted at. For the world to know it, the second Person of the Blessed Trinity became a man, and lived in this world; this was the first step toward a perfect knowledge of God. But for the Son to be more truly known, the Holy Spirit, the third Person of the Holy Trinity, had to come to us. (Conference, Sept. 25, 1937)

THE HOLY SPIRIT

And who is the Holy Spirit? The flowering of the love of the Father and the Son. If the fruit of created love is a created conception, then the fruit of divine Love, that prototype of all created love, is necessarily a divine "conception." The Holy Spirit is, therefore, the "uncreated eternal conception," the prototype of all the conceptions that multiply life throughout the whole universe.

The Father begets; the Son is begotten; the Spirit is the "conception" that springs from their love; there we have the intimate life of the three Persons by which they can be distinguished one from another. But they are united in the oneness of their nature, of their divine existence. The Spirit is, then, this thrice-holy "conception," this infinitely holy "Immaculate Conception."

Father Kolbe was very much an original thinker in calling the Holy Spirit the "uncreated conception" in God. Whatever conception takes place in God must always be thought of in terms of an eternal begetting. There can be no question of things happening in time in the nature of the Blessed Trinity. The Father is eternally begetting the Son. The Holy Spirit is always the love springing forth from the first two Persons within the Trinity. As Father Kolbe said, the Holy Spirit "is the flowering of the love of the Father and the Son."

As I mentioned earlier, in Scripture there is seen a tenderness in God that is both fatherly and motherly. The love of God is compared by the prophets sometimes to a father's love, sometimes to a mother's love. It was this motherly love in God that brought forth from the Creator the heart of a mother and his greatest masterpiece in this respect, the Immaculate Heart of Mary.

The thoughts of Father Kolbe may be deep, but their beauty is so precious coming from this very special Marian saint that we cannot afford to pass them up in considering the Immaculate Heart of Mary and the Holy Spirit. The Holy Spirit is seen to have a maternal place within the Blessed Trinity and a maternal role in our supernatural life. The Holy Spirit is the Love personified between the Father and the Son. An affinity is seen between the personal properties characterizing the Holy Spirit and those which characterize a mother.

There is no more precious love, no more disinterested, selfless love than the love of a mother. No other love can compare to the love a mother gives us. No other person is given to us on earth like our mother. Likewise, on the supernatural plane, the Holy Spirit is the Gift of God to us, the depths of the Trinity's own love and activity within Itself. At the Last Supper Jesus revealed the third divine Person as the Spirit of truth and love (see Jn 14-16).

When Father Kolbe called the Holy Spirit the "uncreated conception" he was not thinking of physical conception as in humans. The conception is only an analogy, a similarity of which the Holy Spirit is the prototype. In the Blessed Trinity the Holy Spirit is not simply like the conception of an idea by the intellect. It is more like conceiving a deep affection for another, which is an act of the will.

God the Father begets God the Son, who is the Word. The Holy Spirit is the Love conceived by both the Father and the Son for each other. The Son is the Word spoken by the Father. The Holy Spirit is the Love conceived by both of them. The Conception which is the Holy Spirit is eternal and therefore is uncreated. The Conception as applied to Mary is not eternal, because Mary is a creature and had a beginning. At Lourdes, when Our Lady calls herself "Conception," she merely says that she is a creature. While the Holy Spirit is the *uncreated* Immaculate Conception, Mary is the *created* Immaculate Conception.

" 'Immaculate' [means] that from the beginning of her existence there was not the least falling away from the Will of God. The Immaculata, the creature most elevated among creatures, is the most perfect creature . . ." (Father Kolbe, Conference, July 26, 1939).

Father Kolbe saw a special relationship between the conception of Mary and that of the Holy Spirit. The only created conception like that of the Holy Spirit is the conception of Mary. The name Mary gave herself at Lourdes, "the Immaculate Conception," is the name of the Holy Spirit. It calls to mind the title frequently used by medieval theologians, "Spouse of the Holy Spirit."

As Father Kolbe wrote, "If among creatures the bride receives the same name as that of her husband because she belongs to him, is united to him, becomes like him, and in union with him initiates the creative activity of life, how much more so the name of the Holy Spirit, 'Immaculate Conception,' is the name of her in whom He lives with a love so fecund for the entire supernatural order."

Father Kolbe came to a startling conclusion, considered bold theology, when he wrote of a quasi-incarnation of the Holy Spirit taking place in Mary. The "marital union" is not strong enough a

comparison for Father Kolbe. He compares the union of Mary
and the Holy Spirit to the union of the Word and human nature, af-
firming that the Holy Spirit is "almost incarnate" in the Immaculata. Father Kolbe was careful to distinguish that the person
of Mary is a created person distinct from the uncreated Person of
the Holy Spirit. He writes:

> The Second Person of the Most Holy Trinity came upon the
> earth and gave us the proof of His love. The Third Person of the
> Trinity is not incarnated. Nevertheless, the expression "Spouse
> of the Holy Spirit" is very much more profound than human
> concepts can express. In a certain sense, we can affirm that the
> Immaculata is the incarnation of the Holy Spirit. . . .
>
> He [the Holy Spirit] is in the Immaculata as the Second Person
> of the most Holy Trinity, the Word, is in Jesus Christ — with
> this difference: in Jesus we have two natures, the divine and the
> human; but the nature and person of the Immaculata are dif-
> ferent from the nature and the person of the Holy Spirit. It is an
> unexplainable but perfect union by reason of which the Holy
> Spirit does not act except through the Immaculata, his spouse.
> She therefore is the Mediatrix of all the graces of the Most Holy
> Spirit.

Jesus Christ is the incarnate Word of God. Mary is *not* the
Holy Spirit, as Jesus is the Word. However, the Holy Spirit came
to dwell so intimately in Mary as His very special sanctuary, in
her very being as woman and mother, that she is the closest the
Holy Spirit could come to being incarnated without actually being
able to say, "The Holy Spirit was made flesh" as we can truly in
faith say, "The Word was made flesh." While Father Kolbe says,
"The Holy Spirit never took flesh," he then declares that "in a
certain sense . . . the Immaculata is the 'incarnation' of the Holy
Spirit."

How profound and beautiful all this is, beyond our imagination to appreciate — the wonder of the close union between the
Immaculate Heart of Mary, the total person of the Mother of
God, and the Third Person of the Blessed Trinity, who is Love. It
is with the will faculty of the soul that man loves. In Mary there
was never for an instant the least falling away of her created will
from the infinite, uncreated will of God. So closely was the love of
Mary's heart united to the Love which is the Holy Spirit that she
alone of all human persons is Immaculate.

With such intimate union of the Immaculate Heart and the Holy Spirit, the power of our Mother's intercession to obtain for us the Gift of the Holy Spirit is greater by far than most men could ever imagine.

If the moon be so bright, how radiant must be the sun.

CHAPTER 4

† The Word, the Immaculate Heart, and the Pope †

AMONG THE MANY beautiful and proper titles of the Blessed Virgin Mary is to be found "Mother of the Word Incarnate." The Son of God, Jesus Christ, is revealed in the Sacred Scriptures as the "Word of God."

> In the beginning was the Word,
> and the Word was with God,
> and the Word was God. . . .
> The Word became flesh
> and dwelt among us,
> full of grace and truth;
> we have beheld his glory:
> glory as of the only Son from the Father.
> (Jn 11:1, 4)

God the Father, first Person of the Most Blessed Trinity, is infinite Intellect. He knows all things. He is the first Source of all knowledge, power, and beauty. The Word of God spoken by the Father gives expression to all His wisdom. God, being infinite, is also simple. This simplicity of God enables Him to give expression of himself perfectly in *One Word*, which is the Son of God. That Word made flesh is Jesus Christ. That Word became flesh through the action of the Holy Spirit and the will of Mary's Immaculate Heart. That Word of God is revealed in the "light of the gospel of the glory of Christ, who is the likeness of God" (2 Cor 4:4). God prepared the world for this revelation of the Son during thousands of years.

When the people of Jerusalem were in exile, after the destruction of their city in 587, the Prophet Jeremiah uttered the great oracle of the "new covenant," sometimes called "The Gospel before the Gospel." The Old Testament had for its purpose preparation for the coming of the Christ, "the Word made flesh." Mary, of course, is the bridge between the old and the new, as in the Word made flesh we have the new covenant of which Mary is the Ark. These words of Jeremiah are the landmark of the Old Testament:

> "Behold, the days are coming, says the LORD, when I will make a new covenant with the house of Israel and the house of Judah, not like the covenant which I made with their fathers when I took them by the hand to bring them out of the land of Egypt, my covenant which they broke, though I was their husband, says the LORD: I will put my law within them, and I will write it upon their hearts; and I will be their God, and they shall be my people. And no longer shall each man teach his neighbor and each his brother, saying, 'Know the LORD,' for they shall all know me, from the least of them to the greatest, says the LORD; for I will forgive their iniquity, and I will remember their sin no more." (Jer 31:31-34)

Jeremiah always delivered all the words God commanded of him, even when he was tempted to hold back. The word of God gradually became a fire within him so that he said: ". . .There is in my heart as it were a burning fire shut up in my bones, and I am weary with holding it in, and I cannot" (Jer 20:9).

No one pondered God's words more than Mary. She was a woman of the old covenant too, preserved from Original Sin and full of grace from the first moment of her conception. She sat in the synagogue and heard God's word, and it penetrated deeply, open as she was to the Holy Spirit. She recognized that God was visiting His people. Mary's heart yearned for the day when the Promised One would come to restore God's people and the entire world would know His saving power.

In her great humility, Mary never imagined that she herself would one day be the Mother of the Messiah, the long-awaited One of Israel. There is scriptural evidence for her vow of perpetual virginity. No one thought a Messiah would come without a human father. Even as a young girl, Mary longed for God's Anointed to be present to His people. The great prayer of God's people was for the coming of the Messiah. They never dreamed it would be the Word of God made flesh. God's people before the coming of Christ were not conscious of three Persons in One God. In waiting and looking for their Savior, God's people never imagined for a moment God would become a Brother to the whole human race.

There were centuries when the poor and humble, the great and holy, longed for the fulfillment of that promise first made in Genesis 3:15: that the woman would be at enmity with the serpent, that there would be enmity between her seed and its seed and the head of the serpent would be crushed. All the longing that God stirred up in His people became concentrated in the heart of Mary as she prayed for the Messiah of God among His people. When the Prophet Hosea looked forward to a new covenant, these words were never fulfilled more perfectly than in Mary: "I will betroth you to me in faithfulness; and you shall know the LORD" (Hos 2:22).

Never did Mary dream that she would be the holy temple in which God would marry humanity to himself. When we meditate what the Word made flesh really means and how God accomplished it, there is little wonder that the Fathers of the Church loved to repeat: "Mary conceived the Word in her heart long before she conceived Him in her womb." In saying "Yes" to the Angel Gabriel, Mary truly became the Mother of the Word made flesh. The Word of God in becoming flesh would teach humanity and give "light to every man" who was disposed in obedience to accept Him. He would empower them "to become children of God" (Jn 1:12).

The centuries of preparation and longing finally culminate in the heart of Mary. If Jeremiah experienced the word of God as a burning fire in his heart, what then of Mary's Immaculate Heart, wedded to the Holy Spirit? In the symbol, one sometimes sees Mary's heart issuing flames, commonly thought symbolic of her holy and pure love, and rightfully so. Still, can't we also envision in these flames Mary's great desire, burning to present the Word of God become her very own Son to the world? It was Mary's great faith that prepared her to become the Mother of the Word.

This, before all else, we should see in Mary's Immaculate Heart. As Jesus invited each one of us to become His mother, to mother the Word of God within our spirits, in Mary's flaming Heart we behold our greatest inspiration for conceiving the Word of God. One must know before one can love. One must first know the Word of God, accept it in faith. Obedient to God's Word, the soul then conceives Him in love. We become transformed into His likeness. Such is the invitation of Mary's own Immaculate Heart.

The Mother of the Word, through faith lived in perfection upon the earth, a faith now replaced by vision in glory, lives still as Mother and Spouse of Love, which is the Holy Spirit. She would beckon the Holy Spirit, whose perfect temple she was and remains, to descend into our lesser temples, our bodies and souls. There, within us at Mary's desire, the Word conceived again is given birth to increase members of the Mystical Body of Christ, the Church. Mary too is a member of the Mystical Body, its Mother.

What do Mary, the Mother of the Church, and the Pope, the visible head of the Church, have in common? The Pope, guided by the Holy Spirit to keep the Church infallible in its official teachings, has as a chief function to teach the Word, to teach Jesus Christ. His role is to be exercised in a paternal way, after the example of Jesus Christ. Mary, spouse of the Holy Spirit, according to a maternal role, brings us the Word as well. Mary presents the Word made flesh, as does the Pope.

Pope John Paul II has been traveling the world proclaiming, "JESUS CHRIST IS LORD." On October 12, 1984, Pope John Paul II came to Santo Domingo on pilgrimage to inaugurate a "novena of years" in preparation for the fifth centenary of the discovery and evangelization of America, to be observed in 1992-93. In Santo Domingo one can visit the tomb and monument of Christopher Columbus.

On the way to Santo Domingo, Pope John Paul stopped off in Zaragoza, Spain. There he visited the Shrine of Our Lady of the Pillar. He said, "Here, in the solid and ancient tradition of the Virgin of Pilar, the apostolic dimension of the Church shines out in all its splendor."

To appreciate the significance of the Pope's action and words in going to Zaragoza, we should recall that the first recorded apparition of our Lady took place there, according to tradition. It was during her own lifetime and so was actually a bilocation. The Apostle St. James, brother of John, had gone to Spain to evangelize the people and bring them Jesus Christ. As he was lonely, far from his native land, suffering opposition, persecution, and discouragement, our Blessed Lady came to St. James to encourage him. The Mother of the Word was solicitous for the apostles in carrying the Good News of the Word made flesh to all the nations.

So that St. James would not think afterward that he had only dreamed our Blessed Lady had visited him, she left with him a small stone pillar which to the present day is enshrined at Zaragoza in what is one of the most magnificent Marian shrines in the world. I've personally visited this shrine and experienced the perfume that comes from the pillar given St. James.

Pope John Paul II spoke of the apostolic, missionary, and Marian dimension of the Catholic Church in Spain as it evangelized the Americas and Philippines. He said that in Mary's company he "gathered at this Pillar of Zaragoza, which symbolizes the firmness of the faith of the Spanish and their great love for the Virgin Mary."

> This meeting is not accidental. The Marian faith of the Spanish missionaries quickly took root in those latitudes under the form of devotions and prayers which continues to be the guiding star for the believers of those countries. To say Spain is to say Mary. It is to say Pilar, Covadonga, Aranzazu, Montserrat, Ujué, El Camino, Valvanera, Guadalupe. . . .
>
> The Puebla Conference, in its reflections on evangelization, stated expressly: "Mary must ever more be the teacher of the Gospel in Latin America" (Puebla, 20). Yes, the teacher, she who leads us by the hand, she who teaches us to carry out the missionary service of her Son and to preserve all that she has taught us. Love for the Virgin Mary, Mother and model of the Church, is a guarantee of the authenticity and of the redeeming effectiveness of our Christian faith. . . .
>
> May Mary, the Mother of the Church, continue to guide and enlighten the faith and the path of the peoples in America!
>
> (*L'Osservatore Romano*, Nov. 19, 1984)

See in the following prayer a summary of the doctrine concerning Mary's Immaculate Heart and its meaning which we have been meditating. It was given to us by the great Marian Pope John Paul II, who ends every exhortation with some mention of God's Mother.

Prayer of Preparation for the Fifth
Centenary of Evangelization of America

Most Holy Mary, Mother of our America,
through the preaching of the Gospel
our peoples recognize their brotherhood
and know that you are the Immaculate one, full of grace.

As children with unwavering trust in our Mother,
we know that in your ears the angelic message sounds,
on your lips is the canticle of praise,
in your arms, God as a Child,
in your heart, the Cross of Golgotha,
in your countenance, the light and fire of the Holy Spirit,
and beneath your feet, the vanquished Serpent.
Our Most Holy Mother,
in this hour of renewed evangelization,
pray for us to the Redeemer of man,
that he may ransom us from sin
and from all that enslaves us;
that he may unite us with bonds of faithfulness
to the Church and to the pastors who guide it.
Show your Mother's love to the poor,
to the suffering, and to all who seek the Kingdom of your Son.
Strengthen our efforts to build up
the continent which unites all our hopes, in truth, justice, and love.
We offer heartfelt thanks for the gifts of our faith,
and glorify with you the Father of mercies,
through your Son Jesus, in the Holy Spirit. Amen.

When Pope John Paul arrived in San Juan, Puerto Rico, in the Plaza de las Americas, he said to the people that the provident love of the Father had led them by the hand of Mary along pathways of history. Speaking of the miracle of Cana, recorded in John 2, the Pope said:

The Mother of Divine Providence shows herself again in the words 'Do whatever he tells you.' The essential function of Mary comes to light here, which is to lead men to the will of the Father as it is manifested in Christ. That is, to lead her children to the heart of the saving mystery of the Redeemer of mankind.

By her words, but above all by her example of perfect obedience to the plan of Providence, Mary continues to point out to every man and to society the road to follow: 'Do whatever he tells you.' In other words: listen to what He says, because He is the one sent from the Father (cf. Mt 3:17); follow Him faithfully, for He is the way, the truth, and the life (cf. Mt 5:13-16); work for peace, justice, mercy, and purity of heart (cf. Mt 5:1-12); discern in the hungry, the sick, and the stranger the presence of Christ, who claims your assistance (cf. Mt. 25:31-46).

(*L'Osservatore Romano*, Nov. 26, 1984)

If some theologians have hesitated to speak of Mary as teacher, Pope John Paul II has not failed to do so. He spoke of her as "teacher of the Gospel." When he went to Fatima on May 13, 1982, in his sermon delivered on the occasion he agreed with Pope Pius XII in calling Fatima "a reaffirmation of the Gospels." Mary's example in the Gospels would be sufficient to accept her as a teacher.

On November 2, 1984, when Pope John Paul went to the Sanctuary of Our Lady of the Mountain in Varese, he invoked our Blessed Mother:

> O Mary, we pray to you. . . . Teach us recollection and the interior life; give us the disposition to listen to the good inspirations and the Word of God; teach us the need for meditation, for the personal interior life, for the prayer that God alone sees in secret.
> Mary, teach love.
> We ask love of you, Mary, the love of Christ, the only love, the highest love, total love, the gift of love, sacrificing love for our brothers and sisters. Help us to love this way.
> Obtain for us, O Mary, faith, supernatural faith, simple faith, full and strong, sincere faith, drawn from its true fountain, the Word of God, from its unfailing source, the Magisterium, instituted and guaranteed by Christ, living faith.
> O "Blessed who have believed," comfort us with your example, obtain for us this charism.
> (*L'Osservatore Romano*, Dec. 3, 1984)

On October 31, 1942, Pope Pius XII consecrated the Church and the entire world to the Immaculate Heart of Mary. Two years later, on May 4, 1944, the same Pope instituted the Feast of the Immaculate Heart of Mary.

In his 1956 Encyclical on the Sacred Heart of Jesus, Pope Pius stated:

> In order that favors may flow in greater abundance on all Christians, even on the whole human race, from devotion to the Sacred Heart of Jesus, let the faithful see to it that to this devotion, that of the Immaculate Heart of the Mother of God is closely joined. . . . It is, then, entirely fitting that the Christian people, after they have paid their debt of honor to the most loving Heart of Jesus, should also offer to the most loving heart of their heavenly Mother the corresponding acts of piety, affection, gratitude, and expiation. . . .
> Entirely in keeping with this most kind and wise disposition of

divine providence is the memorable act of consecration by
which we ourselves solemnly dedicated Holy Church and the
whole world to the spotless heart of the Blessed Virgin Mary.
                                                  (*Haurietis Aquas*)

In June, 1929, Our Blessed Lady appeared again to Sister
Lucia in what is often called "The Last Vision" of Fatima. Our
Lady asked for the collegial consecration of Russia to her Immaculate Heart "promising by this means to prevent the spreading of its errors and to bring about its conversion." Eleven years
later, December 20, 1940, Sister Lucia was authorized by her bishop to write the Holy Father, Pope Pius XII, asking for this consecration.

Sister Lucia described the vision in a letter as follows:

> Suddenly the whole chapel was illumined by a supernatural
> light, and a cross of light appeared above the altar, reaching to
> the ceiling. In a bright light at the upper part of the cross could
> be seen the face of a man and his body to the waist (Father), on
> his breast there was a dove also of light (Holy Spirit), and
> nailed to the cross was the body of another man (Son). Some-
> what above the waist, I could see a chalice and a large Host sus-
> pended in the air, onto which drops of blood were falling from
> the face of Jesus Crucified and from the wound of His side.
> These drops ran down onto the Host and fell into the chalice.
> Our Lady was beneath the right arm of the cross (. . . it was Our
> Lady of Fatima with her Immaculate Heart. . . in her left hand
> . . . without sword or roses, but with a crown of thorns and
> flames. . .). Under the left arm of the cross, large letters, as of
> crystal-clear water which ran down over the altar, formed
> these words: "Graces and Mercy."
>
> I understand that it was the Mystery of the Most Holy Trinity
> which was shown to me, and I received lights about this Mys-
> tery which I am not permitted to reveal.
>
> Our Lady then said to me: "The moment has come when God
> asks the Holy Father, in union with all the bishops of the world,
> to make the Consecration of Russia to my heart, promising to
> save it by this means."

According to Sister Lucia, the request of heaven was especially for the Consecration of Russia to her Immaculate Heart. It
must also be collegial, that is, done by the Holy Father in union
with the bishops of the world, so that people might realize the intercessory power of Mary's Immaculate Heart.

Ten years after his 1942 consecration of the Church and the world to Mary's Immaculate Heart, Pope Pius XII came closer to what Sister Lucia claimed was requested. On July 7, 1952, Pope Pius XII consecrated the Russian people to the Immaculate Heart of Mary.

While all this was pleasing to God, the missing element was that the Pope acted alone rather than in union with the bishops of the world in conducting the consecrations.

Millions of petitions through the years went to succeeding popes asking for a collegial consecration of Russia to the Immaculate Heart of Mary. The petitions came from throughout the world, including a special one from the bishops of Poland promoted largely by Cardinal Karol Wojtyla before he was elected pope some years later.

On November 21, 1964, the Feast of the Presentation, in the presence of the bishops of the world gathered for Vatican II and the promulgation of the important *Dogmatic Constitution on the Church* (*Lumen Gentium*), with its famous eighth chapter dedicated to Mary, Pope Paul VI did something striking. He renewed the consecration to the Immaculate Heart of Mary which Pius XII had made in 1942. In the presence of the Council Fathers, over two thousand bishops from throughout the world, Pope Paul VI proclaimed Mary Mother of the Church, renewed the consecration of the world to the Immaculate Heart of Mary, and announced that he was sending a "mission to Fatima."

For a time it was thought that the action fulfilled the request of Sister Lucia for collegial consecration. In the last analysis it was determined it was still an action by the Pope alone, done merely in the presence of the world's bishops. The consecration must be collegial, as Sister Lucia said our Lord had "insisted" that it be exactly as requested because He wanted "My entire Church to know that it is through the Immaculate Heart of My Mother that this favor [of Russia's conversion] is obtained."

On May 13, 1965, Pope Paul VI, through a representative, presented a golden rose at Fatima, confiding "the entire Church" to her protection. Fatima means essentially the Immaculate Heart of Mary. When a pope sends a golden rose to any Marian Shrine it is a sign of special papal approval and spiritual joy.

Two years later, on May 13, 1967, Pope Paul VI himself went

to Fatima and called all the world to renew consecration to the Immaculate Heart of Mary. Many had hoped that the collegial consecration would take place at this time. It did not occur. Apparently there was not sufficient favor from bishops for such an action, even though one single petition had included up to five hundred signatures of bishops.

On May 13, 1981, shots were fired in St. Peter's Square, in front of the Basilica, and heard around the world. Pope John Paul II had been shot, in fact with more than one bullet. The Pope was near death as he was rushed to Gemelli Hospital. At the time the Pope was shot, a message he had sent to the hundreds of thousands of pilgrims at the Sanctuary of Fatima in Portugal was being read. The pope later confessed that his first thought upon regaining consciousness was of Our Lady of Fatima. He detected a direct connection in the attempt on his life on the anniversary of Our Lady's first appearance in the Cova da Iria, where she asked for devotion to her Immaculate Heart as the will of God.

The following May 13, 1982, Pope John Paul II went to Fatima himself. Before going, he wrote a letter to the bishops of the world announcing that he intended to renew the consecrations of Pius XII made in 1942 and 1952, the consecrations of the world and of Russia. The bishops were invited to join him.

The Pope spoke at Fatima of that special bond he had with the world's bishops which made them constitute "a body and a college, in the same manner as, according to the will of Christ, the apostles were united to Peter." The consecration concerned not only the Church but the whole of humanity, and even explicitly in the mind of the Holy Father, "the men and the nations who have a special need of this offering and this consecration."

We can be encouraged by reports coming out of Russia of youth turning to God, youth brought up under atheistic methods of education. In December of 1984, China, the largest country under communism, confessed that many of its programs of Marxism had not worked. We may believe that the conversion of Russia and the triumph of Mary's Immaculate Heart have begun.

Below are some of the pertinent paragraphs of the collegial consecration:

Hail to you, Mary, who are wholly united to the redeeming consecration of your Son!

Mother of the Church, enlighten the people of God along the paths of faith, hope, and love. Help us to live in the truth of the consecration of Christ for the entire human family of the modern world.

In entrusting to you, O Mother, the world, all individuals and peoples, we also entrust to you this very consecration of the world, placing it in your motherly heart.

Immaculate Heart of Mary, help us to conquer the menace of evil, which so easily takes root in the hearts of the people of today, and whose immeasurable effects already weigh down upon our modern world and seem to block the paths toward the future.

From famine and war, deliver us.

From nuclear war, from incalculable self-destruction, from every kind of war, deliver us.

From sins against human life from its very beginning, deliver us.

From hatred and from the demeaning of the dignity of the children of God, deliver us.

From every kind of injustice in the life of society, both national and international, deliver us.

From readiness to trample on the commandments of God, deliver us.

From attempts to stifle in human hearts the very truth of God, deliver us.

From the loss of awareness of good and evil, deliver us.

From sins against the Holy Spirit, deliver us.

Accept, O Mother of Christ, this cry laden with the sufferings of all individual human rights, laden with the sufferings of whole societies.

Help us with the power of the Holy Spirit to conquer all sin: individual sin and the "sin of the world," sin in all its manifestations. Let there be revealed once more in the history of the world the infinite saving power of the redemption: the power of merciful love. May it put a stop to evil. May it transform consciences. May your immaculate heart reveal for all the light of hope.

> — *from the Act of Entrusting the World to Mary*
> *by Pope John Paul II*

In his homily at Fatima, May 13, 1982, Pope John Paul said: "If the Church has accepted the message of Fatima, it is above all because that message contains a truth and a call whose basic content is the truth and the call of the Gospel itself."

On the evening of May 12, 1982, Pope John Paul II went to the Chapel of Apparitions in the Cova da Iria, at the very spot where God's Mother appeared. In his greeting to the thousands of pilgrims, the Pope said: "The Message of Fatima indicates the Rosary, which can rightly be defined as 'Mary's prayer'; the prayer in which she feels particularly united with us. She herself prays with us. The Rosary prayer embraces the problems of the Church, of the See of Saint Peter, the problems of the whole world. . . ."

Pope John Paul continued his greeting: "The Rosary is and will always remain a prayer of gratitude, of love and faithful entreaty — the prayer of the Mother of the Church. And do you want me to teach you a 'secret' to keep your faith? It is simple, and it is no longer a secret: pray, recite the Rosary every day."

As theologians have meditated and studied the message of Fatima, they have more explicitly understood that central to the message is the Immaculate Heart of Mary in all its meaning. This book is not an attempt to explore and explain the message of Fatima in detail. That has been done in other volumes. A book dedicated to the Immaculate Heart of Mary, however, could not be complete if it ignored "the explosion of the supernatural" at Fatima, in which God has manifested that He desires devotion spread in the world to the Immaculate Heart of His Mother. While more than one pope has spoken of the message of Fatima as a reaffirmation of the Gospel, this book attempts to show that the foundation for devotion to the Immaculate Heart is biblical, divinely inspired in Sacred Scripture, which Fatima only reaffirms.

Pope John Paul II spoke of the consecration of the world to Mary's Immaculate Heart *henceforth*. Having invited the bishops of the world to join him in the act of consecration, the Pope made it clear that the consecration was to be for all times.

The seriousness of the Pope in intending that the consecration be truly a collegial act of the successor of St. Peter was seen when, for the Feast of the Annunciation, March 25, 1984, he asked the Bishop of Leiria-Fatima that the miraculous statue from the Chapel of Apparitions, which usually stands at the very spot where our Lady stood in the Cova da Iria, be brought to the Vatican. Furthermore, well before the Feast of the Annunciation, he sent a letter to the world's bishops so they would receive it in plenty of time. In the letter the Pope asked the bishops to join him in a renewed act of consecration to the Immaculate Heart of Mary, such as he had made at Fatima on May 13, 1982. He enclosed a copy of the consecration he intended to use at the Vatican.

There, in St. Peter's Square, Pope John Paul II knelt before the miraculous statue from Fatima on March 25, 1984, and prayed: "We have recourse to your protection, holy Mother of God! O Mother of individuals and peoples, accept the cry which we, as though moved by the Holy Spirit, address directly to your heart. Embrace with the love of the Mother and Handmaid, this human world of ours, which we entrust and consecrate to you, for we are full of disquiet for the earthly and eternal destiny of individuals and peoples. In a special way we entrust and consecrate to you those individuals and nations which particularly need to be entrusted and consecrated."

During the same visit of the miraculous statue of Fatima to the Vatican, the Pope had the statue placed on the tomb of St. Peter, beneath St. Peter's Basilica. There Pope John Paul II also knelt in prayer to Our Lady of Fatima.

On this occasion, when the Bishop of Leiria-Fatima brought the statue of Our Lady of Fatima to the Vatican, Pope John Paul II gave this bishop from our Lady's land the bullet with which he was shot on May 13, 1981. Pope John Paul also desired that a special statue of Our Lady of Fatima be made in Portugal and brought to the Vatican. Subsequently, the famous sculptor Avelino Moreira Vinas was chosen to carve a statue of Our Lady of Fatima in ivory for the Pope at the Vatican. I asked the same sculptor to carve the statues in white marble for the Fatima shrine in my parish, St. Mary of Mercy in Alexandria, South Dakota.

The Church would never act as Pope John Paul II and the world's bishops did in the act of consecration unless it was in harmony with the Gospels. The devotion that God wants established in the world is something that must now develop in the heart of each of us. To be devoted to Mary's Immaculate Heart, as will be examined in forthcoming chapters, will involve entrusting and consecrating ourselves as individuals. It will involve a daily living of that consecration.

CHAPTER 5

† Witnesses to the Immaculate Heart †

THE GREATEST witness to the Immaculate Heart is the Church itself. The Church sees in Mary a perfect image of itself in its final destiny when perfected in glory. Since in the fullest sense the object of devotion is not simply the physical heart but Mary's spiritual heart, the total person of Mary, then everything the Church officially has said of Mary has been said of Mary's Immaculate Heart.

Devotion to Mary's heart includes the love of her entire inner life, her virtues, her purity, her humility, her affections, her sorrows. The roses that often surround the representation of Mary's Immaculate Heart are symbolic of her virtues, the sweet perfume of her holiness. The sword represents her sorrows. The virtues Mary lived to perfection are really different expressions of her pure love. Mary lived the beatitudes of the Christian life to their fullest perfection. The spiritual heart of Mary refers to her whole inner life.

While the seed for the development of Marian doctrine is to be found in public divine revelation as recorded in the Sacred Scriptures, from the earliest centuries the Fathers of the Church, both of East and West, bear witness of devotion to the person of Mary. By Fathers of the Church is meant early ecclesiastical writers, known for their holiness and the wisdom with which they taught the truths of the faith, whose writings have been approved by the Church.

The *Apostolic Fathers* are those of the first and second centuries, known as "apostolic" because of their proximity to the original apostles. Having some connection with the apostles, they reflect their teachings in a special way. Those who wrote in the first three centuries are sometimes called *Early Fathers*.

Those who wrote in the fourth through the eighth centuries are known as *Later Fathers*. The last Father in the West is St. Gregory the Great (d. 604). The last Father of the East is St. John Damascene (d. 749). In the traditional teachings of the Church, if the Fathers accepted a teaching this indicates it belongs to the *deposit of faith* which Jesus Christ left to the original apostles. The deposit of faith was complete with the death of the last apostle. However, there remained the development of doctrine. This means there can be growth in the Church's understanding of the truths of divine revelation. It is a gradual unfolding in the Church's explanation and our understanding of what God has revealed. The substantial truth of a mystery revealed by God remains unchanged. The only thing that changes is the depth of the Church's subjective grasp of the revealed truth.

The development of doctrine takes place through the prayerful reflection of the faithful, especially the Church's saints and mystics; or the study and research by scholars and theologians recognized by the Church as being in harmony with magisterial teachings; or finally, the practical experience of living the faith among the faithful. Always it must involve the approved teaching of the Church's hierarchy under the Bishop of Rome. Implicit in the development of doctrine is the will of God that the faithful in general assent to the revealed truth being grasped more deeply, and that they grow in clarity and certitude as they appropriate the understanding of divine faith into their own lives. This has been happening with regard to the real meaning of devotion to the Immaculate Heart of Mary.

It is natural that the position of Mary as presented by the Fathers of the first three centuries would be small by comparison with later centuries. The fact that early Fathers mention Mary at all is proof that the seed of the faith is revealed by God. Patristic writers contain no formal treatises on Mary, as these early Fathers are deeply involved in explaining the fundamentals of Church doctrine, drawing from the primary truths of divine revelation. They must explain the nature of God, the oneness of God in three Persons, something entirely new in man's understanding of God with the coming of Jesus Christ. The early Fathers must spend their energy on the Incarnation, the divinity of the Word made flesh, something utterly startling to people since Old Testament days, that God should become man. There would be many questions and many misunderstandings. Christ must be seen as the Word made flesh, true God and true man, not simply a man in whom God dwelt.

The early Church Fathers must develop doctrines concerning the personality of the Holy Spirit and the relationship of this third Person to the Father and the Son. The unity of the Church and its universality, which caused it to become known very early as the "Catholic Church"; the doctrines of original sin and grace; the meaning of the Scriptures — all these things and much more occupied the time of the early Church Fathers. It was Cardinal Newman who said that the early Fathers spoke of Mary when her own story was necessary for Christ's.

The adjective "Catholic" was attached to the ancient Church of Christ already by St. Ignatius of Antioch in the year 110 when he wrote, "Where Jesus Christ is, there is the Catholic Church" (*Ad Smyr.* 8:2). The same Father has five references to our Lady as Virgin and Mother in his writings. His letters (110-115) are explicit on Mary: "Do not listen to those who refuse to confess that Jesus Christ, the son of David, was born of the Virgin Mary."

St. Justin Martyr (d. 165) is considered the first to write fully about the Blessed Virgin Mary. He refers to the Eve-Mary typology, which is picked up by St. Irenaeus (d. 202). While Eve was disobedient, Mary is obedient. While Eve was unbelieving, Mary made up for it with her great faith. St. Irenaeus saw Mary as the Mother of the new humanity in whom God makes a new beginning.

The Fathers of the third century deal with the divine motherhood of Mary and her perpetual virginity, a virginity existing *before, during*, and *after* the birth of Jesus Christ. St. Cyprian (d. 258) praises Mary's virginity and speaks of her as "the tree that produced the marvelous fruit, the house possessed by the Holy Spirit, the door of the Savior, the guarded sanctuary of the Holy Spirit, the abode of Christ's humanity, the house of sanctity which the Third Person of the Most Blessed Trinity willed to adorn, and the vessel of election in which the Divinity poured the fullness of grace."

Two Marian characteristics have become a part of authorized

Church teaching on Mary by the end of the fourth century, that of her divine motherhood and her perpetual virginity. The spiritual implication of Mary's virginity is seen in the words of Clement of Alexandria: "Mary's fruitful virginity is comparable to that of the written Word of the Lord. The Scriptures are fruitful because of the light that shines from them and the truth that they bring to the world; but they still remain virginal as they enclose the mystery of the Truth in a pure and holy vessel."

The works of the early Church Fathers still provide a rich mine for Marian teachings. An early-Fathers researcher, T. Livius, has written: "Saving a very few differences on points of lesser moment, the Fathers of the first six centuries unanimously held Our Blessed Lady in the same high appreciation as she has been held by Catholics of all subsequent ages. . . . Everything that the Church has at any time defined or sanctioned with regard to her privileges and the honor that is due her — together with all that saints and theologians of medieval and modern days have uttered in her praise — is to be found substantially, and at least in principle or germ, in the writings of the great Fathers."

Vatican Council II, in its eighth chapter on Mary in the *Dogmatic Constitution on the Church*, cites fourteen Church Fathers. Paul VI, in his magnificent Apostolic Exhortation *Marialis Cultus*, has twenty references to the Fathers. Pius IX frequently referred to the Fathers in his encyclical presenting the solemn definition of the Immaculate Conception as a dogma of faith. Pius XII, in defining the Assumption of Mary into heaven, quotes John Damascene, Germanus of Constantinople, and Modestus of Jerusalem.

From the fourth century on, the Fathers of both the East and West began to place great emphasis on the holiness of Mary and her role as model or exemplar for all Christians. St. Augustine already wrote of Mary as being free of original sin and said she is "Mother of all the members of the Divine Head." St. Gregory of Nyssa (d. 394) notes the first recorded apparition of Mary to St. Gregory the Wonder-Worker. This demonstrates the beginning of devotion to Mary not simply as the historical Mary of the Bible but reigning now in power and glory with her Son, Jesus, in heaven. St. Ephrem (d. 397) composed many prayers and hymns to Mary calling upon our Lady's powers of mediation with her divine Son and the Father. "O Immaculate Virgin, protect us and guard us beneath the wings of your tender pity."

By the end of the patristic age, the place of Mary is secure in all areas of Church life — the theological, liturgical, and devotional life of the faithful — in both East and West. The roots or seeds for Mariology given us in public divine revelation have not only sprouted but are beginning to flourish by the end of the times we speak of as belonging to the Fathers of the Church.

By the sixth century the Fathers of the Church had affirmed the bodily assumption of Mary into heaven. The last Father in the East, St. John Damascene, wrote of Mary as follows:

> It was fitting that she, who had seen her Son upon the cross and who had thereby received into her heart the sword of sorrow which she had escaped in the act of giving birth to Him, should look upon Him as He sits with the Father. It was fitting that God's Mother should possess what belongs to her Son, and that she should be honored by every creature as the Mother and as the handmaid of God.

The principal object of the Immaculate Heart devotion is the person of Mary, and the Fathers of the Church did a magnificent job, as shown in summary above, of making known her holiness, purity, faith, obedience, divine motherhood. At the same time, on the practical level among the faithful, devotion to Mary was spreading. The Order of Our Lady of Mount Carmel claims continuity with the hermits on Mount Carmel from ancient times, even to the prophet Elijah. A group of hermits who believed themselves to be the spiritual sons of Elijah lived on Mount Carmel in Palestine in Old Testament times when God's people were awaiting the coming of the Messiah. They pondered the Word of God in their hearts. When Jesus founded the Church, these hermits also developed a deep devotion to the Mother of God. They became known in time as "The Brothers of Our Lady of Mount Carmel."

According to pious tradition, a number of men who walked in the footsteps of the holy Prophets Elijah and Elisha, and whom John the Baptist had prepared for the coming of Jesus, embraced the Christian faith. They erected the first church to the Blessed Virgin on Mount Carmel, at the very spot where Elijah had seen a cloud rising, a figure of the fecundity of the Mother of God. On

Mount Carmel to the present day one can visit the Cave of Elijah and a beautiful church built over it honoring Our Lady of Mount Carmel.

On July 16, 1251, Mary appeared to St. Simon Stock, the superior general of the Carmelite Order headquartered at Aylesford, England. Our Lady placed in the hands of this saint the habit and scapular of the Carmelites. She gave him a great promise: "Whosoever dies wearing this scapular shall not suffer eternal fire . . . it shall be a sign of salvation, a protection in danger and a pledge of peace."

Both Pope Pius XII and Sister Lucia, the living survivor of the three children to whom Our Lady of Fatima appeared, have said that wearing the brown scapular is a sign of one's consecration to Mary's Immaculate Heart. In the final apparition at Fatima, October 13, 1917, our Lady appeared robed as Our Lady of Mount Carmel and held the small brown scapulars down toward the world. Sister Lucia interpreted this to mean that after all these centuries our Blessed Mother still wants us to wear her scapular.

One cannot be devoted to Mary without being devoted to Jesus Christ. Devotion to the Blessed Virgin Mary has long been considered a sign of salvation. Our Lady of Mount Carmel, according to the promise made to St. Simon Stock, affirmed this belief by saying that wearing her brown scapular is a "sign of salvation." Notice that our Lady did not say it was the source of salvation, for that is always Jesus Christ.

According to the teachings of the Church, the divine liturgy is the model of our devotion to the Mother of God. Mention of Mary occurs daily in the divine liturgy. Feasts of Mary occur throughout the year. Vatican II did not do away with devotion to Mary. It asked for a balanced devotion in relationship to Christ and the Church. The Second Vatican Council took note of the development of doctrine regarding Mary by the early Fathers, culminating in the Council of Ephesus (431) under the leadership of Cyril of Alexandria (d. 444).

> Mary was involved in the mysteries of Christ. As the most holy Mother of God she was, after her Son, exalted by divine grace above all angels and men. Hence the Church appropriately honors her with special reverence. Indeed, from most an-

cient times the Blessed Virgin has been venerated under the title of "God-bearer." In all perils and needs, the faithful have
fled prayerfully to her protection. Especially after the Council
of Ephesus the cult of the People of God toward Mary wonder-
fully increased in veneration and love, in invocation and imitation, according to her own prophetic words: "All generations
shall call me blessed; for he who is mighty has done great
things for me" (Lk. 1:48). . .(66).

But this Synod earnestly exhorts theologians and preachers of
the divine word that in treating of the unique dignity of the
Mother of God, they carefully and equally avoid the falsity of
exaggeration on the one hand, and the excess of narrow-mind-
edness on the other. Pursuing the study of sacred Scripture, the
holy Fathers, the doctors, the liturgies of the Church, and under
the guidance of the Church's teaching authority, let them rightly explain the offices and privileges of the Blessed Virgin which
are always related to Christ, the Source of all truth, sanctity,
and piety (67).

                    (*Dogmatic Constitution on the Church*)

Pope Paul VI applied the message of the Second Vatican
Council to the Rosary and Scapular in appointing Cardinal Silva
his legate to the Santo Domingo Marian Congress in March of
1965. In doing so, Pope Paul cited Vatican II: " 'Let the faithful
hold in high esteem the practies and devotions to the Blessed Virgin approved by the teaching authority of the Church in the course
of the centuries:' . . . the Rosary of Mary and the Scapular of Carmel are among these recommended practices. . . ."

The Council of Ephesus (431), mentioned by Vatican II, condemned Nestorianism, which denied the real unity of the divine
and human natures in the Person of Jesus Christ; defined *Theotokos* ("Bearer of God") as the title of Mary, Mother of the Son
of God made man; and condemned Pelagianism, which reduced
the supernatural to the natural order of things.

In the city of Ephesus the faithful waited anxiously outside
the hall while the Council Fathers, one hundred fifty to two hundred bishops, deliberated inside regarding the role of Mary,
whether she could truly be accepted in faith as the Mother of God.
The concern involved faith in Jesus as the Son of God, the Word
made flesh, even more than it involved Mary, for Mary's role is
always in relationship to Jesus. When it was announced to the
people waiting outside that Mary must truly be believed to be the

Mother of God (Theotokos), the joy of the people was expressed in cheers, and dancing ensued on the streets of Ephesus.

While the person of Mary has been venerated in the Church from ancient times, the specific expression of this devotion in the form of her heart cannot be found before the thirteenth century. The first known considerations of the heart of Mary are found in the writings of St. Mechtilde of Hackeborn (1241-1298), St. Gertrude (1252-1302), Tauler (1361), St. Bernardine of Siena (1380-1444), Justus Landsberger (1539), and emphatically in the writings of St. Francis of Sales (1622).

After the sixteenth century, theologians and spiritual writers make ever-increasing mention of devotion to the heart of Mary. St. John Eudes (1601-1680) was renowned as a preacher and ascetic writer promoting the Sacred Heart of Jesus and the heart of Mary. This saint quoted twelve Jesuits whom he called "the twelve apostles of the divine heart of Mary." The most famous witnesses he mentioned are St. Peter Canisius, Suarez, Nierenberg, and Cornelius à Lapide.

St. John Eudes is credited with giving decisive impulse to the devotion to Mary's heart. Preaching popular missions, he spread the devotion in about twenty dioceses of France. He wrote a great work recognized to the present day, *The Admirable Heart of the Holy Mother of God*. He composed a Mass and an Office in honor of Mary's heart but never succeeded in obtaining from Rome the institution of a feast. That was to come as a universal feast long after his death when heaven itself would intervene in calling for devotion to the Immaculate Heart of God's Mother.

But it is St. Bernardine of Siena who is called the "Doctor of the Heart of Mary." In her heart he sees, symbolically, seven burning furnaces that give rise to seven flames which are the seven acts of love expressed in the seven "words" of Mary found in the Gospel.

The apparitions of the Sacred Heart of Jesus at Paray-le-Monial and early apostles of this devotion led to considerations of the heart of Mary. St. Margaret Mary, Blessed Claude de la Colombière, Bouzonié, and Croiset, all early apostles of devotion to the Sacred Heart of Jesus, were also devout clients of the heart of Mary.

In 1669, a Jesuit named Penamonti contributed to the

spread of devotion to Mary's heart in Italy by writing a book on the devotion.

Papal approval of a feast in honor of Mary's heart came gradually. In 1799, Pope Pius VI authorized a feast for the diocese of Palermo. In 1805, Pope Pius VII granted the same privilege to any diocese that asked for it, but the Office and Mass were to be the same as for Our Lady of the Snows. In 1855, just one year after defining the dogma of the Immaculate Conception, Pius XI approved a special Mass and Office in honor of Mary's heart. In 1944, Pope Pius XII established a feast for the universal Church under the title of the Immaculate Heart of Mary with a new Mass and new Office.

Another witness to the Immaculate Heart of Mary was St. Catherine Labouré, through whom the world was given the miraculous medal on November 27, 1830. The medal contains the images of the Sacred Heart of Jesus and the Immaculate Heart of Mary.

Shortly afterward a Father Desgenettes was assigned as pastor of the Church of Notre-Dame-des-Victoires and became completely discouraged by the lamentable condition of his parish. On December 3, 1836, feast of St. Francis Xavier, during the celebration of Mass, this priest thought he heard an inward voice which said twice: "Consecrate your parish to the most holy and Immaculate Heart of Mary." The priest hesitated a long time. Finally he obeyed the call and established a confraternity to honor the Immaculate Heart of Mary in a special way so as to obtain the conversion of sinners through her intercession.

The new association met with great success. Sinners began returning to Jesus Christ in great numbers. In a short time the parish was completely transformed and revitalized. Pope Gregory XI learned of it. He was struck by the marvelous result and raised the confraternity to the rank of an archconfraternity for the universal Church by 1838. Confraternities of the Immaculate Heart of Mary became affiliated with it, so by 1890 there were already more than 19,000, with 30,000 members. Everywhere they were founded, there could be recorded miracles of conversion. Pope Pius IX called the archconfraternity "a heavenly inspiration, a work of God, a source of blessings for the Church."

While our Lady did not mention her Immaculate Heart at Lourdes in 1854, she did make reference to her entire person, which devotion to the Immaculate Heart of Mary is about. To St. Bernadette Soubirous she said, "I AM THE IMMACULATE CONCEPTION." Witnesses to the Immaculate Heart of Mary have continued to multiply. What mighty witness the Church had given just four years before when it defined Mary's Immaculate Conception as a dogma of faith.

Early in this century the authenticated apparitions in the Cova da Iria to Jacinta, Francisco, and Lucia have given worldwide attention to the Immaculate Heart of Mary. On October 13, 1917, our Lady herself gave witness to 70,000 people gathered at the Cova in the parish of Fatima and to people for 35 miles around. Mary had announced on July 13, 1917: "God wishes to establish in the world devotion to my Immaculate Heart." During the same apparition she said, "In October I will tell you who I am and what I want and I will perform a miracle so that all may believe."

The miracle our Lady performed "so that all may believe" was the spinning of the sun in three phases. It appeared to many that the end of the world had arrived. I have personally interviewed people who were in the Cova da Iria on October 13, 1917, when our Lady performed a miracle at the time foretold months in advance. Atheists were converted on the spot. People who had come to mock left the Cova that day believing. The major newspaper of Portugal objectively reported the unexplainable phenomenon of the spinning of the sun. For the thousands who came to believe that God's Mother had actually appeared in the Cova, no explanation was necessary.

In the apparition of July when our Lady said that she would perform a miracle at noon, she mentioned her Immaculate Heart at least four times. The preceding month, June 13, 1917, our Lady had said that she would take Jacinta and Francico to heaven soon but that Lucia must remain upon earth for some time. "Jesus wishes to make use of you to make me known and loved. He wants to establish in the world devotion to my Immaculate Heart."

Lucia asked our Blessed Lady: "Must I stay here alone?" "No, my child. And would that make you suffer? Do not be disheartened.

"I will never leave you. My Immaculate Heart will be your refuge and the way that will lead you to God."

Sister Lucia has written that as our Lady said those words she opened her hands and communicated to the children a second time an immense light which enveloped her. "In this light," Sister Lucia wrote, "we could see ourselves submerged in God. Jacinta and Francisco seemed to be in the light which rose toward heaven, while I was in that which poured out over the earth. In front of the palm of our Lady's right hand there was a heart encircled with thorns which pierced it. We understood that it was the Immaculate Heart of Mary, outraged by the sins of humanity, and that she wanted reparation."

Lucia was in the light that "poured out over the earth." It represented that Lucia must remain in the world as a witness to devotion to the Immaculate Heart of Mary. Sister Lucia wrote that Jacinta was given a special grace, a special light to appreciate devotion to the Immaculate Heart. In writing and telling about the children's spiritual transformation and the role of the Immaculate Heart of Mary in bringing them into closer intimacy with the Most Blessed Trinity, Sister Lucia has been witnessing to the Immaculate Heart of Mary as she has by the life of reparation which she has lived.

Shortly before going to the hospital in Lisbon, Jacinta said to Lucia:

> It will not be long now before I go to heaven. You will remain here to announce that God wishes devotion to the Immaculate Heart to be established in the world. When you are to say that, do not hide yourself; tell everybody that God concedes us His graces through the Immaculate Heart of Mary; that people should invoke her, that the Heart of Jesus wishes the heart of Mary to be venerated at His side. Let them ask for peace through the Immaculate Heart of Mary, for God has given it to her. Ah! If only I could put into people's hearts the flame that is burning within my own heart and making me love the hearts of Jesus and Mary so much!

Our Lady communicated to the children a light in which they saw themselves submerged in God. What powerful witness to the meaning and purpose of the Immaculate Heart of Mary! Her mission in heaven is to lead us to God. The Second Vatican Council called us to imitate the virtues Mary lived perfectly during her life on earth. The Council Fathers also considered Mary's role in relation to us here and now, as so vividly demonstrated in the lives of the Fatima children:

> This motherhood of Mary in the order of grace continues uninterruptedly from the consent which she loyally gave at the Annunciation and which she sustained without wavering beneath the cross, until the eternal fulfillment of all the elect. Taken up to heaven she did not lay aside this saving office but by her manifold intercession continues to bring us the gifts of eternal salvation. By her maternal charity, she cares for the brethren of her Son, who still journey on earth surrounded by dangers and difficulties, until they are led into their blessed home.
>
> (*Dogmatic Constitution on the Church*, 62)

This chapter began by saying that the Church itself is the greatest witness to devotion to the Immaculate Heart of Mary. When the Vatican's Sacred Congregation of Rites (May 4, 1944) extended the Feast of the Immaculate Heart of Mary to the universal Church, it said: "By this cult the Church renders to the Immaculate Heart of the Blessed Virgin Mary the honor which is due to her, since, under the symbol of this Heart, she pays homage to her eminent holiness and particularly to her ardent love for God and her Son Jesus, and to her maternal love for men, redeemed by the Blood of God."

The Church, in giving witness to devotion to the Immaculate Heart of Mary, tells us to venerate not only Mary's love for God but her love for us. The Church desires to arouse our trust in Mary's powerful intercession. The formal object of devotion to Mary's Immaculate Heart is then the love she has for God, for her divine Son Jesus Christ, and for all her children in heaven and on earth.

We owe the Heart of Jesus to the heart of Mary. Her Immaculate Heart conceived Him first and then bore Him incarnate in her holy womb. Thereby we have the human Heart of Jesus Christ.

We owe the heart of Mary to the Heart of Jesus. The Heart of God, this is to say the entire Blessed Trinity, acted to give us the heart, the person, of Mary. The Father willed to send His Son made flesh into the world through Mary. The Holy Spirit overshadowed Mary and gave us the Son Incarnate. To give us a worthy first tabernacle for the Sacred Heart of Jesus, God gave us the Immaculate Heart of Mary. This is why God asks that both these hearts be held together in our love.

It was a natural conclusion, then, in choosing St. Margaret Mary to make devotion to the Sacred Heart of Jesus better known, that God would also point to the heart of His all-holy and pure Mother.

Jesus himself instructed St. Margaret Mary to make His Sacred Heart and the Immaculate Heart of His Mother the double object of her homage and devotion. In showing the saint her own heart between His Sacred Heart and that of His Mother, Jesus said: "Thus it is that My pure love unites these three hearts forever."

In 1684 during Advent, St. Margaret Mary recommended to her novices the following practices:

> You will offer five times to the Eternal Father the sacrifices which the Sacred Heart of His Divine Son offers Him by Its ardent charity on the altar of the Heart of His Mother, asking of Him that all hearts may return to Him and devote themselves to His love. You will make this aspiration as often as possible: "I adore and love You, O Divine Heart of Jesus living in the Heart of Mary; I conjure You to live and reign in all hearts, and to consume them in Your pure love."

St. Margaret Mary repeatedly urged Father Croiset to place in his book on Devotion to the Sacred Heart the Litany of the Most Pure Heart of Mary.

Blessed Claude de la Colombière, spiritual director to St. Margaret Mary, ended one of the meditations in his retreat journal with this prayer:

> O Hearts, really deserving to possess all hearts, to rule over all hearts of angels and of men! You will henceforth be my rule, and in similar situations, I shall try to make Your sentiments my own. It is my will that henceforth my heart should only be in the Hearts of Jesus and Mary, or that the Hearts of Jesus and of Mary should be in mine, that they may impart to it their feelings, and that it be only moved in conformity with the impressions which it receives from these Hearts.

Father Croiset, who had a profound spiritual relationship with St. Margaret Mary, said that devotion to the heart of Mary was the most efficacious means of arriving at the love of Jesus. He wrote:

For the sacred Hearts of Jesus and Mary are too much alike
and too much united for one to have access to the one and not to
the other, with this difference, however, that the Heart of Jesus
admits only extremely pure souls, and the Heart of Mary
purifies, by the graces which she obtains for them, those that
are not pure, and enables them to be received in the Heart of
Jesus!

St. Louis-Marie Grignon de Monfort (1673-1716) never wrote
of the Immaculate Heart of Mary precisely, but it is his manner
of consecration to Mary which has become understood as a most
fitting form of total consecration to her Immaculate Heart. No
modern essay on witnesses to the Immaculate Heart of Mary
would be complete without some mention of this great apostle of
Mary. His great work explaining total consecration is titled *True
Devotion to the Blessed Virgin Mary*. Popes and theologians
in one generation after another have called this book a classic.

St. Louis de Montfort foresaw that the devil would not want
his *True Devotion* to become known and lived. For more than
one hundred twenty-five years his book was lost to the world. This
is what the saint had written of the book. "I clearly foresee that
raging brutes will come in fury to tear with their diabolical teeth
this little writing and him whom the Holy Spirit has made use of
to write it; or at least to envelop it in the silence of a coffer, in order that it may not appear."

St. Louis de Montfort died in 1716, and his work on *True Devotion* was not found until 1842, seemingly by accident, by one of
the priests of his congregation of St. Laurent-sur-Sèvre.

The message of St. Louis de Montfort was to consecrate everything to Jesus through Mary. This means our property, our
prayers, good works, family, everything is given to Mary to do
with as her immaculate will desires. Another chapter of this book
will explain in greater detail the consecration to Mary's Immaculate Heart.

A modern witness of devotion to our Blessed Mother is found
in the life of the stigmatist Padre Pio da Pietrelcina, the Capu-
chin priest who died in 1968 after having borne the bleeding
wounds of Christ and their pain for just over fifty years. While
much has been written about Padre Pio, there are few of his personal writings in publication.

Quoted below are some excerpts from his meditation on Mary Immaculate.

Eternal Love, Spirit of Light and Truth, make a way into my poor mind and allow me to penetrate, as far as it is possible to a wretched creature like myself, into that abyss of grace, of purity, and of holiness, that I may acquire a love of God that is continually renewed, a love of God who from all eternity planned the greatest of all the masterpieces created by His hands: the Immaculate Virgin Mary.

From all eternity Almighty God took delight in what was to be the most perfect work of His hands, and anticipated this wonderful plan with an outpouring of His grace. . . .

Protected by grace by Him who was to be the Savior of mankind that had fallen into sin, she escaped all shadow of evil. She sprang from the mind of God as a pure ray of light, and will shine like a morning star over the human race that turns to her. She will be the sure guide who will direct our steps toward the Divine Sun which is Jesus Christ. . . .

Clothed in light from the moment of her conception, she grew in grace and comeliness. After Almighty God, she is the most perfect of creatures; more pure than the angels; God is indeed well pleased in her, since she most resembles Him and is the only worthy repository of His secrets. . . .

She loved and served Him in the most perfect manner as He never until then had been loved and served on this earth.

The Holy Spirit poured His love into her; she was the only creature worthy or capable of receiving this love in unlimited measure because no other had sufficient purity to come so near to God; and being near to Him, could know and love Him ever more. She was the only creature capable of containing the stream of love which poured into her from on high. She alone was worthy to return to Him from whom came that love. This very love prepared her for that "Fiat" which delivered the world from the tyranny of the infernal enemy and overshadowed her, the purest of doves, making her pregnant with the Son of God . . . .

Dear Mother, make me love Him! Pour into my heart that love that burned in yours for Him.

Padre Pio touched the souls of millions with his holiness and his great devotion to the Mother of God. He was sometimes referred to as a living crucifix. The perfume from his wounds was experienced throughout the chapel as he offered the holy Mass. To participate in the Eucharistic Sacrifice offered by Padre Pio was to be reminded vividly that the Sacrifice of the Mass perpetuates the Sacrifice of the Cross.

There is another man, deeply devoted to the Immaculate Heart of Mary, who is still living at this writing and bears in his body the wound marks of Jesus Christ. His name is Father Gino Burresi, O.V.M., the stigmatist of San Vittorino in Italy. This stigmatist has been investigated by the Vatican more than once. The Church never makes a judgment on the supernatural character of the happenings to a person who is still living. Such was the case with Padre Pio. Such is the case with Father Gino. The Vatican, however, found nothing in connection with Father Gino that needed suppression, authorizing his ordination to the holy priesthood on May 8, 1983.

When I asked permission to write the first full-length book on the life of Father Gino, the authorities who govern the Oblates of the Virgin Mary, the community to which this stigmatist belongs, wanted to know why. The answer that most impressed them was this: "Father Gino appears to be living his consecration to Mary's Immaculate Heart. I should like to demonstrate for readers what can happen to their lives, too, if they consecrate themselves well to the Immaculate Heart of Mary and live that consecration." I was finally permitted to write the book.*

Father Gino constantly witnesses to the Immaculate Heart of Mary. He has been instrumental in having a major sanctuary dedicated to Our Lady of Fatima built at San Vittorino, about twenty miles from central Rome. There pilgrims come from throughout the world, especially Italy. When I asked the stigmatist, "What do you make of all the conversions and healings which reportedly are taking place here at San Vittorino?" the answer came, "I think that the Finger of God is here and that there is the real presence of our Lady."

The mission Father Gino feels compelled to carry out seems closely related to the Virgin's Immaculate Heart as he attempts to imitate Jesus Christ. Mention of the Madonna seems constantly on his lips, but always in relationship to Jesus Christ. This

---

Call of Heaven, Father Gino Stigmatist by Father Robert J. Fox. Christendom Publications, Route 3, Box 87, Front Royal, Virginia 22630.

stigmatist, an excellent painter, once painted a picture for me of the Madonna with the Rosary. He named it "Mother of Sweetness." He explained that he painted the particular picture to inspire the priest to share the sweetness of Our Mother's Immaculate Heart with young people. "The sweetness of her face and the tenderness with which she holds the beads tell that Mary, our Mother, will reveal the sweetness of her Immaculate Heart to those who meditate on the mysteries of her Son in the Rosary."

It is to the Rosary and the Holy Eucharist, to Jesus through Mary, that Father Gino directs youth — all people, for that matter — in the mission he considers heaven has given him on earth. Emphasizing the Immaculate Heart of Mary, the spirituality of Father Gino of San Vittorino also directs souls to unqualified loyalty to the Pope. He takes delight in papal teachings that picture Mary praying the Rosary with us. Father Gino's doctors have described to me the seeming death, stopping the heart of Father Gino, during the three hours each Good Friday.

Father Gino appears to understand the Marian needs of these times as he witnesses to the Immaculate Heart and what it means. He has agreed to serve as a spiritual father in suffering for the Fatima Youth Apostolate, the Cadets of Our Lady of Fatima, for which I am national spiritual director. To youth, the stigmatist has written:

> Through Father Fox, I came to know about your group, so full of good will and wishing to honor the Immaculate Heart of Mary.
>
> Very good, dear young people, take courage in this hour which is particularly difficult for the whole world, tormented as it is by the spirit of materialism.
>
> Let us try to be really devoted to the Blessed Mother, being first in authentically living her great message of salvation and peace. Let us try also to be ahead of all others in taking up the sweet chain of the Rosary that Mary recommended so many times, along with the frequent reception of the Sacraments, both offered for our personal salvation and that of others.
>
> A true devoted son of the Blessed Mother cannot neglect the Holy Eucharist; on the contrary, he should, each day, unite himself with Jesus Christ in this great Sacrament of love.
>
> May the Blessed Mother be your guide forever, in order that you might be the true light able to illuminate constantly this poor earth, so enveloped in darkness.

Let us pray and offer our Communions, our Rosaries, and all our sacrifices so that the Immaculate Heart of Mary may save many of our brothers, victims of the horrible plague of sin, and so that she may finally obtain for the whole world the peace we desire so much, peace in the heart of every man, and peace in each corner of the earth.

I would be delighted to see your group increase in number and produce much good fruit, especially among the youngsters who are slaves of sin, forgetting that sin is really the cause of all evils, physical and moral, because sin always inclines toward hatred and separation, therefore ever pushing peace away.

While multiple witnesses to the Immaculate Heart of Mary could be presented in this chapter, we select one final and chief witness, Pope John Paul II. His witness is constant. We select as a sample the words this Marian Pope spoke in front of Our Lady of the Rosary Basilica in Pompeii, reminding those present that the Annunciation was the beginning of Christ's mission:

The mission of this Son, the eternal Word, begins, then, when Mary of Nazareth, a "virgin betrothed to a man whose name was Joseph, of the house of David" (Luke 1:37), on hearing these words of Gabriel, answers: "Behold, I am the handmaid of the Lord; let it be done to me according to your word" (Luke 1:38). The Son's mission on earth begins at that moment. The Word of the same substance as the Father becomes flesh in the Virgin's womb. . . .

The mission of the Son in the Holy Spirit begins. The mission of the Son and the mission of the Holy Spirit begin. In this first stage the mission is directed to her alone: to the Virgin of Nazareth. The Holy Spirit descends first on her. In her human and virginal substance, she is overshadowed by the power of the Most High. Thanks to this power, and because of the Holy Spirit, she becomes the Mother of the Son of God, though remaining a Virgin. The Son's mission begins in her, under her heart. The mission of the Holy Spirit, who "proceeds from the Father and from the Son," arrives first, too, at her, at the soul that is His Bride, the most pure and the most sensitive. . . .

The Church is missionary entirely and everywhere because this mission of the Son and of the Holy Spirit, which had its historical beginning on earth precisely at Nazareth, in the Virgin's heart, remains continually in her.

This beloved Pope has said further of Mary that the mission of the two Persons of the Most Blessed Trinity "remains continually in her." Mary is always at the very center of our prayer. She is the first among those who ask. She is the "*Omnipotentia sup-plex* (the Omnipotence of intercession)."

Pope John Paul II as a young priest, then as a bishop, finally as Pope, has had for his motto "Totus Tuus" (Totally Yours). In their fullest expression, these two words which summarize the Pope's motto are expanded:

I AM ALL YOURS AND ALL THAT I HAVE IS YOURS, O MOST LOVING JESUS, THROUGH MARY, YOUR HOLY MOTHER.

CHAPTER 6

† Heart Full of Grace †

"HAIL MARY, full of grace." Considering Mary "full of grace" is recognizing her total openness to the action of the Holy Spirit within her. The title recognizes the perfect union of her will with the will of God.

Mary is herself a member of the Church. Our Mother was redeemed. The fullness of grace in Mary has its Source in Jesus Christ. Mary was perfectly obedient to the Father. This grace was merited for her by her Son, Jesus Christ. Jesus Christ is God-man, and the human nature of Jesus was perfectly obedient to His Father. Although the obedience, the perfect conformity of will in Mary with the will of the Father, precedes in time that of her incarnate Son, yet within the Blessed Trinity there is no such thing as time. This fullness of grace in Mary, so full that she is conceived immaculate, is dependent on the infinite merits of Jesus Christ.

In giving us the Immaculate Heart of His Mother, God gives us a model for all members of the Church. Hers is a heart full of grace from the moment it was created, and yet it grew in grace. We may not look at the fullness of grace in Mary as a quantity. If we consider grace in Mary quantitatively, we place a limit on her capacity to grow; Mary's grace is rather a quality, a participation in God's own divine life from the first moment of her creation, and a brilliance of her being that increased in beauty and luster.

What is holiness? Essentially holiness is the possession of sanctifying grace. It is made present in a person from the moment of baptism, making one resemble God. This is why the New Testament speaks of the faithful as "saints." We grow in holiness by doing the will of God once His sanctifying grace is implanted in our souls at baptism. Then everything done for the love of God makes one grow in grace. An increase of grace is achieved by every good work, every prayer, every loving act. The soul grows in sanctifying grace (holiness) especially by the reception of the sacraments and participation in the holy Sacrifice of the Mass.

Not all grow equally in grace when supernaturally motivated by good works, prayers, or reception of the sacraments. Those better disposed grow in grace more abundantly. Better disposition comes from the will. There is greater love in some individuals because the faculty of the will is more closely united to the will of God. There is a purer motive in some than in others.

> . . . [Jesus] sat down opposite the treasury, and watched the multitude putting money into the treasury. Many rich people put in large sums. And a poor widow came, and put in two copper coins, which make a penny. And he called his disciples to him, and said to them, "Truly, I say to you, this poor woman has put in more than all those who are contributing to the treasury. For they all contributed out of their abundance; but she out of her poverty has put in everything she had, her whole living."
>
> (Mk 12:41-44)

Jesus was God. Whatever Jesus did came from His divine Person, the second Person of the Most Blessed Trinity, and therefore had an infinite value. In strict justice, it was not necessary that Jesus suffer and die on the cross for our salvation. One drop of His precious blood would have been more than enough to redeem a million worlds. But in His providence God willed that His incarnate Son should shed the last drop of His sacred, precious blood for our salvation.

In this way God demonstrated His great love for us. In this way Jesus expressed the greatness of His love for the Father and for the brothers and sisters He came to save. It was the will of God the Father that Jesus die on the cross. As the obedient Servant, He gave up His life to death on the cross. This also demonstrated the malice of sin, while it revealed the beauty of a human will perfectly joined to the divine will.

> All that the Father gives me will come to me; and him who comes to me I will not cast down. For I have come down from heaven, not to do my own will, but the will of him who sent me. . . . (Jn 6:38)

> Greater love has no man than this, that a man lay down his life for his friends. (Jn 15:13)

> For God so loved the world that he gave his only Son, that
> whoever believes in him should not perish but have eternal life.
> (Jn 3:16)

Now in Jesus Christ there are two natures, one human, one divine. But there is only one Person, the second Person of the Most Blessed Trinity. Jesus is not merely a man in whom God dwells; He is God the Son become man. Jesus has a human body, a human soul. Therefore He has a human intellect by which He knows, and a human will by which He loves. At the same time, to this human body and soul of Jesus is joined in one substance the eternal Son of God. It is a deep mystery, of course. It is something we must fully accept in faith if we are to be true Christians. The divine Person of the Son of God has taken a human body from Mary. His human soul was created by God the Father.

Hypostatic union is the term the Church has used to help express our beautiful faith in the Word made flesh, Jesus Christ, of whom Mary is Mother. The Council of Chalcedon (A.D. 451) declared that the two natures of Jesus Christ are joined "in one person and one hypostasis." (Hypostasis means whole substance.)

This Jesus, true God and true man, is the One born of Mary after she was overshadowed by the Holy Spirit. It is this Jesus who came to save us, to give us grace. Always, we must remember that sanctifying grace is a quality of the soul that gives us a share in the life of God. Jesus said, "I came that they may have life, and have it abundantly" (Jn 10:10).

The life that Jesus came to give all mankind, that He gave His Mother "abundantly" from the first instant of her creation, was not human life. Mankind had natural human life before the coming of Christ. Jesus is speaking of supernatural life, a life above the nature of men. Such is grace. Such is a sharing in the very life of God.

Consider the levels of creation: mineral, plant, animal, man, angel, God. In each case one kind is supernatural, or above the nature of the life or creature below it. There is not an equality of steps. For God to have become man was a greater condescension than it would be for a man to become a snake or an insect. The step between man or angel and their God is infinite. And yet, in the case of the angels who passed their test, or of baptized man in the process of passing his test by living in sanctifying grace, there is a real participation in the divine life. We share in the life of God.

Multiple quotations could be drawn from Scripture to remind us of the meaning of grace that Jesus Christ came to give more abundantly.

In him was life, and the life was the light of men. (Jn 1:4)

He who believes in the Son has eternal life; he who does not obey the Son shall not see life, but the wrath of God rests upon him. (Jn 3:36)

Truly, truly, I say to you, he who hears my word and believes him who sent me, has eternal life.'' (Jn 5:24)

I am the bread of life. (Jn 6:35)

He who eats my flesh and drinks my blood has eternal life, and I will raise him up at the last day. . . . As the living Father sent me, and I live because of the Father, so he who eats me will live because of me. (Jn 6:54-57)

But these are written that you may believe that Jesus is the Christ, the Son of God, and that believing you may have life in his name. (Jn 20:31)

When we speak of sanctifying grace in the soul, we speak of something so magnificent we scarcely realize what we say. All comparisons would fail, for when one is speaking of the spiritual life every example limps.

Good angels possess the grace of God too. The angel of peace, the angel of the Holy Eucharist, who appeared to the three Fatima children in 1916, was described by Sister Lucia with these words:

"We saw . . . a light whiter than snow, revealing the form of a young man, transparent and much brighter than crystal pierced by the rays of the sun."

Sister Lucia described our Lady in these words: "A beautiful lady dressed in white, poised over a holm-oak sapling very near us. She was more brilliant than the sun, radiating a sparkling light. . . . We were so near that we were bathed in the light that radiated from her person to a distance of about three feet." While pronouncing the words, "the grace of God," Sister Lucia writes, "Our Lady opened her hands for the first time, shedding on us a light so intense that it seemed as a reflection glancing from her hands and penetrating to the inmost recesses of our hearts, making us see ourselves in God, who was that Light, more clearly than we could see ourselves in a mirror."

During our Lady's entire life on earth, she continued to grow in grace. Her share in the life of God continuously increased. "Fullness" of grace in Mary then was not absolute but relative, indicating an overwhelming abundance of supernatural endowment, proportionate to her calling to become the Mother of God. Mary was predestined to be worthy of this, and the initial fullness of grace was given as a fitting preparation from the first moment of her existence.

Since the sixteenth century, theologians have considered a comparison between our Lady's grace and that of other creatures. In summary, this is what they have said: 1) Our Lady's first grace received at the moment of her conception was greater than the initial grace of any saint or angel. 2) That first grace was greater than the *final* grace of any saint or angel taken separately. 3) Our Lady's initial grace was greater than the initial grace of all the saints and angels taken collectively. 4) Her initial grace was greater than the *final* grace of all the saints and angels taken collectively.

Support for such views is seen in the papal bull *Ineffabilis Deus*, wherein Pope Pius IX defined the dogma of the Immaculate Conception of Mary:

> From the beginning and before the ages God chose and appointed a Mother for His only-begotten Son . . . and on her He showered so much love, in preference to all other creatures, that only in her case was He pleased with a most loving complacency. He, therefore, enriched her with an abundance of all heavenly gifts drawn from the treasury of the divinity, far more than all the angelic spirits and all the saints, in such a wonderful manner that she . . . all beautiful and perfect, might display a fullness of holiness greater than which none is at all conceivable under God, and which no one, with the exception of God, can even grasp.

This must be kept in mind. All this grace, which we cannot comprehend or imagine, is due to Mary's unique dignity in having been chosen to be the Mother of God. In no way does such beauty and magnificence of grace detract from Jesus Christ. It adds to Him. Jesus is her Redeemer too. Jesus is the Source of Mary's grace too. Her special grace adds dignity to the entire Church.

St. Louis de Montfort was conscious of the incomprehensible infinity of God when he began his great treatise *True Devotion to the Blessed Virgin* with these words:

> I behold, with the entire Church, that, in comparison with the infinite majesy of the Most High God, Mary is no more than a mere creature formed by His hand; that, in the light of such a comparison, she is less than an atom — nay more, that she is nothing, since only He Who Is has existence as of himself. Consequently, this great Lord, eternally independent and sufficient unto himself, had absolutely no need — and still has no need — of the Blessed Virgin for the fulfillment of His designs and for the manifestation of His glory. He has merely to wish, and all is fulfilled.

In Jesus Christ, always, it is God we are encountering, God become man. In Mary we encounter the one God used to become man so that we might become like God, sharing His divine life. Mary is entirely created in her person. The Person of Christ, uncreated, is the eternal Word. "In him was life, and the life was the light of men" (Jn 1:4). Just before that, the apostle wrote under divine inspiration that "all things were made through him, and without him was not anything made that was made" (Jn 1:3). Mary, coming into being in fullness of grace, immaculately conceived, came into being in Him. Jesus later said: "I am the way, and the truth, and the life; no one comes to the Father, but by me" (Jn 14:6). "I am the vine, you are the branches. He who abides in me, and I in him, he it is that bears much fruit, for apart from me you can do nothing" (Jn 15:5).

All these words of Christ apply to Mary, as a member of the Church fully redeemed in an eminent way. She who is full of grace, perfectly attuned to the will of God as is needful for great holiness, goes to the Father through Jesus Christ. Mary too lives in Jesus. Without Jesus, Mary can do nothing.

In the eternal counsels of the Blessed Trinity, God deigned to become man, as He had in mind from eternity. He always knew Jesus Christ. What unfolds for us in time is always in the eternal mind of God. In seeing Jesus, the Word made flesh, everlastingly, God saw the woman by whom He would accomplish the incarnation! "All things were made through him. . ." (Jn 1:3).

Each member of the Church in grace is so not because he first loved God but because God first loved him. "God is love, and

he who abides in love abides in God, and God abides in him. . . .
We love, because he first loved us" (1 John 4:16, 19). In comparison to Mary, the grace we have is meager, although the least
amount of grace is worth more in the sight of God on the supernatural level than the whole created universe.

God first loves us. If we respond in faith to His love, we grow
in grace. That grace first given children in baptism is entirely out
of the goodness of God's heart, with no act of faith or response on
their part. The same was true of Mary in an eminent way. Mary
did not merit her Immaculate Conception. God saw in this woman
one He deigned worthy to be His Mother and one He loved more
than all angels and saints collectively — much as a good husband
and father loves his bride, the mother of his children, more than
all of his children taken together. Although a father loves each of
his children, he loves their mother more than all of them.

The grace in our souls is in proportion to the love God has for
us. To those whom God loves more, He gives more. God has loved
His Mother more than all of creation, natural and supernatural.
This is why Mary is called God's masterpiece. He has given this
woman a dignity worthy of His Mother, with more grace than all
saints and angels taken together.

This is what God presents to us in the Immaculate Heart of
His Mother — the person of Mary in Christ, without whom she can
do nothing. Through grace, as St. Paul says, "I can do all things in
him who strengthens me" (Phil 4:13). What great things can
Mary do with the fullness of grace that grew every moment in
her. Her will was never anything but perfectly in line with the
divine will whose every thought, word, and act was performed in
love.

What growth of grace took place in Mary at the Annunciation! The time of the Annunciation was pivotal in the history of
salvation. Mankind was in the balance, and Mary spoke for humanity on whether it would accept its Savior. Admittedly God
could have done it in another way; absolutely speaking, God did
not need Mary. God chose to use her Immaculate Heart to accept
the Savior in freely agreeing to become the Mother of the Most
High, the Word incarnate, the Messiah, the long-awaited One.

St. Bernard speaks glowingly and poetically of this moment
when the whole world awaits Mary's reply:

You have heard, O Virgin, that you will conceive and bear a son; you have heard that it will not be by man but by the Holy Spirit. The angel awaits an answer; it is time for him to return to God who sent him. We too are waiting, O Lady, for your word of compassion; the sentence of condemnation weighs heavily upon us.

The price of our salvation is offered to you. We shall be set free at once if you consent. In the eternal Word of God we all came to be, and behold, we die. In your brief response we are to be remade in order to be recalled to life.

Tearful Adam with his sorrowing family begs this of you, O loving Virgin, in their exile from Paradise. Abraham begs it, David begs it. All the other holy patriarchs, your ancestors, ask it of you, as they dwell in the country of the shadow of death. This is what the whole earth waits for, prostrate at your feet. It is right in doing so, for on your word depends comfort for the wretched, ransom for the captive, freedom for the condemned, indeed, salvation for all the sons of Adam, the whole of your race.

Answer quickly, O Virgin. Reply in haste to the angel, or rather through the angel of the Lord. Answer with a word, receive the Word of God. Speak your own word, conceive the divine Word. Breathe a passing word, embrace the eternal Word.

Why do you delay, why are you afraid? Believe, give praise, and receive. Let humility be bold, let modesty be confident. This is no time for virginal simplicity to forget prudence. In this matter alone, O prudent Virgin, do not fear to be presumptuous. Though modest silence is pleasing, dutiful speech is now more necessary. Open your heart to faith, O blessed Virgin, your lips to praise, your womb to the Creator. See, the desired of all nations is at your door, knocking to enter. If He should pass by because of your delay, in sorrow you would begin to seek Him afresh, the One whom your soul loves. Arise, hasten, open. Arise in faith, hasten in devotion, open in praise and thanksgiving. "Behold the handmaid of the Lord," she says, "be it done to me according to your word." (Hom. 4, 8-9: *Opera omnia*, Edit. Cisterc. 4, 1966, 53-54)*

In fact, there was no hesitancy or deliberation on the part of Mary whether to do the will of God. Her will from the moment of her immaculate conception was always one with God's. Any delay was only necessitated by the need for Mary to learn fully the will of God on her behalf. What St. Bernard poetically envisions

*Liturgy of the Hours, Roman Rite, Dec. 20.

on the part of Mary while the angel and world await her answer is more appropriately applied to failings of God's people before Jesus came, to the members of the Church, less perfect than Mary, at times hesitant to do God's will. Mary in fact is the archetype of the Church, the paradigm of the perfect disciple. Mary is being asked to be Mother of the Church. Becoming Mother, she will also be the perfect member, already fully redeemed.

Mary says "Yes." The increase of grace in the soul of Mary when she answers "Yes" for the whole world is unimaginable. The fact that God in His loving providence looked to the free consent of Mary for the Word to be made flesh and dwell among us, gives a Marian quality to every aspect of Christianity.

The moment of Mary's "Yes" was the moment of the Incarnation. Had there been, in divine providence, no Annunciation, there would be no Incarnation, no Redemption on Good Friday, no Easter Sunday, no Ascension and Descent of the Holy Spirit. This is why every aspect of Christianity bears a Marian quality, because in Mary is climaxed the thousands of years of preparation after the fall of the first Eve for this New Eve to say "Yes." At the same time, the greatness of this New Eve stems from the grace of her Son, as God is not bound down by space and time. At the moment of her immaculate conception, Mary received prevenient grace, merited by the redemption of her Son.

Mary is God's greatest gift to the Church, of which Christ is the Head and Source of all grace. We might say Jesus Christ himself is God's greatest Gift to the World, and that is true. The Church is the Mystical Body of Christ. The Church in all is an extension of Christ in all its baptized members. By faith, grace, the indelible character of Christ, baptism brings together, with all the moral and theological virtues, the fruits and gifts of the Holy Spirit, the members of the Church into one.

Christ is the Head of the Mystical Body, the Church. Mary is member and Mother. Mary is not outside the Church, but she is the only one fully redeemed at the exact moment of her creation. Her heart is immaculate. Still, her heart will grow in all the virtues and gifts God bestows upon the human person incorporated into Jesus. Every other created person after Adam and Eve had to await the time of redemption. Mary did not wait a moment. The moment of her first existence in time was the moment of her redemption. Therefore, in virtue of Jesus Christ, Mary is the greatest gift to the Church. The Church was given a Mother so it might have Life.

We have considered the increase of grace in Mary's soul when she responded affirmatively for the human race at the Incarnation. There was then the carrying of the Word made flesh in her holy womb for nine months. She became the world's first tabernacle for the Word Incarnate. Today in the tabernacles of our churches, He is present in the Most Blessed Sacrament. When we receive Jesus in Holy Communion, His body, blood, soul and divinity, we receive an increase of grace according to the dispositions of our soul. Where there is greater faith and love, a greater openness to the Holy Spirit, the coming of Jesus into us at the time of Holy Communion brings with it a greater growth in grace as a result. Mary's perfect faith and openness to the Holy Spirit not only brought the Real Presence of the Word made flesh, but as she carried Him under her heart she continuously grew in grace.

The Scriptures tell us that at the judgment our reward will correspond to how well we served Christ in our least brethren when they were hungry, thirsty, in need of clothing, etc. (Mt 25:31-46). Grace grew in Mary as she nursed the infant Jesus, tended to His growing needs, served Him at table, performed domestic duties. In a human way, she taught Jesus as any good mother teaches her child. Jesus grew in human experiential knowledge, as theologians like to call it lately. (Much can be said for St. Joseph in this regard too.) The angel came to give Jesus human comfort in the garden the night of His agony. Mary was surely a source of comfort to Him, tender beyond telling, during the years of His maturing and the years of His public ministry.

Who would say that Mary completely withdrew from the life of Jesus once she had advanced His hour at the wedding feast of Cana "and his disciples believed in him"! During the approximately three years of His public ministry, Mary was there, not in the foreground by any means, but there, believing, loving. Jesus could know that if many rejected Him, refused to put faith in Him, there was always one who believed most perfectly, that model of everything the Church would ever become that He came to earth to found.

The Scriptures mention an occasion when Mary and relatives of Jesus stood outside the house where He was teaching (see Mk 3:31-35). Mary had become His Mother because the Father had made her heart so immaculate, one with the will of God. Jesus used the occasion to teach that we all may become His Mother by doing the will of God, by receiving the Word into our hearts in faith and love.

Mary was with Jesus to the end as He hung dying on the cross, redeeming the world. As grace was merited for all the world, abundant grace flowed into her Immaculate Heart during those hours beneath the cross of redemption. It was the will of the Father that His only begotton Son die on the cross for love of mankind. He died for Mary too. He died for the Church's greatest gift, a Mother full of grace, full of faith, full of love.

The angels in countless numbers were in awe at Jesus' dying on the cross. "For to what angel did God ever say, 'Thou art my Son, today I have begotten thee'? Or again, 'I will be to him a father, and he shall be to me a son'? And again, when he brings the first-born into the world, he says, 'Let all God's angels worship him' " (Heb 1:5-6). The angels had been given no second chance. God had not become an angel, who is higher in nature than man. God not only became man but then died for man. The good angels are in total awe and adoration at this mercy of God. The man on the cross is their King. The woman beneath the cross is their Queen. The grace in the millions of angels does not equal the degree of grace in the Immaculate Heart of God's Mother.

Jesus, in His perfect obedience to the Father, even to death, made it possible for all of us to be inserted into His life so that His life of justice becomes that of the members of His Mystical Body; first of all, most perfectly of all, of His Mother and our spiritual Mother, Mary. This quality of perfect obedience in Christ is seen by God the Father as belonging to humanity since His Son became man. In Mary God sees its perfection in a member of the human race who is not hypostatically one with the divine nature but wholly created.

In Mary, then, we see our greatest glory before God for a member of the human race, a descendant of Adam and Eve, who is not, as Christ is, one substance with the Father. "I and the Father are one" (Jn 10:30). The eternal life which God poured into the heart of Mary was given by Jesus Christ. When Mary assists in the distribution of graces, she is not giving them from herself but from Jesus Christ.

The Second Vatican Council recognized Mary's title as Mediatrix of Grace. This intercessory power of Mary that grace may be granted to her spiritual children in no way enhances the value of Christ's redemptive acts or His role as the Mediator between God and men. It means that graces are granted by God to all men from Christ in union with Mary's intercession. Her Immaculate Heart acts in union with the Sacred Heart of her Son. The grace that has its source in Jesus is most perfectly received in Mary in her role as member and Mother of the Church. Her heart wills that it be granted and shared with all members of the Church.

Christ's own divine life is shared with us. Mary mediates redemptive graces through her perfect prayers, through the love of her Immaculate Heart for God, for Her Son, for all the other members of the Church. Through baptism, Christ shares His divine life with us, incorporating us into himself in union with all other believers in grace, His Mother the first among them.

Mary does perfectly in her heart what each of us is called to do. We too are called to be intercessors — always in, with, through Jesus Christ, the one essential Mediator, the one Source of all grace. Mary mediated when she answered "Yes" to the angel. It was the sign of her perfect receptivity to grace. That was Mary's first mediation for all of humanity, associating her with the Redemption.

Mary's entire life was one constant receptivity to grace. As already shown, it was ever growing. Mary's involvement with the distribution of the graces of Jesus Christ is not restricted to the moment of her "Yes" at the Annunciation. Mary's role is ongoing. It is constant. It is universal. It is now. She is always our Mother in time and in eternity. "Pray for us now and at the hour of our death."

The mediation of Mary, asking for the dispensations of graces, is of the highest degree. It is not a different kind from that of every Christian, but it is the greatest, for she is the closest to Christ. She is the Mother of the God-man, the Mediator. She is the greatest in grace. Her love is greatest of all. Her power of intercession is the most influential of all.

Such is the glory of the Immaculate Heart of Mary for God and for our happiness.

Mary grew in grace after the Ascension of Christ by the reception of her divine incarnate Son in Holy Communion. After the redemptive acts of the Cross, the Apostle John took her into his own home (see Jn 19:27). We may be sure that our Blessed Lady received the Holy Eucharist frequently, even daily, as was the practice of the early Christians (see Acts 2:46). She lived with John the priest, the beloved disciple.

Since baptism incorporates one into the Church, we may believe Mary received it, not to deliver her from original sin but to mark her with the special sign of Christ, the sacrament's indelible character. As for confirmation, which grants another indelible mark of Christ and outpouring of the Holy Spirit, this is what happened in the life of Mary in a more eminent manner. Her soul was flooded with the plenitude of the Holy Spirit and His gifts on Pentecost (see Acts 1:14). The Holy Spirit came upon Mary when she conceived the Christ Child. Now that the Church is to be identified as Christ's Body, with the Holy Spirit as its Soul, this Spirit of Love descended upon all in the upper room and found a special temple adorned for His presence in Mary's heart.

"And there appeared to them tongues as of fire, distributed and resting on each of them. And they were all filled with the Holy Spirit" (Acts 2:3-4).

From all eternity, in Christ, God had singled Mary out. God's Son, sent as man to redeem mankind made in God's own image and likeness, would achieve His greatest accomplishment in the woman who was to be His Mother. She would be associated with Him in His work of redemption as every Christian must be, but Mary would be most fully redeemed, full of grace, more radiant in beauty than all the rest of the Church.

Such magnificent beauty, such radiant brightness of the light of life, we see in Mary's Immaculate Heart.

CHAPTER 7

† The Immaculate Heart and the Interior Life †

THERE IS nothing greater we can ask of the Mother of the incarnate Word than that she form Jesus within us by communicating to us her faith and love. That is what the Christian life is about, having Christ formed in us, making Him live within us. "My little children, with whom I am again in travail until Christ be formed in you!"(Gal 4:19). Whom better could we call upon to assist us in having Christ formed within us than Mary, in whom Christ was first formed most perfectly?

The call to devotion to the Immaculate Heart of Mary is a call to live a rich interior life modeled after the faith and love of Mary. It is a call to have Christ formed in us as He was in His Blessed Mother. Again it must be remembered, as the Fathers of the first centuries knew so well, that it was not her physical motherhood that made Mary so great, but her first bearing the Word by faith and love.

It was through Mary that the incarnate Word became a member of our human race. To become man, the Word did not have to be born of Mary. God could have created for the Second Person of the Blessed Trinity a humanity like that of Adam on the day the first man was created. In that way, Christ Jesus could have been fully human, but He would not really have been of our race. In joining himself directly to us by a human birth to Mary, the Word Incarnate became our very brother.

In effect, God said to our human race, through Mary, "Give Me your human nature and I in return will give you a share in My divine nature." The plan of God was to give the divine nature in its fullness to the humanity of Jesus Christ so that we could draw from this fullness. "And from his fulness have we all received, grace upon grace" (Jn 1:16).

God willed that Mary should be the Mother of this humanity to which He would unite himself, so closely as to be one with it, that it might be the instrument of His grace to the world. Because God asked us for our humanity through Mary and she gave it to Him, Mary is inseparable from the mysteries of Jesus Christ. It is why in Mary we find the perfect model of the interior life. While Jesus is the Son of God for all eternity, it is above all in the mysteries of His childhood and hidden life that He is revealed as the Son of Mary.

It is through His humanity that Jesus saves us. God the Father is not our Savior. God the Holy Spirit is not our Savior. The Son is our Savior through the instrumentality of His humanity, the Word made flesh. This Son, sent into the world by the Father, conceived by the Holy Spirit, reveals His humanity through Mary. Those who do not know Mary, who ignore her, risk not knowing Jesus Christ. They risk not understanding in faith the mysteries of the humanity of Jesus. For a better understanding of the interior life to which we are called, that Christ be formed in us, let us consider this divine Motherhood of Mary ever united with her Son.

Jesus has the fullness of grace (see Jn 1:16). It is His by right of His divine nature. Mary is "full of grace" by participation. Mary *receives* all her grace. Jesus *has* it in plenitude in virtue of His divine, eternal Person. The measure with which Mary participates in the divine nature, in the life of God, is measured only by her dignity of having been chosen to become the Mother of God. This greatness of Mary is best expressed in the *Magnificat* which Mary sang, inspired by the Holy Spirit, and which we her children have sung ever since, for the gifts given her were for us too:

> *My soul magnifies the Lord,*
> *and my spirit rejoices in God my savior,*
> *for he has regarded the low estate of his handmaiden.*
> *For behold, all generations will call me blessed;*
> *for he who is mighty has done great things for me,*
> *and holy is his name.*
> *And his mercy is on those who fear him*
> *from generation to generation.* (Lk 1:46-55)

It was the interior life of Mary's heart that enabled her to identify with the first mystery of Christ at the Annunciation when she answered "Yes": in effect, "your will is my will." We adore the incarnate Word in Mary's womb. She, enlightened by the Holy Spirit, adored the Son of the Most High within her as she carried him as in a tabernacle for nine months.

The same Word of God who lived in Mary's heart and was made flesh in her womb dwells in us by faith, and we share His divine life when we are in the state of sanctifying grace. God has said, "You must be holy as I am holy," but He remained hidden in inaccessible light. Then He came down to become visible and live among us. He lived our life so that we might live His life, so that we might ascend to Him and become holy with His holiness.

Just as this interior life of Mary, the union of her will with His, accomplished that "the Word became flesh and dwelt among us," so our living an interior life like Mary's can enable the Word to take up His abode in other souls. Becoming a mother to Christ, the Word living in souls, is more than welcoming Him into our own soul. We are called to be missionaries. We are called to become mother to Him in other souls as Mary did in ours. Mary's role will always be unique and unsurpassed as Mother. Still, she is our model.

The whole world is called to be Christian. When the world comes to recognize Christ as its sole Savior, it will have come at the same time to recognize Mary, His Mother. Mary will play a special role in the union of Christians among themselves and the bringing of the world's non-Christians to Christ. Islam means literally to surrender oneself totally to God's will. Sincere Muslims are unflinching in their faith in God and their desire to accept the will of God. Often they put Christians to shame. Muslims in great numbers are faithful in prayer, some going to the mosque five times a day. They spread their prayer-mats and perform their prayers without embarrassment. Muslims fast during the month of Ramadan, surpassing what many Christians do during Lent. They have a devotion to Mary and even speak of the Immaculate Conception without realizing the divinity of Christ her Son.

Significant that when God's Mother came to Fatima, Portugal, saying that God desired devotion be established in the world to the Immaculate Heart of His Mother, she thereafter became known as "Our Lady of Fatima." The daughter of Mohammed was Fatima. Mohammed is credited with founding the religion of

Islam, which combines paganism, Christianity, and Judaism. Since the essence of both the Immaculate Heart of Mary and Islam is to surrender oneself totally to God's will, we can anticipate the place the heart of Mary will have in the conversion of millions of people to the Heart of Jesus Christ.

"Behold, I am the handmaid of the Lord; let it be to me according to your word. . . . And the Word became flesh and dwelt among us. . . ."

As there was no hesitancy in the will of Mary at the Annunciation, so too it was revealed that Joseph and Mary would have to go to Bethlehem, to the town of David for the enrollment ordered by Caesar just when "the time came for her to be delivered. And she gave birth to her first-born son and wrapped him in swaddling cloths and laid him in a manger, because there was no place for them in the inn" (Lk 2:6-7).

Mary had greater faith than all the just people of the Old Testament. She saw her God in her Son. Beholding the Word made flesh of her own flesh, we cannot conceive the depth of the spirit of faith and adoration that was Mary's in relation to the Mystery of the Incarnation. Added to this faith and adoration was love, both natural love — the human love of a mother — and supernatural love, the charity that was in her as one "full of grace."

"God is love" (1 Jn 4:8). Every mother in some way reflects this love of God. Even though the love a mother has for her child is but a spark compared to the love God has for us, yet it is a most precious and tender image of God's love. If this is true of every normal mother, how magnificently then did the Most Blessed Trinity fashion the Immaculate Heart of the woman chosen to become the Mother of the incarnate Word.

There exists in the Immaculate Heart of Mary the perfect harmony of a creature who loves God perfectly and loves her Son in like manner. How much any one of us loves God is measured by the degree of grace in the soul. With the degree of grace in Mary's soul, according to great spiritual writers like St. Thomas Aquinas, surpassing all the angels and saints collectively, we can only fathom in a weak manner by poor comparisons the magnitude of Mary's grace. According to the children of Fatima, when our Lady projected herself on the sun, she was brighter than the sun. In the light that emanated from her body they saw themselves in God. Sanctifying grace is a *sharing* in the life of God. It empowers the soul to love in a way surpassing ordinary human powers.

The Holy Spirit never found any obstacle to the unfolding of divine grace in the sweet heart of Mary, always docile to His inspirations, always full of life and love. According to Pope Pius XII, the human soul of Jesus had the beatific vision of the Blessed Trinity from the time of its creation, from the time His body was being formed in the holy womb of Mary. After the joy in the soul of Jesus contemplating the love the Father had for Him within the Trinity, the joy He received from His Mother's love was the most profound.

The human soul of Jesus, united to the eternal Person of the Son of God, always had the *immediate* vision of the Most Blessed Trinity, seeing the divine essence of God even as He is. This beatific vision existed from the first moment of the creation of His human soul and continued without interruption throughout His entire earthly life. The Holy Office of the Vatican declared in 1918 that the contrary could *not* be taught. Pope Pius XII, in his encyclical on the Church as the Mystical Body (*Mystici Corporis*, 1943), stated:

> That knowledge which is called vision He possesses in such fullness that in breath and clarity it far exceeds the beatific vision of all the saints in heaven. . . . In virtue of the beatific vision which He enjoyed from the time when He was conceived in the womb of the Mother of God, He had forever and continuously had present to Him all the members of His Mystical Body (the Church) and embraced them with His saving love.

The love Jesus found in the Immaculate Heart of His Mother was more than sufficient to compensate for all the indifference through the centuries in the millions of souls He came to redeem. This is not to say that Jesus is indifferent to those who decline faith and love for their Savior, only that in the heart of His Mother is a love so ineffable, enkindled by the ever-growing grace of His Spirit, that it is the greatest love between persons after that love between the Persons within the Most Blessed Trinity. Had Mary only responded to grace, her great nobility alone would have sufficed for God to become man.

In each baptized Christian in the state of grace, the Holy

__nity dwells. Invocations to the Trinity long approved for use in the Church are:

(a) "O Most Holy Trinity, I adore You who are dwelling by Your grace within my soul."
(b) "O Most Holy Trinity, who are dwelling by Your grace within my soul, make me love You more and more."
(c) "O Most Holy Trinity, who are dwelling by Your grace within my soul, sanctify me more and more."
(d) "Abide with me, O Lord, be Thou my true joy."

While such prayers to the Holy Trinity dwelling in a soul in the state of grace are proper for any Christian, we can well contemplate the love and joy the Blessed Trinity found within that most pure temple of Mary's heart.

When Jesus was forty days old, she and Joseph presented the Child in the Temple of Jerusalem. Coming into the great Temple, little did onlookers realize that this unique Child was in reality the God they worshiped. The act of Mary's heart offering her Son in the Temple was surpassed only by the oblation that Jesus the High Priest made of himself to the Eternal Father from the moment of the Incarnation in Mary's womb, consummated on the cross.

Every Jewish mother had to present herself in the Temple within a few weeks after the birth of her child. She was to be purified from the legal stain contracted in consequence of original sin. In the case of a firstborn son, the child must be presented to the Lord to be consecrated to Him as to the sovereign Master (Lk 2:23). But the birth of Jesus was miraculous, as was His virginal conception. All was pure and Mary herself knew no sin, not even original sin. The angel had said so: "The child to be born will be called holy, the Son of God" (Lk 1:35).

The heart of Mary was nonetheless guided by the Holy Spirit to present herself in the Temple. Her heart was in perfect conformity with the Heart of her Son. That is seen in the first act of the human will of Jesus expressed to His Father on coming into the world: "I have come to do thy will, O God" (Hebrews 10:7). That act of will of Jesus coincided with the will of His Mother at the same moment. "I am the handmaiden of the Lord; let it be to me according to your word" (Lk 1:38). Mary willed to engage in this ceremony in the Temple, as it expressed the depth of the submission of her will. Together with Joseph, Mary presented Him who was to remain her only Son while becoming "the first-born among many brethren" (Rom 8:29).

The great St. Gertrude related that one day when she heard the chanting of the Divine Office, the words "the firstborn Son of the Virgin Mary" as found in the Gospels caught her attention. She began thinking: "The title of Only Son would seem more befitting for Jesus than that of Firstborn." While she contemplated this, our Blessed Lady appeared to her. "No," said Mary to the nun, "it is not 'Only Son' but 'Firstborn Son' which is most befitting; for, after Jesus, my sweetest Son, or more truly, in Him and by Him, I have given birth to you all in my heart and you have become my children, the brothers and sisters of Jesus."

The Temple of Jerusalem was a Wonder of the World. It was the pride of Israel. The original Temple was built by Solomon in the tenth century B.C. (see 2 Chronicles 1-5). For over a thousand years, the Temple was the center of religious life for Jews all over the world. Annually the parents of Jesus visited Jerusalem for the Passover.

When Mary and Joseph present the Christ Child in the Temple, they come as poor people, for they bring no lamb, the offering of the rich. They bring the offering of the poor, two pigeons. Jesus comes to the Temple as a hidden God. "Truly, thou art a God who hidest thyself, O God of Israel, the Savior" (Is 45:15). The Holy Spirit enlightens the old man Simeon and the prophetess Anna so that they recognize the Messiah in this Child. Scripture (Lk 2:25-38) records no surprise in the hearts of Mary or Joseph at these revelations of Simeon and Anna.

The light of the divinity of Jesus remains hidden as He is presented in the Temple. His own Body *is* the Temple that will be offered on the cross one day. At this presentation in the Temple, Jesus renews the offering of himself made at the moment of His Incarnation. Mary offers too. She offers her Son in the Temple where thousands upon thousands of offerings have been made — all the sacrifices and holocausts of the old covenant. But now, at this moment, more glory, more adoration, more homage is given to God the Father than in all other offerings combined. Now it is His Son, Jesus Christ, who offers infinite adoration, thanksgiving, reparation, and supplication. The only Victim worthy of God is offered to the Father here as the entire heavenly court gazes in awe. Mary offers too, for she is inseparable in her Immaculate Heart from the divine mysteries of her Son, Jesus Christ.

The woman of perfect faith, the Mother of perfect Love, full of grace, is inspired by the Holy Spirit who lives in her as in a temple. The Spirit leads Mary to the Temple of Jerusalem to present the infinitely perfect Victim, after which no other holocaust and sacrifice of animals would be necessary. The Immaculate Heart of Mary is at one with the inner dispositions of the Sacred Heart of Jesus.

At each holy Sacrifice of the Mass today we present Christ in offering to God the Father. The Mass perpetuates the Sacrifice of the Cross. No Christian, no ordained priest, has ever presented the Gift of Jesus to God the Father with such great faith and pure dispositions as Mary did that day in the Temple of Jerusalem. Mary acted as one with the Heart of Jesus, and her own all-pure heart was forever joined in the sacrificial offering of Jesus Christ.

This is what is meant when it is said that we ought to assist at the holy Sacrifice of the Mass and offer the Gift-Victim of Jesus Christ to God the Father together with Mary. Mary is our Mother and model of adorers. We should unite our weak faith to the intense faith of our Lady. By such faithful love, our offerings become pleasing to almighty God. This first offering made in the Temple must be lived through the years as Mary joins her life interiorly to that of Jesus.

While the Gospels record only briefly the flight into Egypt, a strange and unknown land to the Holy Family, it was no mean feat but required a prompt correspondence of the wills of Joseph and Mary to the will of God. Surely Mary and Joseph learned not only of the wrath of the tyrant Herod but of the murder of the innocents. We can contemplate the intense sorrow in the heart of Mary at the slaughter of innocent children. Her heart was truly the heart of a mother of sorrows. Simeon had foretold that a sword would pierce her heart because of her close identity with the mysteries of this Child. Could Mary have thought the sword would come so soon?

For thirty years Jesus lived close to Mary. His public life was just three years; His hidden life took thirty. Before three years of manifestation to the world He came to redeem, thirty years were spent intimately with Mary, whom He redeemed most perfectly and fully from the first instant her all-pure heart was created.

How seldom the veil is lifted from Jesus' hidden life. How full of mystery the events are when revealed, and always in association with Mary. In His infancy, the call of the wise men to faith, as they observed "his star in the East" (Mt 2:2), is expressive of the call of the nations of the world to true faith in Jesus Christ. They "saw the child with Mary his mother" (Mt 2:11). The call to faith contains a call to eternal happiness, when we shall see God "face to face" (1 Cor 13:12) even as He is. Faith lived will bring us to the beatific vision.

The rare instance of the veil being lifted during the long hidden years Jesus spent with His Mother is when He was twelve years old. At that age young Israelites began to be subject to the precepts of the Mosaic Law. This meant going to the Temple three times a year, the feasts of the *Passover* (to commemorate the deliverance of the Jews from the bondage of Egypt), *Pentecost* (Jewish Feast of Weeks, which fell on the fiftieth day after Passover, when the first fruits of the grain harvest were offered to the Lord), and *Tabernacles* (to thank the Lord for the harvest and commemorate the sojourn in the desert, finding a home in the Promised Land and the building of the Temple as a permanent place of worship of the one true God).

The fact that Jesus was circumcised expressed His will to bear the yoke of the Law until He had enacted the New Covenant on Calvary. Then, at the age of twelve, Jesus went with His Mother, Mary, and virginal father, Joseph, to the Holy City.

Jesus entered the Temple. He mingled with the crowd. The crowd did not know that this Boy walking in their midst, beginning His adolescent years, was the God they adored in the Temple. Jesus took part in the ceremonies, chanted the psalms. God himself, through the prophets, had laid down the details of the liturgy conducted in the Temple. No one had ever participated so perfectly in the Temple rites or understood more profoundly their deep significance, perpetuated today in the Sacrifice of the Mass and the sacraments of the Church. Jesus saw the symbolism of what He had yet to do in redeeming the world.

The Holy Spirit, who inspired all of Sacred Scripture, had a most serious reason for sharing this incident of Jesus going to Jerusalem and then Mary and Joseph losing Him. "And when the feast was ended, as they were returning, the boy Jesus stayed behind in Jerusalem. His parents did not know it" (Lk 3:43). It was the custom that young people walking in caravans to and from Jerusalem were free to be either with the group of men or the group of women. "Supposing him to be in the company they went a day's journey, and they sought him among their kinsfolk and acquaintances" (Lk 3:44). As the caravans moved along, they would visit and sing hymns, as Mary did, thinking Jesus was with Joseph or others. Only when evening came did families rejoin. It was then that the hearts of Mary and Joseph were torn deeply. Jesus was missing.

What hours and days of heartache were those when Mary and Joseph did not know where Jesus was! After three days they found Him in the Temple. The teachers of the Law in Judea would assemble in one of the Temple halls to discuss the meaning of the Sacred Scriptures. Others were free to join them. Jesus came among them, not to teach, for that hour had not yet come — at least, not to teach directly. He was there "listening to them and asking them questions" (Lk 2:46). Doubtless Jesus' questions led the teachers to discover for themselves the meaning of Scripture regarding the appearance of the promised Savior. The Father willed that the Son do so at this particular time, for Jesus always did the Father's will. "I can do nothing on my own authority . . . because I seek not my own will but the will of him who sent me" (Jn 5:30).

And what did these learned men think of the twelve-year-old Jesus? "All who heard him were amazed at his understanding and his answers" (Lk 2:47). When His parents came upon this scene they were astonished.

Isn't it significant that although Joseph was the head of the Holy Family, it is Mary who speaks first when on the third day they came upon him in the Temple sitting in the midst of the teachers? " 'Son, why have you treated us so? Behold, your father and I have been searching for you anxiously.' And he said to them: 'How is it that you sought me? Did you not know I must be in my Father's house?' " (Lk 2:48-49).

These are the first words Sacred Scripture records coming from the lips of the incarnate Word. Perhaps other translations reveal more of Jesus' intent to say that He must always do the will of His Father ("Did you not know that I must be about my Father's business?" "Did you not know that I must be busy with my Father's affairs?").

His answer explains the essence of the whole Person of Jesus and the work His heavenly Father had given Him to do. It reveals that Jesus is the Son of God, not only the Son of Mary. Mary had said, meaning Joseph, "your father and I." Without any offense to Joseph intended, Jesus speaks of another Father, His divine Father by nature. Surely Joseph and Mary above all should be conscious of the origin of Jesus. Why do they need to search? His whole life was about His Father's business. They should have known to come directly to the Temple.

Jesus meant no disobedience to Mary and Joseph, for the Evangelist Luke immediately adds (2:51): "And he went down with them and came to Nazareth, and was obedient to them; and his mother kept all these things in her heart." When they were without Him for three days, however, the will of His heavenly Father was a higher obligation than human duty to Mary and Joseph. Contemplating the mystery that caused Mary to ponder "all these things in her heart," we conclude that whatever God requires of us to accomplish His will must not permit any human considerations to stand in the way.

The Gospel did not conclude the account telling us that Joseph and Mary disagreed with the answer of Jesus but that, at least for the time being, "they did not understand the saying which he spoke to them." Mary quietly submits to the divine will. Within her Immaculate Heart she adores the mystery of the holy words of her Son, the Son of God. Mary never pushes the will of God for an instant answer. She willingly awaits light as God wills to give it.

Faithfulness to the inspirations of grace becomes the source of greater and brighter illuminations. Those who love more will have more given to them. Jesus himself reveals this to us. "In that day you will know that I am in my Father, and you in me, and I in you. He who has my commandments and keeps them, he it is who loves me; and he who loves me will be loved by my Father, and I will love him and manifest myself to him" (Jn 14:20-21). Jesus has told us that those to whom much has been given, and who have received it in faith and love, will receive all the more. No one has been given a greater share in the fullness of grace from the incarnate Word than Mary. No human person has loved more than the Immaculate Heart.

We do not know how long Joseph lived. We know that suddenly he disappeared from the Gospels, and it is thought that Mary and Jesus were left alone before the public ministry of our divine Lord began. Every suffering that man must endure entered the Immaculate Heart of Mary in one form or another. Let us consider some of the chief events.

To the present day, Mother Church celebrates the Feast of the Presentation of the Blessed Virgin Mary. The feast is founded on pious tradition, originated by two apocryphal gospels. Still the event is thought probably authentic. It relates that the Blessed Virgin Mary was presented in the Temple of Jerusalem when three years old, and there she lived with other girls and holy women. The feast was commemorated in the East already in the sixth century. In 1372 Pope Gregory XI kept it in Greece on November 21, and he introduced it at Avignon. Sixtus V extended it to the whole Church in 1585, and Clement VIII raised it to a higher-ranking feast. With such a long tradition, there is doubtless much merit to the belief. Religious communities have been named in honor of the Presentation of the Blessed Virgin Mary. Musn't there be some sorrow in separation from her parents at such a tender age, however meritorious in fulfilling the will of God? Anna, who lived as a widow for so many years and "was constantly in the Temple, worshiping day and night in fasting and prayer" (Lk 2:37), was probably familiar with Mary since her childhood. Anna sees Mary now as a young mother coming into the Temple with the Christ Child, in whom she recognizes the Messiah.

The suffering of Mary's all-pure heart when she had conceived the Child Jesus with Joseph not knowing the Source of her pregnancy cannot be imagined. One would have to have the holiness of our Lady "full of grace" to imagine the intense sufferings it must have caused her when Joseph had a mind to put her away privately. Mary had not been told to reveal to Joseph the Source of the Child she carried. She waited and suffered until heaven informed Joseph not to fear to take Mary as his wife.

Her Child becomes the source of the wrath of Herod when the Magi arrive at Jerusalem one day from the East. The flight into Egypt and living in a foreign land have already been mentioned, as has the poverty of the Holy Family. All may seem romantic in holy art, but in reality, there was intense suffering, always accepted with great faith and love.

Returning to Nazareth, Mary has to run her household with the barest of necessities; her husband had offered two turtledoves. Material goods do not make for happiness. Love in the heart at peace brings happiness. There was never a happier home than that of Jesus, Mary, and Joseph. Still this family was not without suffering. Mary herself spoke of the sorrow when she and Joseph were separated from Jesus during His three days in the Temple.

The death of Joseph meant intense sorrow for Jesus and Mary. Jesus groaned in sorrow at the death of Lazarus, his friend, whom he brought back to life. What must His sorrow have been at the death of the virginal father who was the earthly surrogate of His heavenly Father? As Jesus began His public teaching, He would speak often of His heavenly Father. His virginal father on earth, Joseph, according to the divine will, must leave this world to be with the heavenly Father before such public preaching began.

And when Jesus left home to begin that public ministry, what thoughts must have filled the Immaculate Heart of His Mother! A new state of relationship opens. Mary must now begin to share Him with the world. He came to redeem the world. Now she will often stand at the edge of crowds as He teaches. She will even have to wait outside houses when Jesus is inside teaching. Never would her Immaculate Heart for an instant interfere with the divine will.

"And when Jesus had finished . . . he went away . . . and coming to his own country he taught them in their synagogue, so that they were astonished, and said, 'Where did this man get this wisdom and these mighty works? Is not this the carpenter's son? Is not his mother called Mary?' " (Mt 13:53-55). The Gospel account then speaks of the brothers and sisters of Jesus — not to be mistaken for members of an immediate family, for the faith of the Church is in the perpetual virginity of Mary. In the language of the Bible, the terms used include other relatives.

What humble and silent roles Joseph and Mary have in the Gospels! Yet they are the virginal parents of the Savior of the world. Mary is physically the Mother as well. Joseph's role as virginal father is great too, for he freely chooses to accept the role as husband of Mary, to take Mary as wife, after heaven informs him that the Child Mary has begotten is of the Holy Spirit. The Kingdom of God is not built up in great fanfare but in silence. The Kingdom of God is built up interiorly, in the heart. Thus in many ways it is hidden.

How well the words of the Apostle Paul, written later, describe the life and spirit of Mary's heart. "If then you have been raised with Christ, seek the things that are above, where Christ is, seated at the right hand of God. Set your mind on things that are above, not on things that are on earth. For you have died, and your life is hid with Christ in God. When Christ who is our life appears, then you also will appear with him in glory" (Col 3:1-4).

No one has greater faith in the teachings of Jesus during His public ministry than His Mother. No one but Jesus suffers more than she does when she sees her Son attacked by the hatred of the Pharisees. Mary is witness to the rejection of Jesus even by His disciples. She sees Him delivered into the hands of His enemies. The leaders of God's people, who should have been the first to recognize that He is in fact the Messiah, the long-awaited One of Israel, are in fact the very ones who instigate His crucifixion and death.

Mary stands beneath the cross and hears her divine Son cry aloud: "My God, my God, why hast thou forsaken me?" (Mt 27:46).

She knows, as the sword prophesied by Simeon transfixes her heart, that she is passing into still another state of relationship to Jesus and the people He came to save when she hears the words, "Woman, behold, your son! . . . Behold, your mother!" (Jn 19:26-27).

Mary remains the faithful Virgin even when the apostles have fled, only John remaining with her beneath the cross. When Jesus' lifeless body is taken from the cross and all withdraw as

He is laid in the tomb, Mary remains, full of faith, heart broken but brimming over with undying love.

It is in this interior life of Mary that her greatness is to be found. Through this great faith and love she continued to grow in grace. It is in sanctifying grace that each of us shall find the true source of greatness. It is grace that gives the soul a share in divine life, light, imperishable splendor.

The Immaculate Heart of Mary is for all of us, her children, the perfect Mother and model of the interior life wherein the Kingdom of God will be built into a magnificent heavenly kingdom that shall never end.

The heart of Mary was filled with unutterable joy when Jesus the Redeemer, her Redeemer as well, risen, appeared to her. We are not told all things by the Gospels. We do know that the risen Jesus appeared repeatedly to His disciples and to a crowd of hundreds at one time. Mary's faith and love, which had never weakened, could only have increased during those forty days after the Resurrection. John, who took Mary into his own home after the death of Jesus on the cross, ended his Gospel with: "But there are also many other things which Jesus did; were every one of them written, I suppose that the world itself could not contain the books that would be written" (Jn 21:25). Once Jesus has risen and appeared to Mary with His body still bearing the wound marks but now with spiritual qualities of a glorified body, Mary realizes once again a new, deeper relationship she has to her Son, the Son of God and Risen Christ, and to the countless billions of souls He has redeemed.

After Jesus ascended into heaven, the apostles returned to Jerusalem from the mount called Olivet and went to the upper room, the Cenacle. "All . . . with one accord devoted themselves to prayer, together with the women and Mary the mother of Jesus, and with his brothers" (Acts 1:12-14). Acts 2 describes the descent of the Holy Spirit accompanied by the strong, driving wind. "And there appeared to them tongues as of fire, distributed and resting on each one of them. And they were all filled with the Holy Spirit" (Acts 2:1-4). Mary's association with the mysteries of Christ will continue in the Mystical Body of Christ, the Church.

Mary remained upon earth many years after her Son's ascension and the descent of the Holy Spirit. The Scriptures record the

great effects the outpouring of the Holy Spirit had upon the
apostles to love and witness Jesus in their ministry. The efficacious fruit realized in Mary, the spouse of the Holy Spirit,
cannot be calculated, so we shouldn't try. We know that it was
Mary's unique openness to the Holy Spirit, the faith and love of
her heart, that contributed to her being the worthy tabernacle of
the incarnate Word. Now with the descent of the Holy Spirit upon
the Church of which she is Mother, the power of her influence
would be all the greater. As Queen of Apostles, she continued to
be an example and urge them in openness to the Holy Spirit in
their work within the infant Church. The Holy Spirit, descended
upon Mary at the Annunciation to give us the Head of the Church,
now descended upon Mary as Mother of the Church, and the
Church as the Mystical Body of Christ would begin to give birth to
millions through the centuries.

As the intense interior life of our Mother's Immaculate
Heart, praying with the apostles in the Cenacle, drew forth the
fires of divine Love from the Holy Spirit that first Pentecost, so
the heart of the Mother of the Church continues to plead still for
each one of us.

"This makes Jesus the surety of a better covenant. The for-
mer priests were many in number, because they were prevented
by death from continuing in office; but he holds his priesthood
permanently, because he continues forever. Consequently he is
able for all time to save those who draw near to God through him,
since he always lives to make intercession for them" (Heb
7:22-25).

As Mary was associated in the mysteries of Christ from His
conception to the descent of the Holy Spirit on Pentecost — the
birthday of the Church — now that she is in heaven, she too is associated with Christ Jesus as He "always lives to make intercession" for us. The Sacred Heart of Jesus, the Son with whom
the Father is well pleased, is the Savior, the essential Mediator.
Associated is the Immaculate Heart of His Mother. These two
hearts beat as one.

The Heart of Jesus did not cease to make intercession for
those who approach God through Him once He was ascended.
Scripture assures us of that. As Scripture tells us, after His ascension Mary together with the apostles and some other disciples

"with one accord devoted themselves to prayer" awaiting the fulfillment of the promise of Christ. Since Mary's assumption into
heaven, we can believe that this constant prayer of intercession
of her Immaculate Heart continues to the Father through Jesus.

It is this the Church teaches.

CHAPTER 8

† Consecration to the Immaculate Heart †

THE WORD "devotion" comes from the Latin word *devovere*. It means to devote or consecrate oneself to a person one loves. Each one of us is called to be totally devoted to the love of God. Jesus said that "you shall love the Lord your God with all your heart, and with all your soul, and with all your mind, and with all your strength" (Mk 12:30).

Jesus asked for our love *totally*. We are to love God without reserving anything for ourselves. We are to give ourselves to Him promptly in every possible service that may present itself as the will of God. We should devote our total being, all our activity, to the Person of the incarnate Word.

How then does devotion or consecration to Mary fit into this total giving of self, our whole being, with all our faculties, to the Person of the incarnate Word, and thereby to the Blessed Trinity? Jesus Christ is the Mediator; Mary is model. Mary gave herself totally to Jesus by the perfect surrender of her will to the Word, as already explained in these pages. In the fourth century St. Ambrose spoke to Christian people, expressing the hope that each of them would have the spirit of Mary in glorifying God: "May the heart of Mary be in each Christian to proclaim the greatness of the Lord; may her spirit be in everyone to exult to God." Perfect consecration develops that spirit of Mary within us.

Pope Paul VI, in his Apostolic Exhortation *Marialis Cultus*, issued to the world for the right ordering and development of devotion to the Blessed Virgin Mary, took up this theme: "Mary is above all the example of that worship that consists in making one's life an offering to God. This is an ancient and ever new doctrine that each individual can hear again by heeding the Church's teaching, but also by heeding the very voice of the Virgin as she, anticipating in herself the wonderful petition of the Lord's Prayer — 'Thy will be done' (Mt 6:10) — replied to God's messenger: 'I am the handmaid of the Lord. Let it be to me according to your word' (Lk 1:38). And Mary's 'yes' is for all Christians a lesson and example of obedience to the will of the Father, which is the way and means of one's own sanctification" (21).

In the same document Pope Paul reminded people of the perennial mind of the Church when he quoted St. Ildefonsus: "What is given to the Handmaid is referred to the Lord; thus what is given to the Mother redounds to the Son . . . and thus what is given as humble tribute to the Queen becomes honor rendered to the King."

Why should we consecrate or entrust ourselves to Mary's Immaculate Heart? When Pope John Paul II went to Fatima on May 13, 1982, he reminded us that Jesus Christ himself first entrusted the world to His Mother as He hung dying on the cross. "Woman, behold, your son!. . . Behold, your mother!" No act of Jesus, the Universal Savior dying on the cross, was of private or individual significance. The disciple John represented us all in being given Mary as Mother. As John thereafter took Mary into his care, into his home, Mary too took John and all future members of the Church into her care. In Scripture, the last recorded action of Mary is when she is gathered with the disciples and some others in the upper room after the Ascension praying constantly for the coming of the Spirit.

This devotion, this consecration to Mary, takes its origin and effectiveness from Jesus Christ. It finds its complete expression in Christ. It leads through Christ in the Spirit to the Father.

When one is consecrated, he or she is made sacred by being set aside for the service of God. When one consecrates oneself to Mary, it means giving oneself to Jesus Christ through the Immaculate Heart of His Mother. We are all her spiritual children. As she once presented her Son Jesus in the Temple in the Spirit to the Father, so now, when we consecrate ourselves to Mary, we recognize ourselves as her spiritual children and desire that she present us, united to her Son Jesus in the Spirit to the Father. The spirit of Mary then lives within us and therefore the Holy Spirit dwells within us in a special way, as in a special temple. The Holy Spirit is never separated from His spouse.

Pope John Paul II consecrated the entire world to the Immaculate Heart of Mary. Pius XII had done the same years before, while Paul VI renewed it during Vatican Council II. The Church simply did what Christ did on the cross. It remains for each one of us to unite our individual wills to the will of God reflected in Mary's heart. Mary has not kept anything for herself. She never has. When we as individuals open our wills to hers, she can more effectively present us to her Son, Jesus, and thus in the Spirit to the Father. Each will is free. Mary gathers up our weaknesses. She sees us faltering at times. We make some effort, we do so little, we advance toward her; rather, we go with her to Jesus. She then makes it easy. She shows us to Jesus. In effect, "This is one of my children you entrusted to me from the cross. Accept this one into Your Sacred Heart in a special way. I have come with this child of mine whom you have redeemed by your death on the cross. Present Him to the Father as a member of your Body."

Aren't the expressions above, however poorly put, a feeble explanation of that brief consecration to Jesus through Mary, "I am all thine, my Queen, my Mother, and all that I have is thine"? Or, "I am Thine, O most loving Jesus, through Mary, Thy Holy Mother" . . . or "Come, Holy Spirit, come by means of the powerful intercession of the Immaculate Heart of Mary, Your wellbeloved spouse"?

"Christ is the only way to the Father (cf. Jn 14:1-11), and the ultimate example to whom the disciple must conform his own conduct (cf. Jn 13:15), to the extent of sharing Christ's sentiments (cf. Phil 2:5), living His life and possessing His Spirit (cf. Gal 2:20; Rom 8:10-11). The Church has always taught this and nothing in pastoral activity should obscure this doctrine. But the Church, taught by the Holy Spirit and benefiting from centuries of experience, recognizes that devotion to the Blessed Virgin, subordinated to worship of the divine Savior and in connection with it, also has a great pastoral effectiveness and constitutes a force for renewing Christian living" (*Marialis Cultus*, 57).

Consecration to the Immaculate Heart of Mary is really an effort to live in depth the vows of our baptism. Unfortunately, most Christians fall far short of living up to their baptismal consecration and renunciation of Satan. At baptism we become temples of the Holy Spirit. In fact, the entire Blessed Trinity comes to live within us. The theological virtues of faith, hope, and love are infused into the soul. The indelible character of Jesus Christ, His seal, is forever stamped upon the human soul. In baptism we are called and consecrated to live the life of Christ, to love the Lord with all our heart, all our soul, all our mind, all our strength (see Mk 12:30).

There is only one Christian who has ever fulfilled perfectly everything to which a soul is called and consecrated at baptism. That perfect disciple is Mary. In consecrating ourselves to Mary's heart, then, we express the will to live the perfect life to which our baptism called and consecrated us. Mary, who gave the incarnate Word His humanity, became the most like Him in mind, heart, and soul. Without a flaw, she lived to the full a life of likeness to her Son, who is God and man. Consecration to Mary's Immaculate Heart is expressing the will of the one entrusting to have Christ formed in Him after the pattern of the Lord's perfect disciple, Mary, His Mother. In the act of consecration, one gives oneself to Mary as a secure way of being united to Jesus, for we approach our divine and loving Savior in union with His Immaculate Mother.

Our Lord and Savior Jesus Christ is indeed all loving and merciful. He has become "man in all things except sin." He is the one essential Mediator between God and man, and yet His very Person is the omnipotent God, the "I Am Who Am." In only one human person did the "I Am Who Am" find a perfectly adorned, immaculate tabernacle in which to dwell. That was the heart of His Mother, Mary. How fitting, then, that He who desires to dwell with us and in us and came to us through Mary should have us return to Him through Mary. Jesus came to us in a perfect way, the Immaculate Heart of His Mother.

Mary is, as Vatican Council II stated, the "mediatrix" of grace. The same council added that this title, as others, "is so understood that it neither takes away anything from nor adds anything to the dignity and efficacy of Christ the one Mediator." Vatican II added:

"The Church does not hesitate to profess this subordinate role of Mary, which it constantly experiences and recommends to the heartfelt attention of the faithful, so that encouraged by this ma-

ternal help they may the more closely adhere to the Mediator and
Redeemer" (*Lumen Gentium*, 62).

Consecration to the Immaculate Heart of Mary, understood
in the sense of total consecration, involves Mary as mediatrix,
the way Christ came to us, through whose Heart He still wills to
come to us and have us return to Him united in the Spirit, offering
ourselves to the Father. To put it simply, Mary never keeps anything for herself. Everything she is and has came from and
through Jesus. Everything given her is always returned to Jesus.
Every time we say "Mary," she says "Jesus," who in turn says
"Father." A correct understanding of total consecration to
Mary's Immaculate Heart looks to her role as mediatrix, subordinate to Christ the Mediator, and her part in the doctrine of the
Communion of Saints.

The Communion of Saints expresses the Church's faith in the
unity and cooperation of members of the Church on earth with
those in heaven and those in purgatory. They are united in one
Mystical Body of Christ. Baptized members on earth are in communion with the saints in heaven by honoring them as glorified
members of the Church, invoking their prayers, and striving to
imitate their virtues. While this union we have with all the saints
in heaven, greater and lesser, is real, the efficacy of such invocations, the aid we receive, and the honor we give is greatest, after
Christ, when it involves Mary, the Mother of the Church. St. Paul
wrote of the saved coming to the glory of the Lord's power and
being "glorified in his saints" (2 Thes 1:10). In no mere creature
is God glorified more than in His Mother. When we approach the
"I Am Who Am" become man together with the Immaculate
Heart of His Mother, the Lord sees the insignificant and unworthy
gift that we are in ourselves enhanced by His Mother's love.

In no way can it be rightly said that going to Jesus while placing ourselves within the Immaculate Heart of Mary somehow
makes Jesus less human, less merciful, less approachable, less
powerful. The opposite is true. It is as Vatican II said, so that
they may "more closely adhere to the Mediator and Redeemer."
Approaching Jesus in the company of His Mother, whom we have
accepted with all our heart as our Mother too, can only make the
oblation of self to the Lord more pleasing. The holiness, the beauty, the light of life shining forth from His Mother's heart — such

rays of powerful intercession in the love of His Mother's Immaculate Heart embracing each of us as one of her very own children — can only make us more acceptable.

"The reason the Son of God appeared was to destroy the works of the devil" (1 Jn 3:8) through Mary. When she reveals us to her Son, saying, "They have no wine" (Jn 2:3), how powerful our Mother is to have the desires of her heart fulfilled even if His hour has not yet come! When she is able to show Him that these children are consecrated to her Immaculate Heart, the Lord Jesus, recognizing that heart as the way He came into the world and the place where He found His greatest satisfaction, can only be more disposed toward His brother and sister who have taken their abode in the same tabernacle, Refuge of Sinners. Seeing His Mother's spirit in us, Jesus can only love us profoundly and accept our consecration to Him as His Mother is perfectly consecrated herself.

The Christian who entrusts self to the Immaculate Heart of Mary must not consider that it is accomplished in the mere recitation of a formula. It is living hour by hour, day by day, year after year, a consecration to Jesus through Mary. It is to Jesus we then belong entirely, through Mary. It is the spirit of Mary's total consecration to Jesus we must live.

St. Louis-Marie Grignon de Montfort (1673-1716), who developed this doctrine so beautifully in his book *True Devotion to the Blessed Virgin*, was not the first to advocate or live total consecration to Mary. Nor did he so claim. He spoke of total consecration as an easier and quicker way to union with God. Where there are still difficulties, crosses that only indicate union with the Lord, yet souls in this way "go forward more sweetly and more peacefully. . . . This good Mother and Mistress remains so near and so present to her faithful servants, to enlighten them in their darkness and in their doubts, to strengthen them in their moments of fear, and to sustain them in their combats and their difficulties, that indeed this virginal way leading to Jesus Christ is, by comparison with the others, a way of roses and of honey."

St. Louis de Montfort spoke of saints, not numerous in his time but growing in numbers, who discovered total consecration by special grace. "There are some saints, but not many — Saint Ephrem, Saint John Damascene, Saint Bernard, Saint Bernardin,

Saint Bonaventure, Saint Francis de Sales, etc. — who have reached Jesus Christ by this sweet way, because the Holy Spirit, the faithful Spouse of Mary, revealed it to them through a singular grace.''

Who could deny that the Apostle John, who took Mary to himself from that moment beneath the cross, discovered true and total consecration to the Mother of God and lived it day by day for the rest of his life? John, the apostle of love, who wrote most frequently and profoundly of love, must have learned much of this from Mother Mary.

St. Louis de Montfort recognized that the vast majority of saints known up to his time did not enter into this way of total consecration. "They passed through more raw and dangerous trials and temptations," according to this saint. Yet, he said, this "secure way of reaching Jesus Christ and of acquiring perfection through uniting ourselves with Him . . . is so ancient that . . . it is impossible to give a precise date for its beginning."

He recognized traces of it more than seven hundred years before his time: for example, works of St. Odilon, Abbot of Cluny (d. 1049); Cardinal Peter Damien (d. 1072), since canonized and a Doctor of the Church, spoke of it. The saint mentioned other well-known personalities who had studied and approved of such a consecration, even though at times the devil was effective in attempting to destroy knowledge of it. The same proved true in the great work of St. Louis de Montfort. His book *True Devotion* was hidden from the world for more than one hundred twenty-five years after his death before it was discovered.

While, as St. Louis de Montfort says, "it is impossible to give a precise date" for the beginning of total consecration to Mary, yet the doctrinal foundation for it is implicit in the very nature of Christianity, the Incarnation. The meaning of Christ's words from the cross has become more explicit with meditation over centuries. Evil spirits have not been anxious to have the true role of Mary in relation to the incarnate Word appreciated and lived.

The century leading up to the close of Vatican Council II (December 8, 1965) is recognized as a Marian century. Vatican II spoke gloriously and, according to Pope Paul VI, "more extensively" of Mary than any preceding council of the Church. Yet, for a time after the council, devotion to Mary seemed to wane, only to return by the time of this book, more vigorously healthy and better balanced. The unique role of Mary in Scripture is now recognized, and it is increasingly appreciated that in the Mother of Jesus all Christians have an ideal model to imitate and an intercessor for their every need. The Marian era St. Louis de Montfort foresaw has since witnessed the canonization of many saints deeply devoted and consecrated to Mary.

When one is perfectly consecrated to Mary's Immaculate Heart, it is not a matter of Mary's being far off in heaven interceding for us. Rather, in the Communion of Saints, the very spirit of Mary lives in us, and we in her. We pray together. We live our consecration to Jesus together with Mary in union with the Holy Spirit to the glory of the Father. There is a moral presence of Mary. It is not the same as the presence of the Holy Trinity within the soul in the state of sanctifying grace. Still, as we have a union with the entire Communion of Saints, there is a special union with our spiritual Mother, whose love and grace, after and dependent on Christ, are greater than all.

In living in such close intimacy with the Immaculate Heart of Mary, we are only imitating her Son, Jesus. The thirty years of physical and spiritual intimacy of Jesus with His Mother are unparalleled. After Bethlehem there were the years in Egypt, at Nazareth. After being carried in the tabernacle of Mary's womb, immediately beneath her heart, He was carried in her arms or ever at her side. She spoke to Him with eyes, lips, and heart. During the last three years of His life, when Jesus was so often misunderstood, even by the apostles at times, rejected by the multitudes, surely His own Sacred Heart turned in love to the heart of His Mother, even if she was not physically present. The Bible records how His thoughts turned to His Mother as He hung on the cross, dying that we might live.

Jesus always knew that there was one who understood Him well and loved Him perfectly: His Mother. While he received joy from the love of His apostles, especially John, and from the devotion of many of his disciples and the pure, simple souls who believed and responded, yet all these joys did not equal the joy, the satisfaction, the love He found in His relationship with His Blessed Mother. This, again, is why our own little generosities, our own faith, service, devotion, and loyalty can be only enhanced

and more pleasing to Jesus when we go to Him with and within
the Immaculate Heart of His Mother. See, Jesus, I come to You,
to be one with You, to be Your very brother (sister), and I come
to You under the mantle of Your Mother's heart.

The soul that strives to live in the heart of Mary will thereby
spontaneously work to imitate the virtues of Mary, her humility,
her purity, her deep faith and confidence. Living in such close intimacy with Mary, the soul will discover many things that cannot
be put into writing. Led by grace to Jesus through Mary, one will
discover the secrets of the Mother's heart and thereby those of
Jesus. Since the heart has its own reasons, explanations will not
be needed and demonstrations through teaching-words will not be
possible. United in prayer to Mary, we pray in her and she with
and in us. Jesus is not replaced; Jesus the Mediator is most effectively encountered in this manner. The Holy Spirit, her Spouse, is
active within us. The Father of Jesus is then our Father too.

Mary sees Jesus in each soul consecrated to her. As a member of the Church, Christ's Mystical Body, living in Christ, Mary
sees her Son, Jesus, talking to her when such a soul prays to her.
Whether we desire to speak to God the Father, to the Holy Spirit,
or to Jesus, we may effectively do so in union with Mary. Living
habitually in such close intimacy with Mary's heart, we spontaneously approach the Blessed Trinity with a more profound faith,
confidence, and love for this heart, since its creation has been the
choice temple of the Trinity.

We may reveal to Mary the innermost recesses of our hearts.
Our emotions, our insecurities, our fears, our discouragements,
our indecisions, our many failings — all may be taken to Mary.
We need not speak many words to Mary. Often simply uttering
"Mother" in love will tell her all. Like the child who runs to his
mother and with pleading eyes and an open heart calls her to aid
him, comfort and love him, we can take to our Mother our joys
and happiness as well. She loves to hear our expressions of gratitude and our offerings of all we are and have. Again, the simple
word "Mother" can express it all. The word "Mother," containing our desire to give all to Jesus through her, is often sufficient
to renew our consecration to her Immaculate Heart.

Now our running as children to the heart of our Mother does
not mean that she will keep our little gifts for herself. Rather, she

works to transform us more and more into Jesus. Once upon a time long ago, within her Immaculate Heart the Word of God was conceived perfectly. Now, as all of us — other little Jesuses, as it were — approach Mary, we are transformed more and more within her heart into copies of the one perfect Master and Lord, JESUS CHRIST.

In such an interior union, Mary teaches us well. She leads us well. She transforms us into her All, Jesus Christ, "the Alpha and the Omega" (Rev 1:8). From Mary we learn to think the thoughts of Jesus. In this way we will have in us the mind "which was in Christ Jesus" (Phil 2:5).

Is there danger here in such attention to Mary, as many fear, of detracting from Jesus? I repeat: Not at all. For as we put on the mind of Jesus Christ, we take, as I've said, His thoughts, which even in His public life turned back to Mary. Isn't she the perfect daughter of Zion, the perfect model of the Church? Whatever of His Mother Jesus discovers in us can only be pleasing to Him. Whatever of Mary exists in us can only be directed to the entire Trinity in, with, and through Jesus Christ. Those who fear this approach are trying to limit God, who embraces one in All and all in One.

There will always be the enemy who attempts to keep the likeness of Mary from existing within us so that we may be transformed into her Son, Jesus Christ. The archenemy of the woman was mentioned already in Genesis 3:15. As long as we live upon this earth, each one, through baptism into Christ, must fight the battle against the enemy, the consequences of Original Sin to which we are all subject. Baptism took away Original Sin, imprinted the indelible seal of Christ Jesus upon our souls, put a sharing of God's life (grace) within us for the first time. Baptism also gave us the theological virtues of faith, hope, and love in seed form; they need to grow, develop, and mature in the right soil.

In no soil is the baptized soul better nourished to grow into the likeness of Jesus Christ than within the Immaculate Heart of Mary. The vices will raise their ugly heads: pride, envy, vanity, lack of humility displayed through hypersensitivity and touchiness. All can work as tools of the enemy to weaken faith and keep our souls from responding in love of God. There may be a spirit of ambition that seeks the glory of self rather than the glory of God

and the salvation of souls. There is a spirit of inconstancy to un-
dermine the spirit of perseverance that stays with Christ "in season and out of season" (2 Tim 4:2). There is sensuality, seen in
sins of the flesh, every kind of craving for food, drink, and repose
that is not in balance; in sins of impurity, lacking a sense of
modesty. Recent popes have been saying that mankind is losing
its sense of sin. Pope John Paul II was bold enough to say it has
already lost its sense of sin.

A soul whose interior life is lived in Christ, in union with
Mary day by day, does not fall victim to the enemy. Or if a soul in
a moment of weakness should succumb to the weaknesses of the
flesh, should the soul on some occasion fall away from union with
God, then if that soul has been striving day after day, week after
week, month after month to live in Christ in union with Mary, the
power of Mary's intercession will quickly bring that soul to repentance, to regain and renew its life in Jesus Christ. St. Peter, who
denied our Lord three times, wept bitter tears of repentance. His
great sorrow led him to even greater love of our Savior so that the
day would come when this saint would offer his life in martyr-
dom. "Greater love has no man than this, that a man lay down his
life for his friends" (Jn 15:13).

A soul consecrated to Mary's Immaculate Heart will make
frequent use of the sacraments so as to live constantly in Christ.
Wherever possible, daily Mass with Holy Communion will be part
of such a life. Frequent confession not only purifies the soul more
and more through the absolution of the priest, but gives the soul
added spiritual strength against the enemy who ever battles
against the woman and all her spiritual children.

St. Louis de Montfort, the recognized expert on total consecration to Mary, described the nature of perfect consecration to
Jesus through Mary in his book *True Devotion*:

> This devotion consists, therefore, in giving ourselves entirely
> to the Most Blessed Virgin, that, through her, we may belong
> entirely to Jesus Christ. We must give to her: (1) our body with
> all its senses and members; (2) our soul with all its powers; (3)
> our material possessions and all that we may acquire; (4) our
> interior and spiritual possessions — our merits, our virtues and
> our good works, past, present, and future: in short, all that we
> possess in the order of nature, in the order of grace and in the
> order of glory — and this without the least reserve, not even to

the keeping back of the least good work; and for all eternity. In doing so, we must claim and expect, for our offering and our services, no reward other than the honor of belonging to Jesus Christ through Mary and in Mary, not allowing ourselves to be consciously influenced by the fact that she is at all times the most liberal and most grateful of creatures. . . .

It follows from what has been said that, by this devotion, we give to Jesus Christ all that we can give Him, and far in excess of other devotions in which we give Him a part of our time, or a part of our good works, or a part of our satisfactions and mortifications; that, furthermore, we do so in the most perfect manner — namely, through the hands of Mary. For in this devotion, everything is dedicated and given, even to the right of disposing of our interior excellences, and of the satisfactions which we gain daily by good works. This is something which is not done even in a Religious Order. . . .

Furthermore, it also follows that anyone who has made this complete dedication and sacrifice to Jesus Christ, through Mary, can no longer dispose of the value of any of his good works. All that such a person suffers, everything of good that he thinks, says and does, belongs to Mary, in order that she may dispose of it according to the will of her Son and for His greater glory; it being clearly understood, of course, that this dependence is prejudicial in no way to the obligations of one's state now or at any future time — for example, to the obligations of a priest. . . . It must always be understood that this offering to Jesus through Mary is made in accordance with the order of God and the duties of our state.

Lastly, it follows that we consecrate ourselves jointly to the Blessed Virgin and to Jesus Christ; to the Blessed Virgin as to a perfect means which Jesus Christ has chosen to unite Himself with us and to unite us with Him; and to Our Lord, as to our Last End, to Whom we owe all that we are, as to our Savior and to our God. . . .

This devotion does not prevent us from praying for others, both the living and the dead, provided the application of our good works is left entirely dependent upon the will of the Most Blessed Virgin. Indeed, the contrary holds: this devotion leads us to pray with greater confidence for others. . . . (Part 2, Chapter 1, Article 2, *True Devotion*)

Personally, I do not remember a time in my life when I was not devoted to the Mother of God, having obviously learned it from my mother's knee. However, I confess that in the seminary some years before ordination I lingered and debated for some time before finally making the act of total consecration to Mary.

It is not recommended that anyone would make the act suddenly or without due preparation and prayer. The problem for me was a delay in fully appreciating the generosity of Mary. There was the fear that in giving all to Mary I was somehow hindered in my desire to give all to Jesus. The insight that dissolved the difficulty completely was this: The will of Mary is perfectly one with the will of God. The heart of Mary is one with the Heart of Jesus. Mary wills nothing but what her Son, Jesus, wills. It is impossible for Mary to will anything that Jesus does not already will. By giving all to Mary, I will really be giving all to Jesus through Mary, and she in her motherly tenderness and love will purify whatever is weak and sinful in my humble gift of self. My gift will therefore be more pleasing to Jesus when given in Mary. Mary then will have been more completely and perfectly accepted as my Mother to keep me always one with Jesus.

When a soul objects to consecration to the Immaculate Heart, it is because that soul does not yet fully understand the meaning of the consecration. The person does not yet know Mary as he might. Her heart magnifies the Lord (Lk 1:46). It is an ongoing process to get to know and love our Mother more and more, as it is in regard to Jesus.

When we speak of the beauty of our Blessed Mother, it is not just physical loveliness, not mere material charms we mean. It is a spiritual beauty, a supernatural beauty. However lovely an artist may depict the Mother of God in a work of art, it will still be only a dim reflection, a weak suggestion of the reality of that heavenly creature who is God's Mother and our spiritual Mother by grace. Mary, of course, is both body and soul. Her Immaculate Heart suggests her total person, with all the faculties of her soul, all the grace she possesses, the state of glory in which she now lives.

Consecrating oneself to the Immaculate Heart of our heavenly Mother is a reaching out to identify oneself with Christ through the means God used to come to this world and identify himself with the human race. That heavenly Mother, magnificent while upon earth in perfection of faith and fullness of grace, is now glorified in heavenly existence beyond what has ever entered into the mind of man (see 1 Cor 2:9).

Once all has been given to Mary through consecration, a

peace comes over the soul. No longer will the consecrated one attempt to determine for himself how God might best apply the humble value of his good works, his prayers, his petitions. All is given to Mary to do with as she pleases. One does not forget the charity one should have for all, especially and most immediately for those closest, for whom one is responsible. At the same time, the consecrated person knows that Mary gathers one's every thought, word, and need. Our heavenly Mother possesses all we are and all we have. Her decisions on our behalf, the direction she gives our prayers and good works, will always be far superior to our own — all pure and holy and perfectly one with the will of God.

Each day henceforth will be a living of the prayer, "I am all Yours and all that I have is Yours, O most loving Jesus, through Mary Your holy Mother." And there is something more. This total entrusting to the Immaculate Heart of Mary does not end at the grave. This consecration to Mary's Immaculate Heart is eternal.

When the earth as we know it will be no more, when the present world has passed away and is made over according to God's plan, each one who lived his or her consecration to Mary's Immaculate Heart upon earth will still be living it within the heart of God's Mother before His eternal throne. As the Father, beholding Jesus in the perpetual light of the Blessed Trinity, sees the most perfect likeness of His Word incarnate in the Immaculate Heart of His Mother, He will gaze everlastingly upon that heart in an act of knowledge and love that surpasses all else in heaven. So too in that gaze God will see something of each one especially consecrated to Jesus in Mary's heart.

Those who consecrate themselves to Mary's Immaculate Heart on earth, while living in faith and responding in love, do so for time and for eternity. Mary takes those who so entrust themselves into her heart, already in Jesus, and there she will keep them with a special love for all eternity.

Jesus, the Word incarnate, sits forever at the right hand of the Father. The Holy Spirit, the Spirit of Love, is still breathed forth between the Father and the Son as that Third Person of Love completely envelops and unifies the heart of Mary, the Mother of the Word, into the life of the whole Trinity. Bringing

Mary into that oneness of the Trinity, while she still retains her identity, embraces in the same act all the consecrated souls Mary forever keeps within the love of her heart.

In Appendix 2, at the back of this book, you will find a formula for an *Act of Total Consecration to the Immaculate Heart of Mary*. The entire book should be studied thoroughly before the Act of Consecration should be seriously considered. While reading of this work ought to be of value for greater knowledge and love of our Blessed Mother, those called to *Total Consecration* will be better prepared for making that serious step through prayer and contemplating the thoughts offered in the chapters before this and those yet to come!

CHAPTER 9

† Living One's Consecration †

MARY IS THE Temple of the Trinity. Our Mother's Immaculate Heart is the hearth of the divine fire. As Mother of mercy, she enshrined Jesus, the Source of Life, so that we might all share in divine life.

In Mary the Word of Life was written. In her the Light of Life shines brightest after the Source itself. The Light and Love of God has a burning desire to diffuse itself and share itself with all men made in His image and likeness. "And from his fulness have we all received, grace upon grace" (Jn 1:16).

It is in this Life, this brightness of Light, that we must live our consecration to Mary's Immaculate Heart. Living one's consecration is first and foremost the living of a life consecrated to Jesus in Mary and Jesus through Mary. Consecration, truly to live one's consecration, is a new way of life, a wholly sanctified attitude of mind and will. "For by one Spirit we were all baptized into one body . . . and all were made to drink of one Spirit" (1 Cor 12:13).

We see in Mary's heart the first flowering of the Church and the ideal for which we all should strive. Look again into that miraculous heart. While each one of us receives baptism and confirmation only once, they bestow a vitality that God intends to grow, to intensify, to inflame and enlighten, so that "according to his glorious might" we may "share in the inheritance of the saints of light" (Col 1:11-12). This continuous growth in life, light, glory — this being the one "who first hoped in Christ . . . destined and appointed to hope in his glory," this being "sealed with the promised Holy Spirit," a people God had made his own, "to the praise of his glory" (Eph 1:12-14) — was true preeminently of Mary, the Mother who belongs to us all and intercedes with God to share the same privileges of her inheritance with her children.

To the heart of such a Mother we must attach ourselves. She knows the way, for the Way is her very own Son. As He found His choicest home in her Immaculate Heart, He will also find His dwelling place in the hearts of her children, so that He may be our Brother as well as our Lord, and we His dearest brothers and sisters. He understands our love for and consecration to such a Mother, for He had such a love and was devoted to this same Mother long before we came along. And when Wisdom burst forth in creating such an Immaculate Heart as Its very own Mother, the same act foresaw her motherhood by grace of each one of us. Such a family is the family of God within the Immaculate Heart of God's Mother, joined in the love of the Holy Spirit under the fatherhood of God.

The greatest means God has given us to be ever more enriched with the divine life is "the Bread of Life," taking our Lord's body, blood, soul, and divinity in Holy Communion. There is a relationship between our receiving Jesus in Holy Communion and the indwelling of the Blessed Trinity in the soul. Receiving the Real Presence of Jesus Christ, the God-man, in Holy Communion does not bring a greater indwelling of the Blessed Trinity in the soul that is already in grace. God is simply present in us by grace, Father, Son, and Holy Spirit — not more or less, not in parts or by degrees — God in all three divine Persons, infinitely and perfectly in all His divine Being. Our participation in His life, however, increases and the effects of the divine indwelling of the Three in One intensify by a worthy and loving Holy Communion. Mary, in whom Jesus dwelt, body, blood, soul, and divinity — His body receiving nourishment through her body during the nine months before His birth at Bethlehem — is indeed the model for us to live the Christ-life and be formed more and more into His likeness.

Isn't that what devotion to the Immaculate Heart of Mary is about? While she shares and reflects the brightness of eternal light and love most profoundly, she is powerful to share with us the wine of the new covenant. She intercedes to bring forth Jesus.

While it is true that some may receive Holy Communion with little spiritual effect to the soul, little growth in grace, it should not be so. Such is not the divine intention for this Most Blessed

Sacrament. Just as for most the effects of baptism and confirmation do not reach their full potential — and for some little or none at all because of poor dispositions or response to grace — so too when Holy Communion is received with the minimum of dispositions, or worse yet, unworthily.

Unification in Christ, as our Mother Mary has shown us, is possible for a created human. The Fathers of the Church have described the effect. "Throw melted wax into melted wax," wrote St. Cyril of Jerusalem, "and the one interpenetrates the other perfectly. In like manner when the body and blood of Christ are received, the union is such that Christ is in the recipient and he in Christ. . . . We have the same body, and the same blood." St. Cyprian adds: "Our union with Christ unites affections and wills."

When we receive Jesus in Holy Communion, then, Christ is so entirely in our hearts and souls that our thoughts and affections are also His, if our Communion has been in faith and love. Here again we can see, from all that has been said of the faith and response in love of Mary, how her Immaculate Heart is our perfect model. If one has poor dispositions of heart and soul, with only a little love, Jesus is hindered. He must accommodate himself to the narrow limits of that soul and is prevented from pouring forth His gifts more abundantly. How much we can learn from Mary! Consecrating our very lives to her Immaculate Heart disposes us to a faith and love like her own. We are led to fruitful results in Holy Communion and to a more intense life in union with the Trinity, abiding in us by grace.

Mary's growth in grace during the nine months she was a tabernacle to the unborn infant Jesus is beyond our imagination. Yet she also received Jesus in Holy Communion from the apostles. At the Last Supper Jesus had given the apostles the command, "Do this in memory of me." They offered His Sacrifice of the Mass daily in order to eat of the Bread of Life. Certainly the beloved John, who took Mary into his own home as he was commissioned to do by Jesus from the cross, offered this Eucharistic Sacrifice frequently with Mary present and participating. Biblical accounts and early Christian writings on the faith and practices of the earliest Christians attest to their faith and love centered on the Eucharistic Christ.

We have noted that first fullness of grace in Mary and her profound growth in the divine life as she carried the Author of Life within her. But now our holy Mother drinks deeper of the Spirit after the life, death, resurrection, and ascension of Jesus and the descending of the Holy Spirit upon the Church. With the foundation of the Church of which she is Mother, Mary receives even greater insights, an even profounder grasp of divine revelation now completed. She opens her heart to even greater graces than in her earlier years. Each Holy Communion for Mary meant being plunged anew into the Ocean of Life and Love who made himself one with her by participation. What a divine flame of love must have emerged from the Eucharistic Heart of Jesus into the Immaculate Heart of His Mother! How ablaze must her own being have been as her will and affections became wholly one with those of Jesus! This Temple of the Trinity glows ever brighter and brighter, adding glory to glory for the sake of God. "The unsearchable riches of Christ" (Eph 3:8) continue to multiply with each Holy Communion, each union of hearts.

Such is true to some degree of each one of us who receives Holy Communion in grace. The soul becomes a sanctuary filled with ineffable wonders. The Three Divine Persons are active in the soul. There, God the Father generates His only begotten Son. Together the Father and the Son breathe forth the Holy Spirit. What then of Mary? In an eternal NOW the Father is begetting the Son. "Thou art my Son, today I have begotten thee" (Acts 13:33; see Heb 1:5, 5:5).

Mary begot Jesus only once. The Father begets the Son from and for all eternity. What a profound relationship with God exists in Mary, who begets the Son in the flesh while the Father is thus begetting the Son and the Son and the Father are breathing forth the Holy Spirit. That Holy Spirit, the Spirit of Love, has Mary as spouse. This intense life of the Blessed Trinity is present in everyone in the state of grace. How completely Mary must have entered into this divine life, especially every time she received her Son anew in Holy Communion.

If we have faith — if we are open to that "instinct for God" given us at baptism, that germ of the gifts of wisdom and understanding that was implanted in the soul to grasp the great truths of divine reality; if we realize the greatness of our participation in the life of the Blessed Trinity increased by each worthy Holy Communion — we can look to the Immaculate Heart of Mary as model. We can only marvel at what must be her radiance ever intensifying. We must ever remember that our Mother was free. She lived in faith on earth. No one has received greater grace from Holy Communion than the Mother of Jesus.

Consecrated to Mary's Immaculate Heart, then, we ought to participate in the Sacrifice of the Mass with the spirit of Mary as she stood beneath the cross on Calvary offering her divine Son to the Father. We ought to receive Jesus in Holy Communion calling upon the spirit of Mary's faith and love to assist us in such an intimate and unutterable union. "I am the vine, you are the branches. He who abides in me, and I in him, he it is that bears much fruit" (Jn 15:5).

Jesus said: "If a man loves me, he will keep my word, and my Father will love him, and we will come to him and make our home with him" (Jn 14:23). The soul of one who receives the Word made flesh in Holy Communion becomes as a heaven to the Blessed Trinity. Within the soul of each of us the Father and the Son exchange Their love and equal embrace. Their love for each other breathes forth the eternal flame that is the Holy Spirit. Each of us is such a heaven, such a temple to the Trinity. It is real. It is true. This LIFE is within us, however undeserving and unworthy we may be. How ideal it is for us to approach such a throne of grace in the spirit of Mary.

Didn't Jesus first become one with His Mother so that He might become one with us? And Jesus calls us to do the will of God knowing that Mary first did His will perfectly. Jesus himself prays, asking His Father that we may be admitted into the mystery of the love of the Three in One. "[Father], I do not pray for these only, but also for those who believe in me . . . that they also may be in us" (Jn 17:20-21).

O Blessed Trinity, Three in One, You who came to live in the Immaculate Heart of Mary so fully and so perfectly, come to live in me, become one with me, as You became one with Mary.

It is true that the life of Jesus remains distinct from our life. His divine nature and person are distinct from our human nature and individual souls. We do not lose our identity. Yet an incomparable union of love takes place as He lives His life in us and we become like Him. He brings with Him the entire Trinity into our souls, for one divine Person is never present without all Three.

It is primarily through the Sacrifice of the Mass and the seven sacraments that the sacred humanity of Jesus keeps pouring an inexhaustible effusion of divine grace into our souls. The saints and angels in heaven rejoice. The good angels, having the beatific vision, eternally behold the Mystery of the Trinity — the Father begetting the Son and these Two begetting the Holy Spirit in love. Yet as the angels gaze and will gaze for all eternity, there will always be fresh insights for them into the divine Mystery.

And here the surprise comes for the guardian angel assigned to each of us. He discovers, in that soul to whom he is committed, a reflection and extension of the Incarnation. For each one of us is a baptized and confirmed member of the Mystical Body of Christ. The angel discovers in each one of us something more of the mercy of God, mercy that the angel never directly experienced but which he adores. And when we consecrate ourselves to the Immaculate Heart of Mary and strive to live that consecration, then how the angel rejoices, beholding anew something of the Word made flesh as it applies to us, and as we live in the spirit of Mary's heart. She is the angels' Queen and always their delight, so beautiful and glorious; yet such radiance is not God.

Christ must be our life as He was for Mary. Each time we approach the Lord to receive Him in Holy Communion there is a renewal of the presence of the Three Divine Persons. That is to say, there is a new sharing of the divine life, a fuller grasp of our participation in the Trinity's life of knowing and loving. Each of the Three loves our souls immensely, and the more we share in the life of Jesus the more we are loved by Them.

Our Blessed Mother in heaven now lives an eternal praise of glory, greater than all angels and all men but Jesus. This praise of glory, this living the life within the Trinity, has begun within us even now. What we have on earth is only the beginning of the wonderful joy, a true participation in the praise of glory in heaven which will be one and the same. Now we see by faith. Then we shall see by vision. We shall see God face to face even as He is.

Our devotion to the Immaculate Heart of Mary as we live our consecration should include a consciousness of this union we have with the Trinity, this Presence of God within us. It is her way of life, first in faith, now in glory. Only if we are conscious in faith and love of this divine presence will it bear fruit for eternity. Consider the Apostle John with his head on the breast of Jesus at the Last Supper, discovering the secrets of the Sacred Heart. And what he does not discover directly from that Heart he is to learn later from Mary, as he takes her to his own when Jesus dies on the cross out of love for the whole world. John was consecrated to Mary by Jesus himself. Mary will also teach us further secrets.

Living our life of consecration will not only involve contemplating the union we have with the Trinity through grace, through love, but we must spend ourselves in service of neighbor. Charity to others is living our consecration. "You shall love the Lord your God with all your heart, with all your soul, and with all your mind" (Mt 22:37). We are called to live an active exterior life without diminishing an interior life of union with the Divine Presence. Mary pondered the Word of God in her heart and still served others. Christ said that what we do for the least of His brethren is done to Him (see Mt 25:40).

Sometimes souls who desire to live a spiritual life may either forget the need of charity toward others or think a life of holiness, one of consecration, consists in many external practices. Some think they must say certain prayers each day, this form of prayer, these exact words and exercises, the more Rosaries the better. This is not to discourage the praying of beautiful prayers, and certainly not the Rosary when it consists of a proper praying, namely while meditating on the Mysteries of Christ. The important thing in living one's consecration is not multiplying exercises but a habitual spirit of life, living in union with Jesus Christ and through Him with the entire Trinity, seeing Mary as Mediatrix of Grace and model of the perfect Christian life.

Jesus told us to pray always (see Lk 18:1). This means that everything we do should be offered as a prayer. It is fulfilled if we live the *Morning Offering* where we offer to Jesus our whole day "through the Immaculate Heart of Mary," our prayers, works, joys, sufferings "in union with the Holy Sacrifice of the Mass throughout the world." If the spirit of the Morning Offering is truly the spirit of our day, we live our consecration to Mary's Immaculate Heart.

Perfection requires not being attached to worldly goods. St.

Luke, immediately after relating the love Jesus has for little children, gives the account of the rich man who kept the basic commandments but was attached to the world's goods. Jesus had just said, "Truly, I say to you, whoever does not receive the kingdom of God like a child shall not enter it" (Lk 18:17). Jesus had commanded that the little children be permitted to come to Him. A child believes and loves easily and trusts what he is told. So we ought to believe, trust, and love like a child.

The rich man responded to the commandments Jesus outlined: " 'All these [things] I have observed from my youth.' And when Jesus heard it, he said to him, 'One thing you still lack. Sell all that you have and distribute [it] to the poor, and you will have treasure in heaven; and come, follow me.' But when he heard this he became sad, for he was very rich" (Lk 18:21-23). When St. Matthew told the story he said it was a "young man" and "the young man . . . went away sorrowful; for he had great possessions" (Mt 19:22).

Wisely, then, the spirit of total consecration to the Immaculate Heart of Mary requires giving all our material property to Mary. We may not be called to the life of the Religious who takes the vow of poverty, but we certainly must live the spirit of poverty. "Blessed are the poor in spirit. . ." (Mt 5:3). The poverty of the Holy Family is to be recalled. We must surrender everything to the Lord.

While the person who has a family to support may own property, he must not be attached to it, and he ought to live in the world as though not living in it and use property as though not his own. He uses it only as a reasonable necessity of life. One consecrated to Mary surely should not live in luxurious surroundings for personal comfort or prestige. He ought to share his abundance and keep only what he needs for self-support without a spirit of worldliness.

Then there is Jesus' hidden life of many years. Those were years of preparation and silent worship of the Father until He had reached physical maturity. Then it became time for Him to manifest the entire Blessed Trinity, and himself as Son of God and Savior. When Jesus left Nazareth and began His public ministry, in no way was His interior life of prayer diminished. His consecration to Mary was not diminished either. The same love for

His Father continued and manifested itself in many ways. "My food is to do the will of him who sent me, and to accomplish his work" (Jn 4:34).

As one grows more and more into one's consecration to the Immaculate Heart of Mary, one discovers better how to live the Christ-life as she did. There becomes less and less distinction between time spent in active work and time conversing with our interior Guests. At the very time Mary went in charity to assist Elizabeth, she prayed, "My soul magnifies the Lord" (Lk 1:46). "And whatever you do, in word or in deed, do everything in the name of the Lord Jesus, giving thanks to God the Father through him" (Col 3:17).

Consecration to Mary will not remove sorrows and sufferings from our life. She is the Mother of Sorrows. Simeon foretold at the presentation of the Child that a sword would pierce her heart. She will not be greater than her Lord, Master, and Son; "the Christ should suffer" (Lk 24:46). "Indeed all who desire to live a godly life in Christ Jesus will be persecuted" (2 Tim 3:12). "If any man would come after me, let him deny himself and take up his cross and follow me" (Mk 8:34).

Little wonder the modern Christian so seldom resembles the Master. He does not want penance, sacrifice, the cross. In that case, Jesus tells us, he cannot be His disciple. Mary is the first disciple of Jesus, and there was immense suffering in her earthly life before she, like Christ, entered into glory. So it must be with those consecrated to Jesus through Mary.

Living our consecration must involve embracing the cross that comes into our lives. We do not have to create crosses. We need to accept the duties of our state in life. We need to make everything we do a sacrifice, offering all daily for love of God. If each one, according to his or her state in life, single, religious, married, the priest — if all were true to the duties of their state in life, accepting and offering all for the love of God, how glorious would be the life of the Church. What conversions would result. What saints the Church would have. Isn't it precisely this that Mary did so well in faith and love? It is what we are called to do in consecrating ourselves to her Immaculate Heart. To do one's daily duty is to do the will of God. It is to love. To go beyond our duty is to love more.

". . .Always carrying in the body the death of Jesus, so that the life of Jesus may also be manifested in our bodies. For while we live we are always being given up to death for Jesus' sake, so that the life of Jesus may be manifested in our mortal flesh" (2 Cor 4:10-11).

The suffering of Mary is seen in her title Queen of Martyrs. Like Mary's, when our sufferings are accepted in faith and love, Jesus is permitted to suffer again within us, the members of His Body, and this gives Him the opportunity to offer it up to His Father for the salvation of souls: ". . . in my flesh I complete what is lacking in Christ's afflictions for the sake of his body, that is, the church" (Col 1:24). "For it has been granted to you that for the sake of Christ you should not only believe in him but also suffer for his sake . . ." (Phil 1:29).

But Mary is "Cause of our Joy" too. True joy should come from consciousness of the Blessed Trinity dwelling in our souls. There was joy in Jesus. When He was entering into His final passion leading to His death, He prayed to His Father, "that they may have my joy fulfilled in themselves" (Jn 17:13). We can pray with St. Gertrude: "Joy and gladness be to You, for the most worthy heart and soul of the glorious Virgin Mary, Your Mother, whom You have given me as Mother in the difficulties of my salvation, and who is always opening for me the treasures of her maternal solicitude."

Jesus had sorrow and joy at the same time. The lower faculties of His soul were in anguish while the higher were in joy. So we, though we sorrow in the senses, may rejoice in our intellects and wills since God, the Source of all joy, dwells in us.

It was love for the Father and for us that prompted the Son to become man, be nailed to the cross, and institute the Blessed Sacrament. It was love for God that prompted the will of Mary to accept the request of God through the Angel Gabriel that she become the Mother of the Son of the Most High, share His sufferings, and make it possible for us to receive the same soul, body, and blood of the divine Person she conceived. One who seeks to be like Jesus must first of all love God. This is to say, do His will. That is what consecration to Mary's heart is all about: doing the will of God as Mary did.

The soul is capable of great desires, that is, of great love. The human soul, aided by divine grace, is capable of such intense love as to rise above itself in its transports. The mystic apostle, St. John, who wrote so much about the love of God — that dear disciple whom Jesus loved and to whom His Mother was commissioned on behalf of us all, the one who summed it all up in three words, "God is love" — also wrote, quoting Jesus, "If you knew the gift of God . . ." (Jn 4:10). It was to a sinful woman Jesus spoke those words. For every soul, however lowly in its lack of grace, has the potential to come alive with God and live eternally among His great saints.

In our misery, we could never ask the exalted Blessed Trinity to look upon our souls. However, we may ask the Trinity to look upon Jesus within us and behold His face. In going to Jesus, the Mediator with the Father, we can ask Him to first look upon the face and heart of Mary, to whom we have consecrated ourselves so as to be one with Him. In her we find refuge. Living our consecration, we can pray, "It is no longer I who live, but Christ who lives in me; and the life I now live in the flesh I live by faith in the Son of God, who loved me and gave himself for me" (Gal 2:20).

Jesus said: "As the living Father sent me, and I live because of the Father, so he who eats me will live because of me" (Jn 6:57). The end of receiving Jesus in Holy Communion is to make our heart the Heart of Christ. It is the end of consecration to the heart of Mary as well. How pleasing must be the prayer of one who has received our divine Lord in Holy Communion to say, "O Jesus, living in Mary, come and live in me." How beautiful also at the Consecration of the Mass, where Jesus perpetuates the selfsame Sacrifice He offered on the cross, to join in spirit with Mary as she stood beneath the cross on Calvary. The living of our consecration to Mary's Immaculate Heart has a beauty and power which brings profound awe to the angels of God.

Living one's consecration to Mary's heart requires a constant effort to practice the Christian virtues. We have often mentioned the theological virtues of faith, hope, and charity. There are also the chief moral virtues of prudence, justice, fortitude, and temperance.

A moral virtue is a worthy habit, a steadiness of the will whose immediate object is to be a means by which we attain our final destiny, union with God in eternity. When one is virtuous the will remains constant in spite of difficulties faced in the performance of one's duty.

An entire book could be dedicated to the virtues as one strives to live the good Christian life with Mary as model. Other moral virtues include filial piety, obedience, veracity, patience, humility, and chastity, or purity.

One who truly lives his or her consecration becomes ever more conscious of the indwelling of the entire Blessed Trinity. Since our spiritual Mother is the spouse of the Holy Spirit, living one's consecration to her makes us more alert to discern and ready to do the will of God through the seven gifts of the Holy Spirit, for these gifts are infused with sanctifying grace. The Holy Spirit is never present without His gifts; they are wisdom, understanding, counsel, fortitude, knowledge, piety, and fear of the Lord (see Is 11:2-3).

The supernatural *virtues* help us to follow the guidance of right reason and the true instinct of faith. The *gifts* help us to promptly follow the inspirations of the Holy Spirit. A life consecrated to the Immaculate Heart of Mary disposes one to be truly open to the Holy Spirit, and thus the effects of the indwelling of the Spirit can be truly experienced in the *fruits* of the Holy Spirit and the *beatitudes*.

The fruits of the indwelling of the Holy Spirit will consist of good works performed under the inspiration of the Spirit with a certain delight. Drawn from Sacred Scripture, the twelve fruits of the Holy Spirit are traditionally listed as: charity, joy, peace, patience, benignity, goodness, long-suffering, mildness, faith, modesty, continency, and chastity (see Gal 5:22-23).

The eight beatitudes were given to us by our divine Savior at the beginning of His Sermon on the Mount (see Mt 5:3-10). They are called beatitudes because they will bring us happiness both on earth and in heaven. We must not confuse the intense living of the spiritual life with the kind of happiness the world offers.

The supernatural virtues are rooted in God and always accompanied by the indwelling of the Blessed Trinity and our sharing in the life of God. The indwelling of the entire Blessed Trinity is called "uncreated grace," while our sharing in God's life by various degrees is known as "created grace." The pagan without grace in his soul may have natural virtues and appear very gracious. Grace builds on nature, but there is always the potential for whatever is naturally good in us to be elevated by grace so that all that we are and have becomes Christed, that is, infused by grace grafting us into the Body of Christ (see Rom 11:17).

When we look to the heart of our heavenly Mother as model, as the first and perfect disciple of Jesus Christ, we see one who in every respect was elevated from the natural level to the heights of sanctity and in whom all the virtues, the gifts and fruits of the Holy Spirit, blossomed most magnificently. This is why Mary is considered the "first flowering of the Church."

> But while in the most holy Virgin the Church has already reached that perfection whereby she exists without spot or wrinkle (cf. Eph 5:27), the faithful still strive to conquer sin and increase in holiness. And so they turn their eyes to Mary who shines forth to the whole community of the elect as the model of virtues. Devoutly meditating on her and contemplating her in the light of the Word made man, the Church reverently pene-trates more deeply into the great mystery of the Incarnation and becomes more and more like her spouse. Having entered deeply into the history of salvation, Mary, in a way, unites in her person and re-echoes the most important doctrines of the faith: and when she is the subject of preaching and worship she prompts the faithful to come to her Son, to His sacrifice, and to love for the Father. Seeking after the glory of Christ, the Church becomes more like her lofty type, and continually prog-resses in faith, hope, and charity, seeking and doing the will of God in all things. The Church, therefore, in her apostolic work too, rightly looks to her who gave birth to Christ, who was thus conceived by the Holy Spirit and born of a virgin, in order that through the Church He could be born and increase in the hearts of the faithful. In her life the Virgin has been a model of that motherly love with which all who join in the Church's apostolic mission for the regeneration of mankind should be animated. (*Lumen Gentium*, 65, Vatican II)

Consecration to Mary's heart, then, is the expression of the soul's desire to strive to live the perfect Christian life as Mary did. She intercedes for the Holy Spirit to form Christ in us. How many Christians truly live the beatitudes to perfection? Yet living the beatitudes is the fulfillment of the Christian life preached by Jesus. Living them is required for a true living of one's consecra-tion to Mary's Immaculate Heart. Supernatural happiness exists in the soul regardless of sufferings in this world. As we've stated,

Jesus facing death prayed to His Father that we may all be filled with His joy. As He hung dying on the cross, His soul still had the beatific vision. Mary's soul at the foot of the cross did not enjoy the beatific vision, but the higher regions of her soul were still filled with the happiness of God as the soul of Jesus Christ always was. The sorrowful Mother lived perfectly these beatitudes:

> Blessed are the poor in spirit, for theirs is the kingdom of heaven.
>
> Blessed are those who mourn, for they shall be comforted.
>
> Blessed are the meek, for they shall inherit the earth.
>
> Blessed are those who hunger and thirst for righteousness, for they shall be satisfied.
>
> Blessed are the merciful, for they shall obtain mercy.
>
> Blessed are the pure in heart, for they shall see God.
>
> Blessed are the peacemakers, for they shall be called sons of God.
>
> Blessed are those who are persecuted for righteousness' sake, for theirs is the kingdom of heaven.
>
> Blessed are you when men revile you and persecute you and utter all kinds of evil against you falsely on my account.
>
> Rejoice and be glad, for your reward is great in heaven. . . . (Mt 5:3-12)

It remains for another time and place, perhaps another author, to develop Mary as model in living the beatitudes, a work that could take an entire book. Note, however, that the beatitudes, which entail the living of a perfect Christian life, involve relationships to other people. Authentic Marian piety and living one's consecration to Mary's Immaculate Heart must involve evangelization, concern for the salvation of others. A study of the great Marian apostle St. Louis-Marie Grignon de Montfort reveals not only his personal dedication and promotion of true devotion to Mary but his priestly role as an untiring popular preacher of the Gospel. Modern documents of the Church have demonstrated that evangelization is a duty of every committed Christian.

Spreading in the Church today is a spirit of evangelization and renewed devotion to Mary based on sound doctrine and greater scriptural emphases. Thus begins the realization of the desired fruits of Vatican II, the hailing of an eventual New Pentecost. The Holy Spirit is inspiring in the Church at the same time a rediscovery of Mary and an apostolic spirit reaching out to other souls. While the work of Satan may seem at times to triumph, remember that so it seemed on Calvary on Good Friday afternoon. In reality on Good Friday, Jesus and Mary were triumphing. So it is now.

To evangelize is to "preach the good news of the kingdom of God" (Lk 4:43). To evangelize is to share the incarnation, death, and resurrection of Jesus and the salvation He brings us as the Son of God made man in order that we might become the adopted children of God (see Gal 4:4-5) through baptism and then live as His children. When we evangelize as members of Christ's Mystical Body, we continue the work of salvation for which the Father sent Jesus Christ into the world and for which the Father and the Son sent the Holy Spirit.

Look to Mary as a model in evangelization. She was first to receive the Good News of salvation and devote herself entirely to the Person and work of her divine Son. The first thing Mary does is bring Jesus to Elizabeth and to John the Baptizer. The Child in her arms does not speak yet, but Mary evangelizes the shepherds and the Magi. It was through her direct intervention at Cana that Mary, by her perfect faith, obtained the sign that confirmed the faith of the apostles. She surely must have confided the memories she kept and reflected upon in her heart, aided by the Holy Spirit, to the beloved disciple John, with whom she lived after the death of Jesus. Mary enlightened the faith of the early Church in Jesus as Son of God, Savior. She had the greatest influence on St. John after the death of Jesus on the cross: "from that hour the disciple took her to his own home" (Jn 19:27). That was Mary's home Easter Sunday morning, when Jesus rose from the dead. How could St. Luke write as he does about Mary and the divine infancy without Mary's having shared her knowledge?

Mary Magdalene was first to visit the tomb of Jesus on that first Easter Sunday morning; having found it empty, she ran back to St. Peter and St. John, both of whom then ran to the tomb to be witnesses for themselves of the empty sepulcher (see Jn 20:1-7). It was John, the youngest apostle, who had taken Mary into his home, who was the first apostle to witness the Resurrection in seeing the empty tomb. St. Mary Magdalene was convinced that the body of our Lord had been taken away. St. Peter did not utter a single word. John, having outrun Peter, arrived first; "and stooping to look in, he saw the linen cloths lying there, but he did not go in. Then Simon Peter came, following him, and went into the tomb; he saw the linen cloths lying, and the napkin which had been on his [Jesus'] head, not lying with the linen cloths, but rolled up in a place by itself. Then the other disciple, who reached the tomb first, also went in, and he [John] saw and believed" (Jn 20:5-10).

It was a special grace for St. John, in such an environment, to see clearly what had really happened. Jesus had foretold and Scripture foreshadowed the resurrection of the Christ. St. John, with whom Mary, the most faithful Virgin Mother, had been staying since Good Friday afternoon, wrote the impressive words about himself: "he saw and believed; for as yet they did not know the scripture that he [Jesus] must rise from the dead. Then the disciples went back to their homes."

St. Peter and St. John not only worked closely together, but they lived together, both tenderly cherished by the Blessed Virgin Mary, who after the crucifixion was cared for by St. John. The Acts of the Apostles also mention their staying together (see Acts 1:13). These two worked together and went to the Temple together for their prayers (Acts 3:1). They even preached the Gospel together, as in Samaria (Acts 8:14).

It was St. John who first recognized Jesus at the Sea of Tiberias, standing on the shore and calling to His disciples. St. John was with St. Peter in the boat and said to St. Peter, "It is the Lord!" (see Jn 21:2-14). Then our Lord, having given bread and fish to the few disciples present on that occasion, confirmed in a special way the privileges and primacy of St. Peter in the Church (John 21:12-23), saying to St. Peter: "Feed my lambs. . . . Feed my sheep." St. John had another mission, witness to the primacy of Peter, the apostle of unity of the Church. St. Peter was aware of a special role for St. John, for on that occasion he asked Jesus, "Lord, what about this man?" meaning John. And the Lord answered, "If it is my will that he remain until I come, what is that to you?"

It is well for us, in our consideration of Mary and evangelization, to look a bit at John, the beloved disciple to whom our divine Lord commissioned His Mother in a special way. We see his close collaboration with St. Peter and are reminded how consecration to Mary's Immaculate Heart, as we'll mention again in this book, also requires undivided loyalty to the Church of which Mary is Mother and the Pope is visible head. (*Ubi Petrus, ibi Ecclesia.*) When St. Peter wanted an answer from Jesus at the Last Supper, it was St. John he got to get the answer for him (see Jn 13:23-24).

Mary is concerned about evangelization, as Mother of the Church, the woman of faith to whose heart the entire Church was entrusted from the cross. Entering into the care of St. John from the hour of Jesus' death, Mary must have gone along when St. John went to Ephesus. This departure for Ephesus was apparently early, probably immediately after Christians were driven from Jerusalem, sometime between the years 37 and 42, with the deportation of St. Paul. St. John lived in Ephesus until his death except for the time of his exile on the nearby Island of Patmos, where he received the last Revelation (Apocalypse) of Jesus Christ.

The Fourth Gospel was written by St. John, the apostle and evangelist, the beloved disciple of Jesus and the adopted son of the Mother of God. The apostle wrote the Gospel named after him at Ephesus toward the end of his life, between A.D. 90 and 100. He had been for years in direct association with Mary, and his power as an evangelist is manifest in his Gospel. There St. John witnesses to the Word made flesh, to the divinity of Jesus Christ and His resurrection, to love and faith, the unity of the Church and the primacy of St. Peter. The Gospel of John penetrates the inmost secrets of the Heart of Jesus Christ, the life of God himself, and the mysteries of our redemption. The influence of the Blessed Virgin Mary can be seen in his Gospel and Epistles.

The message of the Immaculate Heart of Mary is one of love. We note in the writings of St. John that he never grew tired of repeating in some way the two great commandments, love of God and love of neighbor. "On these two commandments depend all the law and the prophets" (Mt 12:40). St. Jerome relates that during the last days of his life St. John kept repeating in his sermons, "My dearest children, love one another." One of his disciples, seemingly eager to hear something else, said to his master, "Why do you always keep insisting on this?" He answered, "Because it is our Lord's command, and if only this is observed, it is sufficient."

At a time in history when Christianity struggles with dialectical materialism and international communism, there is great need to practice love for one another as reflected in the teachings of St. John the Apostle and devotion to the Immaculate Heart of Mary. The materialistic race, which pits people against their neighbors in power and earthly riches, dominating others, has no time for the light of life, the true love of God and neighbor. The chapter on the meaning of total consecration to Mary makes clear that it is opposed to the spirit of materialism.

St. John the Evangelist has the eagle for his symbol. The loving Immaculate Heart of God's Mother must have contributed to John's unapproachable heights. John contemplated and wrote of things this Mother had been pondering from the beginning. The evangelists obviously tried to complete their personal knowledge, drawing new and deeper information from every possible reliable source. What better source could they find than the Mother of Jesus? Here we might find the true reason why our divine Lord willed to leave His beloved Mother on earth so long with all her sorrows, after He had ascended into heaven. Mary was left exposed to all the dangers of persecution. Surely the Mother of Jesus was subject to scrutiny and terror after the death of Jesus in the attempt to keep the apostles from spreading the Gospel. That is probably the reason why St. John considered it his duty to leave Jerusalem so soon, before all others, to take the Blessed Virgin beyond danger. That was the primary duty Jesus had placed upon John as our Lord was dying on the cross — to care for Mary.

St. John, looking after the Mother of God, concerned about her care, had to be careful of any public preaching on her Son. With her assumption into heaven, St. John could work freely without putting his choicest treasure in danger. During the life of the Blessed Virgin Mary, John was behind the stage, always living near or with her, caring for her. All the time, in such intimate contact with the greatest witness to the Good News, John had a unique grace to grow in knowledge and love of the Savior. In such close association with Mary, his future work as an evangelist was assuming greater potentials.

There is an ancient saying, *"Ubi Petrus, ibi Ecclesia"* ("Where Peter is, there is the Church"), and there is much truth in another saying, *"Ubi Ioannis, ibi Maria"* ("Where John is, there is Mary"). In living one's consecration to Mary, St. John's intercession should be most powerful, for it was he who carried out his first mission fittingly, caring for the Mother of Jesus and consequently being more powerful in his work of evangelization.

Pope Paul VI in his Apostolic Exhortation *Evangelii Nuntiandi* ("Evangelization in the Modern World," Dec. 8, 1975) wrote: "Evangelization will never be possible without the action of the Holy Spirit. The Spirit descends on Jesus of Nazareth at the moment of His baptism (Mt 3:17). . . . Jesus is 'led by the Spirit' to experience in the desert the decisive combat and the supreme test before beginning His mission (Mt 4:1). It is 'in the power of the Spirit' (Lk 4:14) that He returns to Galilee and begins His preaching at Nazareth, applying to himself the passage of Isaiah: 'The Spirit of the Lord is upon me' (Lk 4:18; Is 61:1). . . . To the disciples whom He is about to send forth He says: 'Receive the Holy Spirit' (Jn 20:22)" (*EN*, 75).

The Church understands that evangelization is not a mere human work but a bringing to birth of the Body of Christ through the power of the Spirit of God. For the model in this, the Church looks to Mary, "temple of the Holy Spirit" (*Marialis Cultus*, 26). In the work of evangelization we must enter deeply into "the mystery-laden bond between the Spirit of God and the Virgin of Nazareth, and their action in the Church" (*MC*, 27). True devotion to Mary is infused with the Holy Spirit, the Spirit of Pentecost, who impels us to evangelize and whom Mary brought forth with her prayers in the Cenacle.

In *Evangelii Nuntiandi*, Pope Paul VI said: "It is the whole Church that receives the mission to evangelize. . . . Evangelization is for no one an individual and isolated act; it is one that is deeply ecclesial . . . in communion with the Church and her pastors" (*EN*, 15, 60).

The spirit of evangelization is a projection of the motherhood of the Church. Jerusalem was the sign of the unity of God's people and the spouse of God called to become mother of a multitude of children (Is 54, 66; Ps 87, etc.). This now has its fulfillment in the Church, our Mother (Gal 4:26-27; cf. Rv 12:17). Through and in

the Church we are born of God and grow into the image of Jesus
Christ. Evangelization, then, is an active participation in the
motherhood of the Church to bring to birth the Body of Jesus
Christ. Within the Communion of Saints, Mary has a major role in
all this.

"The action of the Church in the world can be likened to an
extension of Mary's concern. The active love she showed at Nazareth, in the house of Elizabeth, at Cana and on Golgotha . . .
finds its extension in the Church's maternal concern that all people should come to knowledge of the truth" (*Marialis Cultus*,
28).

As Vatican II said, "In her life the Virgin has been a model of
that motherly love with which all who join in the Church's apostolic mission for the regeneration of mankind should be
animated" (*Lumen Gentium*, 65).

In a modern book dedicated to true devotion to the Immaculate Heart of Mary, it is essential then that we consider other
things under the living of one's consecration to this masterpiece
of the Holy Spirit — not simply one's personal salvation, but the
obligation each one has in the apostolic work of saving other
souls, and the great place Mary, the spouse of the Holy Spirit, has
in this work as our powerful Mother and intercessor.

Because living a consecration to Mary's Immaculate Heart
consists in the life of Christian perfection, we must not narrow
the concept of this consecration to simply the recitation of some
formula of consecration, or a set exercise of prayers or good
works.

It comprises the *whole* of Christian life. That is why one
must grow into the consecration. One cannot give what he
does not have, so while we are all called to evangelize, we must
first live the Christ-life ourselves.

One does not wait to achieve perfection before making the act
of consecration. The Christian life means constant new beginnings. No one among us shall ever reach complete perfection
in this life. The Christian life is like climbing a ladder toward
heaven. The rungs are the virtues that accompany the indwelling
of the Blessed Trinity in the soul and a sharing in the life of God.
We do not reach the top of the ladder in this life. When we die,
however, we must be able to say to our divine Lord, "I did not

reach the top while living the Christ-life upon earth. But when I died, I was still climbing."

Then in heaven, where we will behold what never before entered our imagination, the power of Mary's intercession as we lived the Christ-life in the refuge of her Immaculate Heart upon earth will be revealed to us. On earth God found perfect receptivity in her for the Lord's coming to mankind. She is truly "our tainted nature's solitary boast" (Wordsworth). When God gave himself to us in Jesus Christ, He gave us His Mother as well. In giving ourselves to Mary's Immaculate Heart, we give ourselves to Jesus also. Entrusting ourselves to Mary's heart, we belong to the one in whom the Son is well pleased, as the Father is well pleased with His Son (see Mk 1:11; Lk 3:22). Our growth in holiness and the influence each one of us has in evangelizing will both be enhanced when Mary is implored as Mother and looked to as model.

It was at baptism that the soul entered into glorious spiritual life in the Blessed Trinity as outlined in this chapter. Our baptism consecrated us to Jesus Christ. Baptism takes away Satan's claim on the soul as it applies the effects of Christ's death and resurrection (Acts 26:18).

> Thus, by baptism, men are grafted into the paschal mystery of Christ: they die with Him, are buried with Him, and rise with Him (cf. Rom 6:4; Eph 2:6; Col 3:1; 2 Tim 2:11); they receive the spirit of adoption as sons "in which we cry, Abba, Father" (Rom 8:15) and thus become true adorers such as the Father seeks (cf. Jn 4:23). In like manner as often as they eat the supper of the Lord they proclaim the death of the Lord until He comes (cf. 1 Cor 11:26). That was why on the very day of Pentecost when the Church appeared before the world those "who received the word" of Peter "were baptized." . . . (*Constitution on the Sacred Liturgy*, 6, Vatican II)

Satan tries to reclaim a baptized soul consecrated to Christ. Often he succeeds in getting Christians to break their baptismal promises. When one has entrusted himself to Mary and works at living that consecration, he has the aid of the one Christian over whom Satan never had the slightest success or any claim for even one instant. Mary is the woman who through the fruit of her womb crushed the head of the serpent. This is why the woman is so hated by Satan, and that evil spirit finds our personal consecration to her Immaculate Heart hateful as well. Scripture testifies that Satan tempted Christ. He surely tempted Mary as well, but with absolutely no results.

There are souls who will be tempted not to make a consecration to Mary even after special insights into its meaning have been shown them. They ought to ask themselves the source of their mistrust of consecrating themselves to the Mother of God, whose heart is one with the Heart of Jesus, which is one with the will of the Father. The devil is the "father of lies" and will make adverse motives seem pure and holy, as if such a consecration to God's Mother would diminish one's consecration to Christ.

Once consecrated, one should make a daily renewal of one's consecration to Mary. It should be renewed especially during times of temptation. Renewal of one's consecration implicitly involves the renewal of one's baptismal vows and consecration in Christ when the Blessed Trinity first came to dwell in the soul as in a temple. It is baptism that initiates Christians into the covenant of Christ. Christ's new covenant is struck anew at every Sacrifice of the Mass.

Participation in every holy Sacrifice of the Mass should be viewed as a renewal of one's consecration to Jesus and Mary. Every celebration of the Holy Eucharist renews Christ's own Sacrifice by giving back all things to the Father in Him. In the Mass all things are given to the Father in, with, and through Christ — the world, humanity, ourselves. As Jesus offered all on the cross, and Mary with Him, so too at Mass we renew our consecration, offering all we are and have together with Mary. Keeping nothing for herself, her motherly heart unites in our poor offering of ourselves in Jesus.

CHAPTER 10

† The Reign of Jesus Christ †

JESUS CHRIST, the God-man, our Savior and Mediator with the Father, is Priest, Prophet, and King.

The priesthood of Jesus Christ means that He was sent into the world by the Father to offer sacrifice and prayer for all of humanity, with which He had become one. Jesus was anointed by the Holy Spirit to the office of High Priest of all humanity at the moment of the Incarnation, the moment of Mary's "Yes" to the Angel Gabriel, the very moment when the Word of God assumed human flesh in the holy womb of Mary.

The union of the two hearts of Jesus and Mary is seen clearly at the moment of the Incarnation, when Jesus becomes our Priest and Victim. The moment Mary answers the angel with "*Ecce ancilla*" — "Behold, I am the handmaid of the Lord; let it be done to me according to your word" (Lk 1:38) — coincides with the Incarnation and the soul of Jesus answering the Father with "*Ecce venio*" — "Behold, I come to do your will, O God" (Heb 10:5). Here, at the moment of the Incarnation and the anointing of Christ as Priest, we have the authority of the Word of God for believing that the hearts of Jesus and Mary are inseparable.

The sacrifice of Christ the Priest and Victim was offered in His soul at the moment God created His soul and the beginning of His sacred Body was taken from the body of Mary at her consent. Bossuet wrote, "From the moment He [Jesus] began this great act of oblation He never discontinued it, and remained from His infancy, from His Mother's womb, in the state of victim" (*Elevations on the Mysteries*, thirteenth week, seventh Elevation). St. Gregory the Great wrote, "During the whole mysterious time of His silence and obscurity in Mary's womb, Jesus did not desist from repeating His *Ecce venio*, with an incomprehensible

love for the glory of His Father and an infinite zeal for the love of
our souls" (*Morals*, Bk. xvii, Chap. 30).

St. Denis of Alexandria wrote, "In His Mother's womb our
King was made High Priest and so remained forever. From her
womb came forth the Word, ordained a priest" (*Letter to Paul
of Samosata*).

It is by His love, by His Heart, that Jesus Christ exercises His
Priesthood and immolates himself for the glory of His Father and
for our salvation. It was by the faith and the love of her Immaculate Heart that Mary became the Mother of the High Priest and
Victim. Mary was like the altar where Jesus offered himself in
sacrifice. The cross was the altar upon which the solemn and supreme sacrifice for the redemption of the world was consummated. Nevertheless, before Jesus ever spoke His "It is finished"
from the cross, He had begun His oblation in the immaculate
sanctuary of Mary's bosom, the Letter to the Hebrews tells us
(see 10:5-7).

Mary is not a priest in the strict sense. In 1927 the Church
forbade devotions to "Mary the Priest." She is nonetheless in a
very special way Mother and Queen of all priests. With Mary,
Jesus on the cross offered himself as Victim in priestly reparation. While others were absorbed in the suffering of losing their
Master, Mary, whose heart a sword had also pierced, stood beneath the cross in control of her emotions, fully understanding
that in the mysteries of God this must be for the fulfillment of the
prophecies: the realization of the figures of the Old Testament;
the Great Sacrifice for the salvation of the world; and, thanks to
the institution of the Holy Eucharist by her Son the evening
before, soon to be the perfect and pure Oblation offered to God,
from rising to setting of the sun, to sanctify all mankind as the
Prophet Malachi (1:11) had foretold. Ever open to the action of
the Holy Spirit, His spouse, who had pondered the Word of God in
her heart, knowing her divine Son as Priest, Prophet, and King,
had insights no one else had. Her Immaculate Heart was one with
the Heart of Jesus.

As the reign of Jesus came through His conquest on the cross,
so today His royal reign must come through our turning to its per-
petuation in the Sacrifice of the Mass. The Mass perpetuates the
Sacrifice of the Cross, and Mary's heart continues her interest in

it. The priest at every Eucharistic Sacrifice is still Jesus Christ. The priest we see at the altar is a representative, one who shares in the priesthood of Jesus Christ. But the ordained priest who offers the Mass, the priest who consecrates the bread and wine into the living body, blood, soul, and divinity of Jesus Christ, is acting *in Persona Christi* (in the Person of Christ). Mary is spiritually present too. There is a heavenly liturgy where Jesus is ever presenting to the Father in the Spirit the Sacrifice of His body once made physically on the altar of the cross.

From heaven, Mary unites herself to the entire Eucharistic life of Jesus Christ as she once united herself when He lived His mysteries upon earth. With the priest at the altar today, and with those who participate in the priesthood of the faithful (the priesthood of the baptized), Mary unites herself in adoring, thanking, expiating, in, with, and through Jesus Christ.

Mary is united not only to Christ Jesus as Priest but also as Victim. Was it not Mary who provided the body and blood of the victim? St. Augustine said that Christ's flesh is Mary's flesh. On Calvary Mary, whose heart was one with the Heart of Jesus, offered herself as victim too in union with Him. This is what we too are to do at every holy Mass. It is interesting to note that St. John the Apostle, the only ordained apostle to remain with Jesus and Mary at the cross to the end, gives Jesus the title "Lamb of God" one hundred times in the Book of Revelation, the last book of the Bible. Jesus the Priest becomes the Victim, the Lamb slain for our salvation.

The priesthood of Jesus Christ, which began in the heart and womb of Mary and was exercised by every act of His will, continues now in heaven, where "he always lives to make intercession" for us (Heb 7:25; cf. Rom 8:34). As Mary was one in every offering of Jesus from the womb to the cross, so too in heaven Mary is intimately one with her Son the Priest and Eucharistic Victim in making intercession for us.

Jesus Christ is Prophet. Biblically a prophet was one who spoke, acted, or wrote under the extraordinary influence of God to make known the divine counsels and will. Jesus came as the long-awaited Prophet. He is the very Word of God made flesh, and this Word of God in human form, conceived in Mary by the Holy Spirit, revealed the will of God to us, completing public divine revelation. Mary is associated with Jesus' role as Prophet. Contemplation of her Immaculate Heart, as revealed in the Scriptures and doctrines of the Church, gives us greater insight into the Incarnation, the Word made flesh.

Jesus Christ is King, with authority over all mankind, over all creation. Jesus admitted He was a king but that "My kingship is not of this world. . . . For this I was born, and for this I have come into the world, to bear witness to the truth. Every one who is of the truth hears my voice" (Jn 18:36-37). The Father "delivered us from the dominion of darkness and transferred us to the kingdom of his beloved Son, in whom we have redemption, the forgiveness of sins" (Col 1:13-14).

St. Paul wrote that Christ "must reign until he has put all his enemies under his feet. The last enemy to be destroyed is death. . . . When all things are subjected to him, then the Son himself will also be subjected to him who put all things under him, that God may be everything to every one" (1 Cor 15:25-28).

Jesus gave His Church the power to teach, govern, and sanctify. Before His ascension into heaven, Jesus said: "All authority in heaven and on earth has been given to me. Go therefore and make disciples of all the nations, baptizing them in the name of the Father and of the Son and of the Holy Spirit, teaching them to observe everything I have commanded you; and lo, I am with you always, to the close of the age"(Mt 28:18-20).

Jesus Christ is King of the Universe, both as God and man. In accepting Jesus as King, we recognize His authority as exercised by the Church of which He is the invisible Head.

> The mystery of the holy Church is already brought to light in the way it was founded. For the Lord Jesus inaugurated His Church by preaching the Good News, that is, the coming of the kingdom of God, promised over the ages in the Scriptures: "The time is fulfilled, and the kingdom of God is at hand" (Mk 1:15; cf. Mt 4:17). This kingdom shone out before men in the word, in the works, and in the presence of Christ. . . .
>
> When Jesus, having died on the cross for men, rose again from the dead, He was seen to be constituted as Lord, the Christ, and as Priest for ever (cf. Acts 2:36; Heb 5:6; 7:17-21), and he poured out on His disciples the Spirit promised by the Father (cf. Acts 2:33). Henceforward the Church, endowed with the gifts of her founder and faithfully observing His precepts of charity, humility and self-denial, receives the mission of pro-

claiming and establishing among all peoples the kingdom of Christ and of God, and she is, on earth, the seed and the beginning of that kingdom. While she slowly grows to maturity, the Church longs for the completed kingdom and, with all her strength, hopes and desires to be united in glory with her king. (*Lumen Gentium*, 5, Vatican II)

The reign of Jesus Christ is the ultimate purpose of our consecration to Mary's Immaculate Heart in this life, and subjecting ourselves with Christ our King to God the Father for all eternity in heaven.

The Lord also desires that His kingdom be spread by the lay faithful: the kingdom of truth and life, the kingdom of holiness and grace, the kingdom of justice, love, and peace. In this kingdom creation itself will be delivered from the slavery of corruption into the freedom of the glory of the sons of God (cf. Rom 8:21). Clearly, a great promise, a great commission is given to the disciples: "all things are yours, you are Christ's, and Christ is God's" (1 Cor 3:23). (*Lumen Gentium*, 36, Vatican II)

This — willing submission to and union in Christ — is the reign of Christ toward which our Lady desires to direct us in taking us into her Immaculate Heart. Every time we pray the Lord's Prayer we repeat, "Thy kingdom come, Thy will be done on earth as it is in heaven." We have seen how consecration to Mary's heart involves doing the will of God as Mary did so that Christ may be formed in us, so that His kingdom may come.

The ideal is for each Christian to be personally consecrated to Mary's heart in order to live the Christ-life more perfectly. Then the light of God's Word will permeate all of society — the entire world. Elevated by the grace of Jesus Christ, working in the various vocations of life, members of His body, the Church, should progressively illumine the whole of human society with His saving light.

"God is love, and he who abides in love abides in God, and God abides in him" (1 Jn 4:16). God has poured out His love in our hearts through the Holy Spirit, who has been given to us (cf. Rom 5:5); therefore the first and most necessary gift is charity, by which we love God above all things and our neighbor because of Him. But if charity is to grow and fructify in the soul like a good seed, each of the faithful must willingly hear the word of God and carry out His will with deeds, with the help of His grace. . . .

The Father of mercies willed that the Incarnation should be preceded by assent on the part of the predestined mother, so that just as a woman had a share in bringing about death, so also a woman should contribute to life. This is preeminently true of the Mother of Jesus, who gave to the world the Life that renews all things, and who was enriched by God with gifts appropriate to such a role. It is no wonder then that it was customary for the Fathers to refer to the Mother of God as all holy and free from every stain of sin, as though fashioned by the Holy Spirit and formed as a new creature. . . . (*Lumen Gentium*, 42, 56, Vatican II)

The Immaculate Conception, the Holy Spirit's formation as a kind of new substance and "new creature," took place two thousand years ago. The serpent, symbolic of Satan, who was victorious over the woman in the garden (see Gen 3), will never be victorious over this woman, with whom since her creation he has always been at enmity. Satan, symbolized by the serpent at the dawn of creation, is symbolized by the dragon in the twelfth chapter of Revelation (the Apocalypse). While this Woman of the Apocalypse — clothed with the sun, the moon under her feet, and on her head a crown of twelve stars — symbolizes God's people in the Old and New Testaments and the Church today, we recall that Mary herself is the perfect image of the eventual perfection of the Church "without spot or wrinkle" (Eph 5:27).

This battle between the woman of the Apocalypse and the dragon is taking place in the Church today. It will culminate in the triumph of Mary's Immaculate Heart, which will usher in the social reign of Jesus Christ.

The role of Mary in the economy of salvation, her position as Mother of the Church, and the special power of intercession divine providence has assigned to her, especially in modern times and times to come, are gradually becoming more recognized by Christians.

Satan recognizes this very special power of Mary as well. It is why he attempted to have the role of Mary in the life of Christians downplayed and even succeeded for a while in convincing many that the Church had decided the Mother of Jesus has a lesser role than was once imagined. In reality the official position of the Church, as it has meditated the Gospels through the centuries, has been an ever-increasing appreciation of this unique creature of God who became the Creator's Mother and Mother of us all.

It is a mighty blow to the pride of Satan and his followers, the other fallen angels, to be defeated directly by Jesus Christ, Lord, God, Savior. But when the Lord God uses a humble woman, His Mother, in crushing the head of the serpent of Genesis and the dragon of the Apocalypse, the blow is even more unbearable. It is not that Mary adds any power to Jesus Christ. It is rather that Mary, who is Christ's finest victory, foreshadowing His total victory when all the world will be brought into subjection to Him, becomes an even greater defeat for Satan.

It was a blow to Satan and his followers that God should become man, not angel, and that the God-man should defeat Satan and his fallen angels. And now what is worse to his pride is that a woman who is not God should be more powerful than Satan and all his fallen angels, "terrible as an army with banners" (Song of Songs 6:10). To this woman, wholly human, God gives remarkable power to defeat the evil ones. Such is divine providence. Such is the divine will.

Sensuality and materialism are tools Satan uses to corrupt and attempt to overcome us. He has been successful in winning many souls to his evil. But those consecrated to Mary's heart have reversed the tide of Satan's defeat of souls. Those consecrated to Mary have given body and soul to her. Their souls are now open to the Word of God, to the light of Christ, the will of God. The bodies of such persons offer their senses no longer for sin but for the glory of God. The consecrated have turned over all property to Mary's heart, so the spirit of materialism no longer holds sway over them. All belongs to Mary, and the consecration when lived is the fulfillment of Paul's "all are yours; and you are Christ's; and Christ is God's" (1 Cor 3:23).

In the great battle going on in the world between Mary and the dragon, between the good angels under the direction of Mary their Queen and the fallen angels under the direction of Satan, it is important that each Christian be open to the good angels. It is important that each one be open especially to his guardian angel. While we may be apt to think that the great battle is between man and the devil, it is rather between the good spirits and the evil spirits. But man has a free will, and it is up to each of us whether we open ourselves to good or fallen angels. The most efficacious tool Mary has given us to shackle Satan and his helpers is the Rosary.

It takes humility to pray such a simple prayer. It takes faith to have confidence that Mary has such power through her Rosary. The result of properly praying the Rosary, consisting of meditations on the Mysteries of Christ, the Word of God incarnate, is an increase in love of the truths of our faith — the teachings of the Church about the Person we love, Jesus Christ. The Rosary is such a simple prayer that those who are proud cannot accept it. But to the humble God reveals the truth of His Son, Jesus Christ.

> Already the final age of the world is with us (cf. 1 Cor 10:11) and the renewal of the world is irrevocably under way; it is even now anticipated in a certain real way, for the Church on earth is endowed already with a sanctity that is real though imperfect. However, until there be realized new heavens and a new earth in which justice dwells (cf. 2 Pet 3:13) the pilgrim Church, in its sacraments and institutions, which belong to this present age, carries the mark of this world which will pass, and she herself takes her place among the creatures which groan and travail yet and await the revelation of the sons of God (cf. Rom. 8:19-22). (*Lumen Gentium*, 48, Vatican II)

The Church in Vatican Council II recognized that the ultimate victory of Christ in the Church awaits the time when there will come the restoration of all things in Christ (Acts 3:21). "The Church, to which we are all called in Christ Jesus, and in which by the grace of God we acquire holiness, will receive its perfection only in the glory of heaven" (*Lumen Gentium*, 48). At the same time, the Church recognizes that whereas Christ and Mary have both entered body and soul into the Father's glory, in some manner the ultimate victory is seen in the Church even while still upon earth.

When members of the Church truly live their baptismal vows, when they live the life of Christ in grace, the social reign of Christ is triumphant. This triumph Christ has shared with the Immaculate Heart of His Mother, a gradual triumph being realized day by day as more souls consecrate themselves to her Immaculate Heart and strive to live that consecration more perfectly.

In awaiting the social reign of Jesus Christ through the heart of His Mother, we do not expect the universal triumph before acting ourselves. Rather, each one must so live a life consecrated to Mary that the triumph has already come in individual souls. This is living the act of consecration we first made at our baptism. It is renewed with each Sacrifice of the Mass in which we participate in spirit with Mary, and in each Holy Communion when our King of Love makes entry anew. More and more then does the soul participate in the divine nature. The communion of love between the soul and God is thus intensified.

While it is true that Mary is the perfect model as the first and perfect disciple of Jesus Christ, it is true also that Jesus is our Model and was the Model even for His Mother. The end of each Holy Communion, union with God, is to make our hearts the Heart of Jesus. The Immaculate Heart of Mary, while she was still upon earth, most perfectly assumed the characteristics of the Sacred Heart of Jesus. While God the Son became man so that men might become children of God and like the God-man, it is Mary who first and most perfectly fulfilled the purpose of the Incarnation within her own heart.

God the Father has thought of Jesus and Mary and each of us from all eternity. There was a plan for each one of us always in the mind of God, but always in relationship to Jesus and Mary. While all is summed up in the Word incarnate, we must include Mary first and foremost in Jesus, for Mary is a creature, not God, and yet is the perfect fulfillment of the purpose for which the Word was made flesh. This requires careful meditation.

"Blessed be the God and Father of our Lord Jesus Christ, who has blessed us in Christ with every spiritual blessing in the heavenly places, even as he chose us in him before the foundation of the world, that we should be holy and blameless before him. He destined us in love . . ." (Eph 1:3-5). The Father thought of us from all eternity, and the thought was also an act of His will. The Father spoke a word for each one of us, expressing all we should become in time and in eternity. This word determines the place we should have in the world, the perfection we should reach, the glory we should attain in heaven. This word of the Father for each one of us determines our existence, our vocation in fulfilling God's plan of creation. Each one is free to reject what God had in mind for him, but no one is able to become more than what God has determined in His thought and will from all eternity.

The Father knows us with a knowledge of love. Our daily duty and duty for life is to accomplish the will of our heavenly Father, the thought He had of us from eternity. The Father pronounced a word containing all the joy, sorrow, grace, and glory He had in mind for us. The unfolding of that thought in time is a slow process for us, and in the gradual unfolding we discover His will in the performance of our daily duty. "For those whom he foreknew he also predestined to be conformed to the image of his Son, in order that he might be the first-born among many brethren" (Rom 8:29).

The word that the Father has pronounced in our regard determines the measure in which we are capable of reproducing Jesus for His eternal glory. "He destined us in love to be his sons through Jesus Christ, according to the purpose of his will, to the praise of his glorious grace which he freely bestowed on us in the Beloved" (Eph 1:5-6). We are thus to become like Jesus, become Jesus as members of His Body. His social reign becomes more extensive as more live the Christ-life.

Now Jesus, the Word incarnate, is the universal ideal in which all predestined by love are contained. Jesus is the one Word spoken by the Father which contains all creation in perfection, both natural and supernatural levels. Whether our vocation, as lesser words within the universal Word, be as priests, religious, married, single, every vocation has its perfect fulfillment in the Word incarnate. The fulfillment of the vocation God has for each one of us is in direct measure to our conformity to the Word made flesh, Jesus Christ.

The Holy Spirit is the finger of God, executing the designs of the Father. The Holy Spirit is the Artisan who traces us on the model of the Word incarnate — like a sculptor who first has an idea in his mind and then gradually executes it in stone as a statue. Only we are living stones, made in God's own image and likeness. The Holy Spirit translates the thought of the Father in our regard into the image of the Word. The most nearly perfect masterpiece of such translation of a creature into the image of the Word is Mary. This is why it can be said that Jesus and Mary are both our models. Jesus is the universal Word, and Mary His Mother is the most perfect purely human copy of that Word in her Immaculate Heart.

The Holy Spirit is the Spirit of Truth. If we are to become more like Christ, we must have the fullness of faith and respond in love. "When the Spirit of truth comes, he will guide you into all the truth; for he will not speak on his own authority, but whatever he hears he will speak, and he will declare to you the things that are to come" (Jn 16:13).

One who lives a life consecrated to the Immaculate Heart of Mary is loyal to the teachings of the Church and the Pope in particular. This follows from the need to live in the truth. Jesus said, "I am . . . the truth" (Jn 14:6). Jesus built the Church upon the rock of the papacy (Mt 16:13-19); He promised the Church the Spirit of Truth to keep His Church in the truth, and the Holy Spirit would do this primarily through the papacy. A life consecrated to Mary must be lived in the truth, and this will require true faith as taught by Peter and his successors.

Consecration to Mary's Immaculate Heart, then, is consecration to Jesus, the Truth. Jesus' great priestly prayer for his disciples was: "Sanctify them by means of truth. Thy word is truth. As thou didst send me into the world, so I have sent them into the world. And for their sake I consecrate myself, that they also may be consecrated in truth" (Jn 17:17-19).

In light of these thoughts, which have their basis in God's own word, it is most significant that one pope after another has consecrated the world, all mankind, to the Immaculate Heart of Mary.

It is thereby a consecration to that heart where the Word, the Truth, found its most perfect home and which serves as model for us to be formed into the likeness of the incarnate Word.

For the reign of Christ to take place in souls, a purification is needed. Too often when individuals have special crosses presented to them they are tempted to think that God is rejecting them, that they are less pleasing to Him. In fact, the Lord permits crosses in the lives of each of us as a purification. The purification process is frequently by means other than what we would desire or expect. If we could choose our own crosses we would probably choose the wrong ones, those that would not serve to purify our souls for holiness, for special identification with the Lord. "And he [Jesus] said to all, 'If any man would come after me, let him deny himself and take up his cross daily and follow me. For whoever would save his life will lose it; and whoever loses his life for my sake, he will save it" (Lk 9:23-24).

Each person has a special cross, "his cross." Unless we take up our own particular cross, not someone else's, we cannot be holy in following the Lord. It is not for us to determine what the will of God on our behalf should be. God determined our vocation, our crosses, knowing every sorrow, every incident of our lives when the Father uttered the Word before the creation of the world and spoke a special word for each of us to be identified as an image of the Word incarnate.

The more willingly we carry our cross, however light or heavy, the more we become identified with Christ, who died on the cross for our salvation and eternal life. Jesus took up His cross, dying on it for the purification of the entire world. So following in the footsteps of Jesus, each one must take up his cross daily, identify it with Jesus' cross of redemption, and draw from the infinite ocean of mercy. Without purification there cannot be identification with Christ. We cannot be His disciples unless we walk in His footsteps.

God gives us grace to carry our own particular cross, that cross only. When Jesus was hanging on the cross on Calvary, He was really conquering the forces of evil and becoming King by right of conquest. It was this redemptive death that gave Jesus the right to reign over all souls. It was His Mother's heart, at one with the Heart of her Son, that prepared her to be model of the perfect Christian, the Mother of the total Church, her heart overflowing with grace. Standing beneath the cross, she offered her Son to the Father, one with the will of her Son who hung dying. As we identify with her Immaculate Heart, our own hearts are revealed to the Father in Christ (see Lk 2:35).

St. John Chrysostom wrote of the Apostle Paul, "*Cor Pauli, Cor Christi* (the heart of Paul is the Heart of Christ)." St. Paul himself wrote, "It is no longer I who live, but Christ who lives in me" (Gal 2:20). St. Macarius said, "Christ takes the place of my soul." St. Catherine of Genoa said: "I have neither heart nor soul, my heart and soul are those of Jesus Christ." Jesus said: ". . .my flesh is food indeed, and my blood is drink indeed. He who eats my flesh and drinks my blood abides in me, and I in him" (Jn 6:55-56).

St. Catherine of Siena (1347-1380) tells us that on one occasion she was permitted to see the soul of a person in the state of grace. It was a mystical experience. She said the soul was so bright and lovely that if she had not known there was only one God she would have thought this was another. She asked the angel with her what it was that made that soul so beautiful. The angel answered that it was grace, the soul's sharing in the life of God, that made it so beautiful. This saint chose Jesus for her Spouse. Her only support during prolonged fasts was Holy Communion. She received the stigmata from Christ crucified, and inspired knowledge concerning the most profound mysteries of religion. The exterior identification with Christ such saints have received is possible interiorly for us.

Living a life consecrated to Mary's Immaculate Heart may not bring us mystical experiences like those of the great saints during this early life. Yet something more profound is taking place within souls in grace than could ever be described in human words by any of the saints. The Blessed Trinity is living an intense and infinite life within each soul where dwells the Three in One: the Father is present, generating the Son, the infinite Thought expressed in the Word; and the infinite Love between the Father and the Son is bursting forth in the Holy Spirit. All this within a consecrated heart in grace. Unfathomable mystery!

To give glory to God is our primary work, the purpose for which we were created. This was the reason for the Incarnation and the principal work of the humanity of Jesus on earth and now in the Most Blessed Sacrament. While Jesus came to save our souls, He came as man first to adore and glorify His Father and lead us to the same. Jesus came so we could have more abundant life and be supernaturally happy, but He came primarily so that God could receive from man the fulfillment of His covenant and thereby the glory owed to God by His creation.

Jesus Christ was burning with desire for the glory of the Father. An inexhaustible interior flame of love within Him made Him say: "I came to cast fire on the earth; and would that it were already kindled! I have a baptism to be baptized with; and how I am constrained until it is accomplished!" (Lk 12:49-50). The baptism would be the pouring out of His precious blood, which would redeem the world and restore to God the glory of creation.

At the Last Supper Jesus said: "I have earnestly desired to eat this Passover with you before I suffer" (Lk 22:15). That Pasch, which He wanted to be perpetuated through the Sacrifice of the Mass, was the offering of himself as a holocaust of glory. His intense desire for the glory and love of the Father was expressed on the cross with the words "I thirst" (Jn 19:28).

Jesus looked forward when the adoration, the love He gave His Father would be shared by men everywhere. "But the hour is coming, and now is, when the true worshipers will worship the Father in spirit and truth, for such the Father seeks to worship him" (Jn 4:23).

The Christian's body is a consecrated temple wherein dwells the triune God. His soul is the altar of sacrifice. These aren't mere metaphors. Christ dwells in us as Priest and Victim. Christ is perpetually offering in the altar of our soul the immolated gift of himself to the Father, who also dwells in this temple of our body. There is one liturgy between heaven and earth. We who are united in the Mystical Body to the Communion of Saints are forever participating in this worship, since we are one with Christ the supreme Sacrificer. We are united to every Mass throughout the world, and also to the continued praise of glory in Christ the Priest in heaven. This is the divine liturgy. We are all liturgists by participation, and Christ Jesus is the supreme Liturgist.

It was in such worship, in such a perfect offering, that Mary's heart joined her Son, Jesus, upon earth. Her Immaculate Heart in heaven joins in this constant offering of Christ, forever presenting himself to the Father, the marks of the crucifixion eternally in His glorified body. The Sacrifice offered physically, in a bloody manner, only once on the cross is forever present to the Father in heaven and reenacted daily on our altars.

While Christ alone was enough to make this perfect offering of infinite value, with the infinite satisfaction God deserves, it is the will of the Father that each one of us be incorporated into this offering of Christ. Each one is to offer self in Christ to the Father. This is what the Immaculate Heart of Mary teaches us on Calvary. In offering her Son to the Father, she offered us all as well. We in turn unite with Mary and together with her to Jesus in making the offering of ourselves in Jesus to the Father, a gift sanctified by the Spirit.

Our bodies were made consecrated temples of the Trinity at baptism. From each decent Christian arises a harmony of praise. The greater chords are sung by the higher faculties of the soul united to God, the lesser chords by the body and senses in proper service. Together they form a hymn of praise and living sacrifice. Again, with these analogies of sublime spiritual realities in mind, recall that consecration to Mary's Immaculate Heart is the living of our baptismal consecration.

The New Pentecost awaited by the Church will take place through the triumph of Mary's Immaculate Heart in us, one by one, as each surrenders to the will of God with Mary as model. Christians will live lives of purity and justice. The Holy Spirit will have healed all our wounds with the new wine poured upon our souls accomplishing its purpose of purification in the members of Christ's body, the Church. A new heaven and a new earth will be born as the Spirit of Love fills the hearts of the faithful. The Most Blessed Trinity will be adored, loved, glorified. Mankind will live together in peace and harmony. Christ will reign as King and Mary as Queen of our hearts.

The Church will be renewed in its members. The indestructible Church, which seemed at times to be dying, even dead, will rise anew as Christ rose from the dead that first Easter morning. This renewed Church, this triumph, is coming in Christ through the Immaculate Heart of His Mother.

CHAPTER 11

† True Devotion †

DEVOTION IS an interior act of the will. Religious devotion is an ardor to serve God, the will to give oneself to God in love. True devotion is rooted in faith, with its principal source in the supernatural virtue of love. St. Thomas Aquinas said that "devotion is an act of the virtue of religion," a readiness of the will, therefore of the whole person, in desire to adore and serve God.

St. Thomas said that devotion is a gift of God but also a work of human beings, especially as exhorted to pray, to meditate, to contemplate (*Summa Theologica* II, 2, q. 82). Devotion should characterize our entire life each day. Where there is true devotion in a person, that person radiates interior joy and peace. When one has true devotion there is a joyous dedication of oneself wholly to God and to others for the sake of God. One who has devotion is giving a life response to the gift God first gives of himself. It is a real response to the indwelling of the Blessed Trinity in the soul.

As God is the Beginning of all things, He is the End of all things. " 'I am the Alpha and the Omega [the beginning and the end],' says the Lord God, who is and who was and who is to come, the Almighty" (Rev 1:8). True devotion, then, has God as its Beginning and its End. True devotion to Mary is the burning desire to serve the Mother of God in order to better serve God himself. If one's devotion to Mary is true there is no danger of neglecting the devotion due God, for — as we see throughout this book — true devotion to Mary expresses the Trinitarian and Christological note.

Only for those who do not comprehend a *true* devotion to Mary is there a problem of neglecting the adoration and love of God and the Word incarnate when one has total devotion to the Help of Christians. Everyone with true devotion to the Mother of

God looks to the Blessed Trinity and to the Word made flesh, for apart from that, devotion to Mary is meaningless.

". . .True devotion consists neither in sterile or transitory affection, nor in a certain vain credulity, but proceeds from true faith, by which we are led to recognize the excellence of the Mother of God, and we are moved to a filial love towards our mother and to the imitation of her virtues" (*Lumen Gentium*, 67).

A devotion to Mary that is drawn from the Bible and the divine liturgy can, as Pope Paul VI stated, find ready acceptance among all, even our separated brethren, and lift the faith to total practice of the Christian life.

The reason true devotion to the Mother of God is so important is that one who ignores the place of Mary in the economy of salvation runs the risk of not fully embracing the humanity of Jesus. If one is not devoted to Mary, there is the very great danger of not fully and profitably entering in faith into the mysteries of Christ's sacred humanity which wrought our salvation. It is just as much a sin to ignore or deny the humanity of Jesus Christ as it is to reject His divinity. There is no less sin in rejecting Christ's humanity than there is in denying His divinity.

We must become by grace what Jesus is by nature. In this our holiness consists. We must conform our entire being to the Word of God made flesh. We must participate in His divine Sonship. We can do so only through accepting His humanity. Jesus is Son of God and Son of man, true God and true man. To accept this in faith, we must accept faith in the perpetual virginity of Mary and in her divine motherhood.

The Son of God has eternally existed in the bosom of His Father. The Son is the Word of God and eternal Wisdom. God so loves men, whom he created in His own image and likeness, that eternal Wisdom finds delight in living among men (see Prov 8:31). The Word is God and has lived eternally in infinite light, and yet the Word desired to become one of us.

In the Gospel, Jesus clearly affirms His divinity. He is put to death for making himself equal to the Father. "The Father and I are one" (Jn 10:30). At the same time, in the Gospel we do not hear Jesus describe himself expressly in the words "Son of God."

It is rather explicitly and frequently that Jesus calls himself the "Son of man." He is Son of God, Son of Mary, and it is by being Son of Mary that He is Son of man. Jesus insists on this title while never separating it from His divine Sonship. Jesus claims for the "Son of man" a power that belongs only to God: ". . .That you may know that the Son of man has authority on earth to forgive sins. . ." (Mk 2:10).

When Caiaphas, the Jewish high priest, orders Jesus to tell under oath before the living God whether He is the Messiah, the Son of God, Jesus forcefully admits that He is both God and man. Jesus immediately adds: "But I tell you, hereafter you will see the Son of man seated at the right hand of Power, and coming on the clouds of heaven" (Mt 26:64). Even here Jesus does not say "Son of God," but that the "Son of man" will be seen seated at the right hand of the power of God and coming on the clouds. Jesus joins His title as man to that of God, for these two titles are inseparable. The hearts of Jesus and Mary are inseparable to assure His two realities: Son of God, Son of man. All who claim the name Christian must beware lest they reject the "Son of man" in denying devotion to Mary. "God sent forth his Son, born of woman" (Gal 4:4). Here we are at the very root of the importance of devotion to Mary.

The union between Jesus and Mary is indissoluble. For all eternity Jesus will be Son of God, Son of man, Son of Mary. It is as Son of man that the Son of God comes to save the world. The Word predestined Mary to be mother of His humanity and in doing so filled her with grace and associated her in His mysteries. With her heart and soul, she enters into the mysteries of her Son. In imitating Jesus in all things we imitate Him in this, love for His Mother, true devotion to His Mother. In loving Jesus our Lord, we cannot fail to love His Mother.

Since Jesus commands us to love all the members of His Mystical Body, the Church, in that command He surely gives first place to the one who gave Him His human nature so He could become the Body's Head. Next to Christ, the command involves loving the Mother of the humanity He uses to give us grace. In fact, the teachings of the Church which instruct us to pay homage (*dulia*) to all the saints, at the same time tell us we owe a special homage (*hyperdulia*) to the Mother of the incarnate Word because of her eminent dignity.

St. Thomas Aquinas wrote of the Blessed Virgin Mary: "The

nearer a thing approaches to its principle, the more it experiences the effects produced by this principle. The nearer you come to a furnace, the more you feel the heat which radiates from it. Now, Christ is the principle of grace, since, as God, He is the Author of it, and, as man, He is the instrument of it; and the Blessed Virgin being the nearest of any creature to the humanity of Christ, Christ having taken this human nature from her, she has received from Him higher graces than any creature. But each one receives from God grace proportionate to his providential destination. As Man, Christ was predestined and elected in order that, being the Son of God, He might have power to sanctify all men. Therefore He, and He alone, was to possess such plenitude that it might overflow on all souls. 'Of his fullness we have all received.' The fullness of grace received by the Blessed Virgin had for its end to bring her nearer than any other creature to the Author of grace; so near, indeed, that she enclosed in her womb the One who is Author of grace, and in giving Him to the world by bringing Him forth, she, so to speak, gave grace itself to the world, because she gave Him who is the source of it" (*Summa Theologica* III, q. xxvii, a. 5).

In true devotion to Mary, we draw near to Jesus so as to draw from the fountain of divine life. The Church has long applied the words to Mary: "For he who finds me finds life, and wins favor from the LORD" (Prov 8:35). Mary received from Jesus the grace to be the Mother of the Church. Having received His humanity from her, Christ has associated her in all His mysteries to give perfect glory to the Father from humanity and bring grace for salvation to mankind. Seeing Mary in all those mysteries, from the Annunciation to the Presentation in the Temple to Jesus' redeeming act on the cross on Calvary, whereby He merited all grace, we ought to associate Mary in drawing grace from His mysteries and in worshiping the Father.

This is true devotion to Mary. It is not sentimentality, but accepting things God's way. It is going to the Source of our salvation. Our Savior came to us through Mary, and we go to our Savior through Mary. In this way we are in no danger of forgetting or denying the humanity through which He merited our salvation. If Eve was "mother of all living" (Gen 3:20) in her association with Adam, then when it comes to our salvation, Mary is truly associated with the new Adam, Christ, as the "Mother of all the living."

When one has true devotion to Mary, then deeply rooted in his entire spiritual life is a Marian quality. He then thinks of Jesus always in association with Mary, and Mary always in association with Jesus. This is not making Mary equal to Christ; it is remembering in faith that Jesus is Son of God, Son of man, and for salvation we must not reject either of these titles or the realities behind the titles. True devotion to Mary is consecration to the Son of God as Son of man.

When one's consecration to Mary is total, true devotion in its ideal form, then a consciousness of Mary becomes habitual, almost second nature to one's mind and soul. All is done in union with Mary. The mysteries of the sacred humanity of Christ are constantly present, in one way or another, to the spiritual individual when he turns his thoughts frequently to Mary. Since the Rosary properly prayed consists in meditation on the mysteries of Christ's humanity, and since Mary keeps us mindful of that humanity, it should be easily understood why the Rosary is an ideal prayer. Since Mary is inseparable from the mysteries of Christ, the Rosary by design has us meditate on these mysteries of our salvation, with which Mary was associated in time and now is associated in application as Mediatrix of all graces.

This concept of Mary is a consideration of the mysteries of Christ in their essence, a more complete view of Christianity. Looked at this way, devotion to Mary is not a mere form of piety among many forms of piety from which one may choose as one is inclined. The humanity of Jesus is essential to our faith and our salvation. So is Christ's divinity. So devotion to Mary's Immaculate Heart is more than a devotion in the sense men frequently consider devotions. There are thousands of devotions, not all of which appeal to everyone. But what is meant by devotion to Mary in the final analysis — faith and love for the Christ, Son of God, Son of man, and the mysteries of faith through which the sacred humanity merited our salvation — is not something we can pick or refuse. If we reject the role of Mary, we reject the humanity of Jesus Christ, the essential source of our salvation.

Granted, many who claim to be Christian and ignore the homage they owe Mary may not be doing so in malice. Implicitly, in believing that Jesus was born of a woman and that He is Son of God, they have a basic faith for salvation. Yet they have deprived themselves of a fuller appreciation and model in accepting the Christ, the Son of the living God made man.

History has shown that when Mary is neglected often men have eventually come to reject the divinity of Christ. When the Mother is forgotten, the Son is not properly understood. To separate Jesus from His Mother in our devotion is to divide Christ; it is to lose perspective on the essential mission of Christ's sacred humanity in the distribution of divine grace. Many who have rejected devotion to Mary so as not to derogate from the dignity of the one Mediator have ended in losing faith in the divinity of Jesus. The quality of "Son of man" must never be separated from that of "Son of God" lest we lose sight of one or the other and eventually both. Mary occupies an essential and unique place in Christianity, and so she must in our devotion.

Let the heart pour out its love for Mary. The only reason one can find for paying great homage to Mary is that she is the Mother of God, the one who gave the Son of God a human nature whereby He redeemed the whole world. Jesus Christ is our Savior, our one essential Mediator, our elder Brother because He has taken our human nature. We can resemble Him perfectly and love Him most sincerely only by having a special devotion to the woman from whom He took His human nature. That is to say, if one thinks he can accept Jesus without Mary, something is lacking in what he accepts of Jesus.

The devotion that we have to Mary must be an enlightened devotion. True devotion to Mary can never be separated from the mysteries of the sacred humanity of Jesus Christ, Son of God, Son of man.

By being conceived in Mary, by uniting himself to humanity and developing in all the stages of human growth — from conception to birth to nursing in infancy, childhood at the knees of Mary and Joseph, adolescence and growth into manhood — the incarnate Word sanctified every stage of human growth and development. To sanctify human life, the Son of God was not created from nothing but born of a woman. Infinite Wisdom made this identity of the Word with human nature subject to the free consent of the woman.

It is not an exaggerated fancy to see a similarity between the *Fiat* ("Let there be") of God at the creation of the world and the *Fiat* of Mary in consenting to the divine plan of redemption. God needed no one's consent to create the world from nothing. But before creating an infinitely higher world, a world of grace, God required the consent of Mary so that the second Person of the Blessed Trinity, the divine Word, might become flesh and dwell among us. From the blood of her Immaculate Heart Mary conceived by the operation of the Holy Spirit. Mary formed and nourished the body of Jesus with her most pure substance. How intimately Mary is involved in this essential mystery of Christianity!

The Eternal Word as man made himself dependent on Mary His Mother. When we her spiritual children make ourselves totally dependent on Mary, she nourishes us, contributes to our growth and development, that we may be formed into the image of her Son, Jesus Christ. Such is the fruit of true devotion to Mary.

In loving Mary, in giving her such unique privileges as being conceived immaculate, without stain of sin, so remaining always "full of grace" and growing from grace to grace, God has never so loved a simple creature; never has a son so loved his mother. Jesus loved His Mother so much as part of His love for all mankind, and thus He gave her to all of us to be our Mother by grace as well. It is essential that we love her in return. This is true devotion.

Remember, Jesus Christ, in loving His Mother, died for her too, to merit her privileges. These singular gifts of Mary were the first fruits of the passion and death of Jesus Christ. How fittingly, then, should we be able to identify with Mary at the foot of the cross as she does with us. On Calvary there is an identification of the Mother and her many children with the Son of God, Son of man, on the cross. Mary is the greatest glory of Jesus Christ because she has received the most from Him. We share in her gifts when we freely accept her as Mother and devote ourselves to her.

How are we to give expression to our devotion to Mary? One who truly loves finds the means in a thousand and more ways. As we said before, one who has true devotion to Mary will often find it sufficient to utter simply, "Mother." The Church itself, so devoted to Mary in its divine liturgy at every Sacrifice of the Mass, has feasts honoring the Mother of the Lord scattered throughout the entire liturgical year.

Pope Paul VI, in his apostolic exhortation to all the bishops in communion with the Apostolic See, wrote on the right ordering and development of devotion to the Blessed Virgin Mary. This, in part, is what he wrote of Marian devotion in the divine liturgy and its general calendar:

2. It distributes throughout the year the whole mystery of Christ, from the incarnation to the expectation of His return in glory, and thus makes it possible in a more organic and closely-knit fashion to include the commemoration of Christ's Mother in the annual cycle of the mysteries of her Son. . . .

11. When the liturgy turns its gaze either to the primitive Church or to the Church of our own days, it always finds Mary. In the primitive Church she is seen praying with the apostles; in our own day she is actively present, and the Church desires to live the mystery of Christ with her: "Grant that Your Church which with Mary shared Christ's Passion may be worthy to' share also in His Resurrection.". . .

14. The commemoration of the Blessed Virgin occurs often in the Missal, the Lectionary and the Liturgy of the Hours — the hinges of the liturgical prayer of the Roman Rite. In the other revised liturgical books also expressions of love and suppliant veneration addressed to the Theotokos are not lacking. Thus the Church invokes her, the Mother of grace, before immersing candidates in the saving waters of baptism; the Church invokes her intercession for mothers who, full of gratitude for the gift of motherhood, come to church to express their joy; the Church holds her up as a model to those who follow Christ by embracing the religious life or who receive the Consecration of Virgins. For these people the Church asks Mary's motherly assistance. The Church prays fervently to Mary on behalf of her children who have come to the hour of their death. The Church asks Mary's intercession for those who have closed their eyes to the light of this world and appeared before Christ, the eternal light; and the Church, through Mary's prayers, invokes comfort upon those who in sorrow mourn with faith the departure of their loved ones. . . .

25. In the first place it is supremely fitting that exercises of piety directed towards the Virgin Mary should clearly express the Trinitarian and Christological note that is intrinsic and essential to them. . . .

39. Finally, insofar as it may be necessary, we would like to repeat that the ultimate purpose of devotion to the Blessed Vir-

gin is to glorify God and to lead Christians to commit themselves to a life which is in absolute conformity with His
will. . . .

41. The Angelus does not need to be revised, because of its
simple structure, its biblical character, its historical origin
which links it to the prayer for peace and safety, and its quasi-li-
turgical rhythm which sanctifies different moments during the
day, and because it reminds us of the Paschal Mystery, in which
recalling the Incarnation of the Son of God we pray that we may
be led "through His Passion and Cross to the glory of His Resurrection." These factors ensure that the Angelus despite the
passing of centuries retains an unaltered value and an intact
freshness. . . .

44. . . . The Gospel inspiration of the Rosary has appeared
more clearly: the Rosary draws from the Gospel the presentation of the mysteries and its main formulas. As it moves from
the angel's joyful greeting and the Virgin's pious assent, the
Rosary takes its inspiration from the Gospel to suggest the attitude with which the faithful should recite it. In the harmonious
succession of Hail Marys the Rosary puts before us once more a
fundamental mystery of the Gospel — the Incarnation of the
Word, contemplated at the decisive moment of the Annunciation to Mary. The Rosary is thus a Gospel prayer, as pastors
and scholars like to define it, more today perhaps than in the
past.

46. It has also been more easily seen how the orderly and
gradual unfolding of the Rosary reflects the very way in which
the Word of God, mercifully entering into human affairs,
brought about the Redemption. The Rosary considers in harmonious succession the principal salvific events accomplished in
Christ, from His virginal conception and the mysteries of His
childhood to the culminating moments of the Passover — the
blessed Passion and the glorious Resurrection — and to the effects of this on the infant Church on the day of Pentecost, and on
the Virgin Mary when at the end of her earthly life she was assumed body and soul into her heavenly home. It has also been
observed that the division of the mysteries of the Rosary into
three parts not only adheres strictly to the chronological order
of the facts but above all reflects the plan of the original procla-
mation of the faith and sets forth once more the mystery of
Christ in the very way in which it is seen by Saint Paul in the
celebrated "hymn" of the Letter to the Philippians — kenosis,
death and exaltation (2:6-11). (*Marialis Cultus*, Pope Paul VI)

The Rosary is an ideal prayer for the individual and the family in its devotion to the Mother of God. The Church, seeing the ex-

cellence of this prayer, wants the faithful to feel serenely free in its regard. Pope Paul VI said, "They should be drawn to its calm recitation by its intrinsic appeal."

Having considered the heart of Mary in this book, we come to a better knowledge and love of Jesus. Who better than Mary knows and reflects the Heart of Christ? Through Mary we come to understand and better love the sacred humanity of Jesus Christ. Devotion to Christ means striving to know, love, and serve the Son of God as He manifests himself to us in His humanity.

Just as devotion to the Immaculate Heart of Mary is devotion to the total person of Mary, so devotion to the Sacred Heart is devotion to the Person of Jesus himself, manifesting His love for all and each of us and presenting His Heart as the symbol of this immense love. Devotion to the Sacred Heart of Jesus is combined with adoration of the incarnate Word in His love for us and our giving Him love in return. The devotion to Mary's heart, which is inseparable from devotion to the Sacred Heart of Jesus, leads us to serve God without fear and live a life of love with Him.

When we devote ourselves, especially through total consecration, to Mary's Immaculate Heart, we are seen by the Father in her heart as her children. As children of Mary, we are brothers and sisters of Christ Jesus. God the Father beholds each of us as sons and daughters of God, His own children, in the Heart of His Son. We ought then to love our Father and let His Love, the Holy Spirit, direct every moment of our lives.

The role of Mary in our supernatural lives is to present to us the incarnate Word. We thereby identify with the mysteries of His sacred humanity. The heart is first of all the symbol of love in both Jesus and Mary. The Heart of Jesus is first a symbol of the created love of Jesus. His Heart manifests to us the depth and tenderness of His human love for us as our Savior. Since this humanity is personally united to the Word, Jesus' created human love has its Source in the uncreated love, the divine love of God for us. All acts of Jesus are inseparable from the acts of the Father. "The Father and I are one." Jesus does all things the Father commanded Him to do, and the love Jesus has for us is the human expression of the love of Father, Son, and Holy Spirit. "I do nothing on my own authority but speak thus as the Father has taught me. . . . I always do what is pleasing to him" (Jn 8:28-29).

The Word of God is the expression of the infinite wisdom of the Father. The Holy Spirit is the infinite flame of love proceeding from the Father and Son. It is this third Person of which Mary is spouse and through whose operation she gave the world the Word incarnate. True devotion to the Immaculate Heart of Mary, enlightened by the Gospel, is Trinitarian and Christological.

To you then, O Mary, Mother of God and my Mother, I turn with heartfelt love. It is you, above all whose tender and loving Immaculate Heart inspires me to give all that I am and all that I have to your Son, Jesus Christ, who is my Lord, God, and Savior. I know that my Lord and Savior Jesus is all love and mercy. But still He is my God. He is the Infinite One. He is the "I Am Who Am" become flesh and blood by taking a human nature from you, O heavenly Mother.

I am totally unworthy to approach my Lord and my God even when He has become my Brother. When I go to Him, when I approach His infinite love and mercy in your company, O Mary, I experience an inner confidence, a firmness of will, an enduring courage, because I know that you are totally created, even as I am created. Only you are perfectly sinless and full of grace. Jesus broke into our human race, becoming one with us so we could become one with Him through you, O Mary. I look to you, my Mother, as the Virgin most faithful, as the Mother most loving, as the Virginal Mother of God who is my Mother in the order of grace.

Because of the perfect faith you had upon earth and the high place you have in heaven, next to Jesus, I believe and trust that with you, O heavenly Mother, I can come with confidence to the throne of grace. I see in you as spouse of the Holy Spirit, a union so intimate and so staggering to my imagination as I contemplate your consequent holiness that I can scarcely contain the light that seems intent to penetrate my mind even while I am upon this earth. I see you as the woman brighter than the sun, the Queen of Heaven and Earth.

O Mother of God the Son, spouse of the Holy Spirit, most favored daughter of God the Father, I come to you to cast myself into the refuge of your Immaculate Heart and thereby to become absorbed into the love of the Blessed Trinity, who created me, who sustains me in existence at every moment, who destined me by the divine will to be forever with God in heaven, my true home.

Protect me, Mary, through your powerful intercession, that I may never offend the good and thrice-holy God. And should I ever for a moment be separated from the divine love, I beg you, my Mother, to hasten to the infinite power of your divine Son to restore me at once to the grace whereby I share in the life of God and have the Blessed Trinity dwelling in my soul.

God become man, Word made flesh, Wisdom incarnate — Jesus takes on special meaning for me, dear Mother, when I look to you, my fellow creature, Seat of Wisdom, the greatest and purest human creation of God. When I look to you, O Mother of Sweetness, then I believe more firmly, trust more confidently, and love more strongly the God who loves each one of us so much that His love does not "cease in the face of our sin or recoil before our offenses, but becomes even more attentive and generous; when we realize that this love went so far as to cause the passion and death of the Word made flesh who consented to redeem us at the price of His own blood, then we exclaim in gratitude, 'Yes, the Lord is rich in mercy,'' and even: 'The Lord *is* mercy.' ''[1]

I turn to you, O Immaculate Heart of Mary, Mother of Jesus, in whom is effected the reconciliation of God with humanity, because you have received from God the fullness of grace in virtue of the redemptive sacrifice of Christ. Truly, Mary, you are associated with God, by virtue of your divine motherhood, in the work of reconciliation.[2]

Into your hands, O Mother, whose *Fiat* marked the beginning of that "fullness of time" in which Christ accomplished the reconciliation of humanity with God, and to your Immaculate Heart — to which the whole of humanity has been entrusted by our Holy Father the Pope and the bishops of the world, a humanity disturbed by sin and tormented by so many tensions and conflicts — I entrust myself. I beg that through your intercession humanity may discover and travel the path of penance, the only path that can lead it to full reconciliation.[3]

---

[1]*Reconciliatio et Paenitentia*, Pope John Paul II.
[2]Paraphrase of the concluding words of *Reconciliatio et Paenitentia*.
[3]Ibid.

And while I offer reparation, especially through participation in the Sacrifice of the Mass, to the august Godhead, I offer reparation also to your Immaculate Heart, O Mary. What offends the Son offends the entire Blessed Trinity. What offends the Word incarnate offends the Mother of the Word. And as the sword pierced your sweet heart, O Mary — the same sword that pierced the Sacred Heart of your Son — it was the sins of the world, my sins included, that caused that one sword to pierce both your hearts together.

The Church of which you are Mother, Mary, is the Mystical Body of Christ, your Son. In my unbending and undying devotion for you, O Mother of God and Mother of the Church, I consequently pledge an undivided loyalty to holy Mother Church. Keep me in the path of truth and holiness. Keep me in oneness of faith with the holy, catholic, and apostolic Church as governed by our Holy Father the Pope and the bishops in union with him. Lead me in my love for your Immaculate Heart to the Sacrament of Love, the Holy Eucharist, where I shall find the Source of everlasting life and love. I join you in spirit at the foot of the cross, O Mary, every time I participate in the Sacrifice of the Mass perpetuating the Sacrifice of Calvary.

Lead me home, dear Mother. Lead me gently home. Lead me to my true and everlasting home in heaven. You, my Mother, spouse of the Holy Spirit, are the heart of my true home. While the Holy Spirit is the Soul of the Church, as Jesus Christ is the Head, you, O Mary, are the Mother.

Lead me to my Father's home in heaven. Unite me through your powerful intercession to the Most Blessed Trinity. I await your everlasting and sweet embrace, O Mary, my Mother. Together with my guardian angel, walk with me one day before the Triune God when my days on earth must end.

It is to your Immaculate Heart, O Mother, Singular Vessel of Devotion, that I entrust my total being with all that I am and all that I have. I am all yours, my Queen, my Mother, and all that I have is yours.

† Summary and Practical Application of Devotion to Mary's Immaculate Heart †

WHEN DEVOTION to the Sacred Heart of Jesus first began under that title, the Heart of our divine Lord was not depicted. Devotees centered their considerations on the thoughts and interior affections of our blessed Lord. The Sacred Heart devotion is then a popular manifestation regarding Jesus Christ as the divine Mediator. Through Him, with Him, in Him, in the unity of the Holy Spirit, all honor and glory to God the Father. All honor and glory we give to God passes through the Sacred Heart of Jesus Christ, the Heart of the one essential Mediator, our High Priest.

Devotion to the Sacred Heart of Jesus involves every phase and every mystery in the life of our divine Lord. One word explains it all: "Love." In like manner, devotion to the Immaculate Heart of Mary involves every phase of her total person and life in association with the mysteries and the life of her divine Son. This book has just shown that extensively. It only remains now in appendix form to answer a few basic questions about implementing devotion to the Immaculate Heart in our lives and the practices this might entail.

Essentially, all that is involved in devotion to the Immaculate Heart of Mary is not really new but centuries old. The development of doctrine has enabled us to appreciate even more its scriptural foundation, that its ideal comes from the Heart of God himself.

We remember how ancient Marian devotion is when we look to the Marian prayer *Sub Tuum* ("We Fly to Your Patronage"). The *Sub Tuum* is believed to be the oldest prayer of petition to the Blessed Virgin Mary. An Egyptian papyrus was found in 1917 containing what many believe is the original version of this prayer. Experts dated the papyrus in the third century. This meant the prayer was being used in Egypt already at that time, even before the Council of Nicaea in 325. The prayer spread from Egypt where the Holy Family had fled (see Mt 2:13-15) to all parts of the Christian world. It became a favorite in Europe for those devoted to Mary.

Scholars look to the *Sub Tuum* as theologically rich, a cry out of the past, from the Age of Persecution, remaining relevant to the present day. The mention of the title "Mother of God" (*Theotokos*) makes this prayer contemporary with the great Trinitarian and Christological Councils:

> We fly to your patronage,
> O holy Mother of God;
> despise not our petitions in our necessities,
> but deliver us always from all dangers,
> O glorious and blessed Virgin.

In that simple prayer we are borrowing from the faith and devotion of God's people as already in the first centuries they regarded Mary, as Mother of God, as holy and living in glory, as Virgin, as powerful in her position to deliver us from all dangers. With such love for Mary developing so early in the Christian era, it was only natural that it would be followed by a devotion to her Immaculate Heart as men meditated and understood more deeply not only the love she has for God but the love she has for her many spiritual children. As one word explains all that is meant by the Sacred Heart of Jesus, involving every phase and every mystery in the life of our divine Lord, so one word, the same word, describes all concerning Mary in her life upon earth and now in heaven: "Love."

But to understand the meaning of that one word, whether of Jesus or of Mary, and to explain our understanding, takes many words. St. John Eudes, who wrote so devotedly in his book on *The Admirable Heart of Mary*, often alluded to the divine Heart of Jesus. "His divine Heart is the one our Lord had from all eternity in the adorable bosom of His Father; He has but one heart and one love with the Father; and with his heart and this love He is the principle of the Holy Spirit."

In God the essential love common to the divine Persons, and the personal love between the Father and the Son proceeds from them as Spirit. It is also the Holy Spirit who activates the love in the human hearts of Jesus and Mary. The depth of this divine love expressed in the human hearts of the God-man and His Mother is so overwhelming that it has taken centuries of meditation on the word of God to comprehend. We await eternity to enter more fully into the mysteries of God as lived in the hearts of Jesus and Mary.

St. Ephrem the Deacon (306-373), in his commentary on the *Diatessaron*, wrote as follows on grasping the word of God:

> Lord, who can comprehend even one of Your words? We lose more of it than we grasp, like those who drink from a living spring. For God's word offers different facets according to the capacity of the listener, and the Lord has portrayed His message in many colors, so that whoever gazes upon it can see in it what suits him. Within it He has buried

manifold treasures, so that each of us might grow rich in seeking them out.

The word of God is a tree of life that offers us blessed fruit from each of its branches. It is like the rock which was struck upon in the wilderness, from which all were offered spiritual drink. As the Apostle says: *They ate spiritual food and they drank spiritual drink.*

And so whenever anyone discovers some part of the treasure, he should not think that he has exhausted God's word. Instead he should feel that this is all that he was able to find of the wealth contained in it. Nor should he say that the word is weak and sterile or look down on it simply because this portion was all that he happened to find. But precisely because he could not capture it all he should give thanks for its riches.

Be glad then that you are overwhelmed, and do not be saddened because He has overcome you. A thirsty man is happy when he is drinking, and he is not depressed because he cannot exhaust the spring. So let this spring quench your thirst, and not your thirst the spring. For if you can satisfy your thirst without exhausting the spring, then when you thirst again you can drink from it once more; but if when your thirst is sated the spring is also dried up, then your victory would turn to your own harm.

Be thankful then for what you have received, and do not be saddened at all that such an abundance still remains. What you have received and attained is your present share, while what is left will be your heritage. For what you could not take at one time because of your weakness, you will be able to grasp at another if you only persevere. So do not foolishly try to drain in one draught what cannot be consumed all at once, and do not cease out of faintheartedness from what you will be able to absorb as time goes on.

St. Ephrem was an example and an inspirer of confident devotion to the Virgin Mary. He was nourished by the Bible in his devotion toward her who gave us the Fruit of life as he looked to her as the model of all Christian virtues. In this Appendix our attention is simply to remind the reader through St. Ephrem how early in the Christian era devotion to Mary developed profoundly and how it can develop yet more profoundly in each of us as it surely will in the Church as a whole to the end of time. St. Ephrem described how, as we go back to the spring of living waters (God's word), and satisfy our thirst once again, we find ever deeper and fresher waters, greater meaning that was often hidden to us before. The treasure is so vast, the gifts so magnificent, that there is too much to see the first time.

Lifted high in devotion in his thoughts on Mary, St. Ephrem once wrote: "You alone, Jesus, and Your mother, You are the only ones perfectly beautiful. There is no taint in You nor is there any fault in Your Mother."

St. Ephrem's nourishment from the Bible is seen in the following:

Mary gave us a fruit filled with sweetness
in place of the bitter fruit
that Eve plucked from the fatal tree;
and the whole world finds delight in Mary's fruit.
The Virginal vine gave forth a grape
whose juice is delightful
and brings joy to the afflicted.
Eve and Adam, overwhelmed with anguish,
tasted of the drink of life
and drew consolation from it.
Holy in body, all-beautiful in soul, and pure in spirit,
sincere of mind and perfect in affections,
chaste, faithful, pure of heart, and proved in trial,
Mary was filled with all virtues.

It is my personal experience that even when some richness of Mary is felt more deeply, it is so charming, so enthralling, that time dulls the memory of the exact insight on a mystery once appreciated profoundly. While the love remains, the light that caused the truth of faith to shine so brightly escapes, and then one must go back to the waters of refreshment and drink again. There one discovers again the truth or truths that first caused one to be enraptured. It is my prayer that as the reader has meditated on these truths of Mary that present her burning heart all the more immaculately and brightly, this book may be picked up again and again to help him or her to meditate on the glories of Mary. There will be books by other authors that describe her beauty in more brilliant tones, and as long as they're in harmony with the teachings of the Church, take them up too, from time to time, mindful of St. Bernard's dictum *"De Maria numquam satis"* ("Never enough about Mary").

As I was writing this book, searching for the truths about Mary enunciated by the Church and sacred writers, from time to time I would go back to pages already finished and discover in chapters laid aside a beauty about Mary not appreciated so keenly at writing. Can it be that the Holy Spirit chooses certain rare times to make our vision less obscure? How marvelous, I thought then, when we arrive in heaven and enjoy the beatific vision, seeing God face to face as He is, that we will behold the Mother of God, brighter than the sun — yet the eyes of our souls will not flinch but rest contentedly in freshness of vision that will never grow dull. Each moment of eternity will reveal the divine mysteries anew as we are swept into the eternal embrace. A million or even a billion — make it any number of trillion — years after that first embrace of eternity will provide a glimpse of delight and beauty as captivating as that first moment of sacred vision when we heard, "Come, blessed of my Father. . ." (Mt 25:35).

Beholding the King and Queen of heaven, together with all the angels and saints, as we enter into their blessed communion of glory, how re-warding it will seem to have made a total consecration of ourselves to Jesus Christ through the Immaculate Heart of Mary. How rewarding to have discovered, through total consecration to Mary, the authentic living of our baptismal vows, depending on Jesus in association with Mary's heart for all things each moment of our life on earth and now for all eternity in glory.

Just as parents do not expect as much responsibility of younger children in a family as they do of older children, so in making a total consecration we promise Jesus through Mary's Immaculate Heart to the best of our ability to live in total dependence on Him. We give Jesus all our actions and property in union with Mary. Now the spirit of living in this total dependence on Jesus through Mary is acquired only gradually. Growth in love makes it easier — you could almost say second nature — for one who lives in grace in a Marian spirit. There is no competition with the love of Jesus, for Mary always sweeps us totally toward her Son as she accompanies us in this. Mary is a magnet drawing us to Jesus.

Some cannot understand total consecration to Mary. While it is true that God desires devotion to the Immaculate Heart of His Mother to be spread in the world, it is something that must always be freely embraced. Knowledge always precedes love. St. Louis de Montfort said of the true devotion he preached, "It will not be equally understood by everybody. Some will stop at what is exterior in it, and will go no further, and these will be the greatest number. Some, in small number, will enter into its inward spirit; but they will only mount one step. Who will mount to the second step? Who will get as far as the third . . . ?"

It is my prayerful hope that this book on devotion to the Immaculate Heart of Mary has in some way helped spread devotion to more souls beyond a mere exterior acquaintance. St. Louis de Montfort said in *True Devotion* that "this devotion is a *secure* way of approaching Our Lord, because it is the property of the Blessed Virgin to guide us safely to Jesus Christ, just as it is the property of Jesus Christ to lead us safely to the eternal Father. Spiritual persons must not be deceived into imagining that Mary would prove a hindrance to their attaining to union with God. For how could it be supposed that she who, for mankind in general and for each individual soul, found grace with God could be a hindrance to a soul seeking the mighty grace of union with Jesus Christ? How could it be possible that she, in whom grace is superabundant, who is so united with God and transformed in God that He was drawn to take flesh in her, would hinder a soul from attaining to perfect union with God . . . ?"

It is important that those who make an act of total consecration to Mary (see formula in Appendix 2) spend some careful time in preparation and intend the consecration to last forever. When we consecrate ourselves totally, we give Jesus through Mary all our thoughts, words, actions, joys, and sufferings without reservations. *Everything* is given to Jesus through Mary: every moment awake or asleep, all works, whether successes or failures, whether great or insignificant. God is pleased not just with great works by human evaluation.

If we were to witness Mary presenting her Son, Jesus, with some small, sweet flower and we had faith and love, we would be touched to the depths of our hearts and souls. Jesus would be well pleased in every case, for it comes from the fullness of Mary's heart. Well, this is what happens when we give ourselves to Jesus in, with, and through the Immaculate Heart of Mary. Perhaps it is some small work, some effort that seems most insignificant in itself compared to other things. Jesus does not see it that way when it is presented through His Mother's heart.

Once we have consecrated ourselves totally to the Immaculate Heart of Mary, so long as we have not withdrawn this gift of self with all that we do and have, even when we do not make a conscious mental note here and now that something is being offered to Jesus through Mary, yet in virtue of our total consecration of offering all, this act, thought, or word is now included. It is recommended that we renew our offering of self, in consecration to Jesus through Mary, on special occasions. Feast days of Mary are occasions reminding us to renew the consecration. We do well to renew the consecration whenever faced by temptation. When special occasions remind us to renew our consecration as we grow into its spirit, the time may come when, like a person who constantly walks in the presence of God, we will also walk always in the company of Mary.

God will never be outdone in generosity. Neither will Mary. As a good mother, seeing that we have entrusted all that we are and have into her Immaculate Heart, she is prompt in accepting our good works, prayers, joys, and sufferings, and she purifies and magnifies them as she presents them to Jesus. What makes the offering so great is not what is offered, but who offers. The Mother of God offers to Jesus.

There is no definite time of preparation required before making an act of total consecration to the Immaculate Heart of Mary. St. Louis de Montfort, in his proposed act of total consecration, presented a thirty-day preparation. The preparation is not of strict obligation and could be lengthened or shortened at will. It is considered advisable to make note of the date of the act of consecration, and renew it annually, even preparing for the annual renewal for three days. It is well to sign the formula of consecration we have used.

A feast day in honor of Mary should ideally be chosen for consecration to Mary, although strictly speaking one may consecrate oneself to

her Immaculate Heart anytime one believes oneself to be spiritually prepared and desirous of doing so. A good confession would be most proper
shortly before the act of consecration, to receive our divine Lord in Holy
Communion on the day of consecration.

Rather than multiply many exterior Marian practices, it is well to
have a few favorites that are performed loyally from the heart. The daily
Rosary, said properly — that is, while meditating on the mysteries of
Christ (the mysteries of the Rosary) — should be a minimum of Marian
practice, along with wearing of the Scapular of Our Lady of Mount Carmel.

Those who truly live lives consecrated to Mary's Immaculate Heart
develop a contempt for the spirit of the world. They avoid immoral mov-
ies, television, immoral literature of any kind. A sense of modesty in
dress and speech naturally follows in the life of one sincerely consecrated to the Immaculate Heart of Mary. The consecrated, realizing
that it is a special grace to be called to consecration and to live its spirit,
does not spread devotion so much by attempting to talk others into the
act of consecration as by honestly living a life in Jesus Christ through
Mary. This is not to say that one does not encourage others to know and
love Mary. It means that we do not pressure others to make the act of
consecration, but that we will lead others to Jesus in Mary more by what
we are than by what we say.

Dedicating Saturday to the Blessed Virgin Mary goes back for centuries. The practice is so old it is difficult to separate legend from factual
tradition. Substantially the account is accurate. After Jesus had died on
Good Friday, the next day found Mary alone in preserving intact her
faith in the divinity of her Son. Today the Divine Liturgy associates Saturday with Mary with a special Mass or Office of the Blessed Virgin
Mary. The Benedictine monk Alcuin (735-804), minister of education at
the court of Charlemagne, contributed substantially to the Carolingian liturgical reform. Alcuin composed six Votive Masses for Mary, one for
each weekday and two for Saturday in honor of our Lady. The practice
was soon embraced by clergy and laity.

The liturgical reform of Vatican II kept intact the traditional practice of celebrating the "Mass of the Blessed Virgin" on the days permitted. The present *Roman Missal* presents three formularies of the
Mass, plus one each for Advent, Christmas, and Easter. In the texts of
these Masses, Mary is seen as the image of the Church praying and
model of the meditative hearing of God's word.

While every Saturday traditionally has a Marian character, in recent times the *first* Saturday of the month has taken on a Marian tone of
special quality. The Church's special regard for the First Saturday of the

month as a Marian day preceded the authentic apparitions of our Lady at Fatima. On July 13, 1917, our Lady promised the three Fatima children that she would come back to request "the Communion of reparation of the First Saturdays." Associated with making the First Saturdays of eucharistic reparation would be the intention of relieving the world of war, hunger, and persecution of the Church and the Holy Father; also the promise of Mary's assistance for salvation at the hour of our death. The apparition for First Saturdays occurred on December 10, 1925, when the Mother of God appeared to Sister Lucia in her convent at Pontevedra, Spain.

> My daughter, look at my heart surrounded with thorns with which ungrateful men pierce it at every moment by their blasphemies and ingratitude. You, at least, try to console me, and say that I promise to assist at the hour of death, with all the graces necessary for salvation, all those who, on the first Saturday of five consecutive months, go to confession and receive Holy Communion, recite five decades of the Rosary and keep me company for a quarter of an hour while meditating on the mysteries of the Rosary, with the intention of making reparation to me.

A book dedicated to the Immaculate Heart of Mary would not be complete without mention of the importance of the First Saturday devotion in reparation to the Immaculate Heart of Mary. If any ask why reparation to Mary, not to Jesus, we can only answer that the hearts of Jesus and Mary are inseparable. The sword that pierced the Heart of Jesus on Calvary also mortally pierced the Immaculate Heart of Mary, as the Prophet Simeon had foretold. The same sword pierced both hearts. Sin is social as well as personal. The overwhelming sufferings in the hearts of Jesus and Mary were caused by the sins of men, our own included. Mary was perfectly sinless, although, as this book has mentioned, the sufferings of Jesus merited her special privilege of always being immaculate. Yet the great sufferings of Jesus were hers too and caused by our sins. We owe Mary reparation as we first owe reparation to Jesus.

Sister Lucia, the child of Fatima who was to remain many years upon earth after the 1917 apparitions, revealed that on May 29-30, 1930, during that night, our Lord informed her of the reasons for *five* First Saturdays, rather than some other number, like *nine* for the nine First Fridays, or *seven* for the Seven Sorrows. Our Lord said:

> My daughter, the motive is simple. There are five kinds of offenses and blasphemies uttered against the Immaculate Heart of Mary: 1) Blasphemies against the Immaculate Conception. 2) Blasphemies against her virginity. 3) Blasphemies against her divine maternity and at the same time refusal to recognize her as Mother of men. 4) Blasphemies of those who openly seek to foster in the hearts of children indifference or contempt and even hatred for this Immaculate Mother. 5) The offenses of those who directly outrage her in her holy images.

Here then, my daughter, is the reason why the Immaculate Heart of Mary has inspired Me to ask this small reparation, the effect of which will be that I will show compassion by forgiving those souls who have had the misfortune to offend her. As for you, strive without ceasing by your prayers and sacrifices to move Me to compassion toward these poor souls.

One consecrated to the Immaculate Heart of Mary ought always to wear the Brown Scapular of Our Lady of Mount Carmel. This scapular was held up by Our Lady of the Rosary at the final vision of Fatima, October 13, 1917. The wearing of this scapular has been referred to by Pope Pius XII as a sign of one's consecration to the Immaculate Heart of Mary. One should be enrolled by an authorized person.

Vatican II charged that devotions toward Mary were to continue to be treasured by the Church as recommended by the teaching authority of the Church in the course of the centuries (see chapter 8, *Lumen Gentium*). On February 2, 1965, shortly after the promulgation of the Vatican declaration on the Church, Pope Paul VI explicitly clarified that the time-tested devotions were to stay: ". . . Ever hold in great esteem the practices and exercises of the devotion to the most blessed Virgin which have been recommended for centuries by the Magisterium of the Church. And among them we judge well to recall especially the Marian Rosary and the religious use of the Scapular of Mount Carmel."

In addition to the exterior practices, there are interior practices of consecration to Mary whereby one performs all actions in, with, through, and for Mary so that all is done in, with, through, and for Jesus. In living our lives totally in union with Mary, we are united through her to Jesus Christ. The main difference in *total* consecration from other kinds of consecration is that one does more than place oneself under the protection of Mary. A person truly and totally consecrated to the Immaculate Heart of Mary has given everything to Mary and thereby through her to Jesus Christ. This means that Mary, receiving all we are and have, has at her disposal all our good works and possessions to eternity.

It is worth repeating that one should make an act of total consecration only after having studied its meaning enough to understand its seriousness and really intend that the consecration be permanent. There is no age limit for total consecration. The humble children of Fatima, who had the angel and our Lady herself to guide them, were only seven, nine, and ten years of age, but their consecration to the Immaculate Heart of Mary was certainly total. Countless Christian souls devoted to Mary, from humble children to great saints and popes, have made the act of total consecration.

Total consecration as understood by St. Louis de Montfort means giving all to Jesus through Mary, freely without restraint. You entrust:

your 1) *body*, with all its senses; 2) *soul*, with all its faculties; 3) *exterior goods of fortune*, whether present or to be in the future; and 4) *interior and spiritual goods*, your merits, virtues and good works, past, present, and future.

One who makes an act of total consecration gives all he has in the order of nature and the order of grace, even the future as it pertains to the life of glory. The purpose of this book has been to help readers understand true devotion to the Immaculate Heart of Mary and to help them prepare for an act of total consecration. One cannot love until one knows. Knowledge of the Immaculate Heart will elicit that response of love that leads to total consecration. It is a personal decision of each soul. At times one may need the advice of a spiritual director, a priest, or dedicated Religious, who is deeply devoted to Mary and understands true devotion. It would make little sense to seek assistance of an advisor not informed on the subject matter.

A form of total consecration, more contemporary perhaps than that of St. Louis de Montfort but essentially the same, is to be found in Appendix 2. What is important is not the precise wording of the consecration but that the act of entrusting oneself to the Immaculate Heart of Mary be truly total, intended to last, without reservations, for all of time and eternity.

† Act of Total Consecration and Prayers to the Immaculate Heart of Mary †

(The Act of Total Consecration that follows may be made after careful study of this book on true devotion to the Immaculate Heart of Mary and after due preparation. A good confession ideally should precede the consecration, which is best made, when possible, before Jesus Christ present in the Most Blessed Sacrament in the tabernacle. The Act of Consecration should be made only when one is prepared to live its spirit henceforth. Ideally, it should be renewed on occasion, especially on its anniversary. The Act may be renewed daily in the shorter form, easily memorized, that follows this longer form. Select a feast of Mary on which to make the Act of Consecration, which may be signed and dated as shown below.)

O IMMACULATE Heart of Mary, I, who have been an ungrateful sinner, today renew and reaffirm, to your holy and glorious person, the vows of my baptism. I reject Satan, his evil works, and his empty promises forever, and I give myself entirely to Jesus Christ, incarnate Wisdom and my Savior, to carry my cross after Him all the days of my life, and to be more faithful to Him than I have ever been before.

In the presence of God the Father, to whom you, Mary, are the most favored daughter; in the presence of God the Son, the Word incarnate, to whom you are Mother; in the presence of the Holy Spirit, to whom you are spouse, and before the entire heavenly court, all the holy angels and saints, I consecrate myself to your Immaculate Heart, O Mary. I intend that the consecration I make today will continue for all time and for eternity.

I entrust and consecrate to you, O Immaculate Heart of Mary, my Queen and my Mother, my body and soul and all my goods, interior and exterior, spiritual and natural. I thereby consecrate to you the value of all my good thoughts, words, and actions, past, present, and future, leaving to you the entire right to dispose of me, and all that belongs to me without exception, according to your holy will, for the greater glory of God in time and eternity.

I consecrate to your all-pure person, O Mary, my eyes, my mouth, my heart, all my senses, my whole person. I am totally yours, my Queen, my Mother, and all that I have is yours.

Heavenly Mother Mary, refuge of sinners, I come to your sweet, most lovable heart, to offer myself to you; to consecrate my entire life, all that has gone before and will follow this day, to your Immaculate Heart. In this consecration of my total person, I offer you my body and soul, with all their miseries and weaknesses; my heart, with all its affections and desires; my prayers, works, joys, and sorrows. I offer you all temptations that come to me, so that my every thought and desire may be purified through your holy intercession.

My Queen, my Mother, I offer you in consecration all pleasures and sufferings that come into my life, both physical and spiritual. I offer you especially my death, with all that will accompany it in my last agony. Accept all this, my Mother, and take all into your Immaculate Heart as I give to you irrevocably all that I am and all that I have, together with all my property and possessions. I offer you my family and all who are near and dear to me. Take them all into your Immaculate Heart and keep everyone in your Son, Jesus Christ.

Keep me ever faithful to God and to the Holy Catholic Church, loyal and obedient to the Holy Father, the Pope. I desire to pray the Rosary properly, meditating on its mysteries. I desire to participate in the Sacrifice of your incarnate Son, perpetuated at Holy Mass, and to receive Him frequently in Holy Communion. I attach special importance to the First Saturday of the month in reparation to your Immaculate Heart, and I will work for the conversion of sinners. I will strive to live constantly the spirit of eucharistic reparation.

O Queen of the angels, my Queen and my Mother, I humbly prostrate myself before you as I approach you with my guardian angel. I desire to join all the holy angels, and especially my guardian, in venerating you always as Queen of heaven and earth. Command my guardian angel to keep me always in your love and in the union of grace with your divine Son, with the entire Blessed Trinity dwelling in my soul. Send forth your angels to assist me in spreading devotion to your Immaculate Heart so that through your intercession there may be peace in the world and in the Church, and the Kingdom of Christ may come on earth as it is in heaven. Amen.

Signed_____

Date:_____

• • •

SHORT RENEWAL OF CONSECRATION TO THE IMMACULATE HEART

O Immaculate Heart of Mary, I am all yours, my Queen, my Mother, and all that I have is yours.

REPARATION TO THE IMMACULATE HEART OF MARY[1]

Immaculate Mother, I come to you to offer my love, my very life, and my confession and Holy Communion in reparation for the sins committed against your all-holy and Immaculate Heart. I desire too to offer the holy Rosary and meditation on its mysteries to your Immaculate Heart.

I offer these acts in reparation to you, O Mary Immaculate, especially for the following reasons:

• In reparation for the blasphemies that are uttered against your Immaculate Conception;

• In reparation for those who deny your perpetual virginity and speak in any way against your holiness;

• In reparation for those who deny your divine maternity, refusing at the same time to accept you as the Mother of all mankind;

• In reparation for those who try publicly to implant in the hearts of children indifference, contempt, and even hatred toward your Immaculate Heart;

• In reparation for those who insult you directly in your holy statues and images.

O Mother of God and Mother of men, Mother mine, take me as your child, grant comfort to my poor sinful heart, even as I desire to grant comfort and offer reparation to your Sorrowful and Immaculate Heart. Amen.

• • •

PRAYER TO OUR LADY OF MOUNT CARMEL

O Lady of Mount Carmel, I wear your brown scapular as a sign of my consecration to your Immaculate Heart. I am your spiritual child and, in accepting to wear this small piece of cloth which comes to me as

---

[1]Recommended for First Saturday devotions along with confesson, Communion, and five decades of the Rosary with at least fifteen minutes of meditation.

a sign of the love of your motherly heart, I believe that your intercession is powerful with your divine Son, Jesus Christ, to obtain for me from Him, everlasting life. Amen.

MOTHER OF HOLY LOVE[2]

Mary, Mother of Christ, Mother of holy Love, do you yourself form us according to the Heart of your Son.

LADY OF THE BEATITUDES[3]

Blest are you, O Virgin Mother of God,
    Who surrendered your spirit entirely to the Lord;
        You now reign with God forever.
Blest are you, O Heavenly Mother Mary.
    God regarded the humility of you His handmaid,
        And now you inherit heaven and earth and all creation.
Blest are you, O Virgin Mother, who hungered and thirsted with your Son to do the will of the Father.
    Full of grace upon earth,
        You now intercede for our holiness.
Blest are you, Mother of Mercy.
    You received the highest mercy in being conceived Immaculate.
        You now obtain for us Mercy from the Heart of your Son.
Blest are you, O Immaculate Heart of Mary,
    Who upon earth were single-hearted in believing and loving.
        You now see God face to face and intercede to lead
        us to the same beatific vision.
Blest are you, Mother and Queen of Peace.
    You pray for peace in the Church and in the world;
        You are the highly favored Daughter of God the Father,
        And care for your sons and daughters still upon earth.
Blest are you, O Mother of Jesus Christ, who were persecuted for holiness' sake.
    What was done to Jesus was done to you, and men still treat you this way.
        The reign of God is yours.

---

[2]Composed by Abbot Marmion.

[3]Composed by Father Robert J. Fox.

LITANY OF THE IMMACULATE HEART OF MARY[4]

Lord, have mercy on us.

Christ, have mercy on us.

Lord, have mercy on us.

Christ, hear us.

Christ, graciously hear us.

God the Father of heaven, have mercy on us.

God the Son, Redeemer of the world, have mercy on us.

Holy Trinity, one God, have mercy on us.

Immaculate Heart of Mary, most like the Sacred Heart of Jesus, *pray for us.*

Immaculate Heart of Mary, whose soul was created without original sin,[5]

Immaculate Heart of Mary, who said to God's messenger, "Be it done to me according to your word,"

Immaculate Heart of Mary, who always remained sinless,

Immaculate Heart of Mary, to whom the angel Gabriel first announced the Good News,

Immaculate Heart of Mary, who awaited the Savior with the greatest love,

Immaculate Heart of Mary, within whom we see the beginning of the Church,

Immaculate Heart of Mary, who remained always a Virgin in giving us Jesus,

Immaculate Heart of Mary, Queen of peace, who gave us the Prince of peace,

Immaculate Heart of Mary, who conceived Jesus in your heart before conceiving Him in your womb,

Immaculate Heart of Mary, who first adored the newborn Savior,

Immaculate Heart of Mary, Mother of love in the Holy Family at Nazareth,

Immaculate Heart of Mary, whose immaculate soul and virginal body were taken into heaven,

Immaculate Heart of Mary, Mother of God and Mother of us all,

Immaculate Heart of Mary, Queen of guardian angels,

Immaculate Heart of Mary, Queen of all angels and saints,

Immaculate Heart of Mary, who kept the Word of God in your heart,

Immaculate Heart of Mary, whose soul Simeon said a sword would pierce,

Immaculate Heart of Mary, praying with the Apostles for the Church,

Immaculate Heart of Mary, desiring sacrifices for the conversion of sinners,

---

[4]Composed by Father Fox and taken from *A Prayer Book for Young Catholics*, OSV.

[5]*Pray for us* is repeated after each invocation.

Immaculate Heart of Mary, comfort to souls at the hour of death,

Immaculate Heart of Mary, at whose request Jesus changed water into wine,

Immaculate Heart of Mary, offering Jesus in sacrifice on Mt. Calvary,

Immaculate Heart of Mary, and our Lady of the Most Holy Eucharist,

Immaculate Heart of Mary, teacher of us in the way of God,

Immaculate Heart of Mary, living example of the love of humility,

Immaculate Heart of Mary, perfect model of adoring the Father through Christ in the Spirit,

Immaculate Heart of Mary, Mother of the Church and spouse of the Holy Spirit,

Immaculate Heart of Mary, Mother of Christ and our Mother in the Communion of Saints,

Immaculate Heart of Mary, crowned as Queen in heaven by the Most Blessed Trinity,

Immaculate Heart of Mary, praying for our salvation,

Immaculate Heart of Mary, full of grace and Mother of grace,

Immaculate Heart of Mary, desiring to give grace to children who ask,

Immaculate Heart of Mary, ever ready to hear the prayers of children,

Immaculate Heart of Mary, wounded in love by the sins of men,

Immaculate Heart of Mary, hope and comfort for merciful forgiveness,

Immaculate Heart of Mary, perfect model of reparation,

Immaculate Heart of Mary, triumph of all who believe in God's word,

V. Pray for us, O holy Mother of God.

R. That we may be made worthy of the promises of Christ.

Let us pray:

O Sorrowful and Immaculate Heart of Mary, Mother and model of the Church, I want to bring comfort to your all-pure heart wounded by sin. I offer this litany, my sufferings and good works of this day in reparation for the sins of the world. Through Jesus Christ, you are the cause of our joy and the means of salvation. I shall try to spread devotion to your Immaculate Heart so that many souls will find salvation in the Sacred Heart of your Son.

R. Amen.

A NEW LITANY IN HONOR OF MARY'S QUEENSHIP

(On March 25, 1981, the Church promulgated the Rite for Crowning an Image of the Blessed Virgin Mary. *Included in the rite was a new Litany of the Blessed Virgin Mary, as printed below. The Triumph of Mary's Heart will involve a recognition of her Queenship as associated with the Redeemer King.)*

Lord, have mercy.
Christ, have mercy.
Lord, have mercy.
Holy Mary, *pray for us.*
Holy Mother of God,[6]
Holy Virgin of virgins,
Chosen Daughter of the Father,
Mother of Christ the King,
Glory to the Holy Spirit,
Virgin Daughter of Zion,
Virgin most pure and lowly,
Virgin most meek and obedient,
Handmaid of the Lord,
Mother of the Lord,
Associate of the Redeemer,
Full of grace,
Fount of beauty,
Summit of virtue,
Most excellent fruit of the Redemption,
Perfect follower of Christ,
Most pure image of the Church,
The new Woman,
Woman clothed with the sun,
Woman crowned with the stars,
Lady most benign,
Lady most clement,
Our Lady,
Joy of Israel,
Splendor of the Church,

Glory of the human race,
Advocate of grace,
Minister of devotion,
Helper of the People of God,
Queen of charity,
Queen of mercy,
Queen of peace,
Queen of Angels,
Queen of Patriarchs,
Queen of Prophets,
Queen of Apostles,
Queen of Martyrs,
Queen of Confessors,
Queen of Virgins,
Queen of All Saints,
Queen conceived without original sin,
Queen assumed into heaven,
Queen of the world,
Queen of heaven,
Queen of the universe,
Lamb of God, You take away the sins of the world; *hear us, O Lord.*
Lamb of God, You take away the sins of the world; *graciously hear us, O Lord.*
Lamb of God, You take away the sins of the world; *have mercy on us.*

---

[6]*Pray for us* is repeated after each invocation.

V. Pray for us, O holy Mother of God,

R. That we may be made worthy of the promises of Christ.

Let us pray:

O God of mercy, hear the prayers of Your servants. We acknowledge Your holy handmaid Mary as our Mother and Queen. Help us to serve You and one another on earth and obtain a place in Your eternal Kingdom. We ask this through Christ our Lord.

R. Amen.

† Select Chronology of Major Marian Events in the Church †

A.D. 30/50 † The Apostolic preaching (some of which is recorded in the early speeches in the Acts of the Apostles — 2:14-21; 3:12; 13:15ff) says not a word about Mary and practically nothing about Christ's earthly life. Reasons: (1) Mary was known to all the faithful of Palestine; (2) her major role in Jesus' life had been carried out during His early years when there were no disciples to know about it; and (3) the role of women in general was always played down in the East of that era.

54/57 † St. Paul provides the first allusion to Mary from among the apostolic preaching — in the Letter to the Galatians (4:4): "God sent his son *born of a woman.*"

65 † St. Mark sketches a portrait of Mary as the Mother of Jesus (3:31ff; 6:3).

70/80 † St. Matthew presents Mary as associated with Jesus in His birth in accord with Old Testament prophecies (including her virginal conception) — a singular role which puts her in a personal relationship with the Spirit (1:16-23; 2:11).

70/80 † St. Luke portrays Mary as the servant of the Lord, daughter of Zion, and closest follower of Christ — who hears God's word and keeps it (1:38, 48; 2:19, 51; 11:28).

70/80 † St. Luke (in Acts) makes mention of Mary gathered in prayer with the apostles in the Upper Room and so hints at her role in the formation of the Church (1:14).

90/100 † St. John portrays Mary as united with Jesus in life (2:1-11) and at His death (19:25) and as His dying gift to His followers (19:26-27).

90/100 † The Book of Revelation puts the finishing touches to the primitive Church's image of Mary, which focuses on her concrete fidelity, deep faith, ecclesial role, and singular grace. Mary is the servant par excellence, who did nothing other than accept, fashion, and offer Jesus (12:1-17).

100/200 † An inscription (found under St. Peter's Basilica) portrays Mary as Protectrix for the departed and their Mediatrix.

110/115 † St. Ignatius of Antioch gives five references to Mary as a Virgin and Mother.

120 † The *Odes of Solomon* mentions the Virgin who gives birth.

145 † Aristedes of Athens cites Mary in a creedal formula.

150/200 † Inscription of Abercius, Bishop of Hieropolis, alludes to Mary's virginity, holiness, and relationship to Eucharist.

150 † St. Justin Martyr is the first to write fully about Mary and he makes use of the Eve-Mary typology.

150 † The *Protoevangelium of James* is the first work to show an independent interest in Mary. It is the "Gospel of Mary."

150/202 † St. Irenaeus of Lyons attributes to Mary a necessary role in the Redemption.

162 † The *Sybilline Oracles* speaks admiringly of Mary.

Before 200 † First paintings of Mary are inscribed on the catacombs.

200/300 † The *Sub Tuum*, the most ancient Marian prayer recorded, is composed, emphasizing Mary's powerful intercession.

200/300 † Inscriptions in Greek, Hebrew, Aramaic, Syrian, and Armenian at the site of the Basilica of the Annunciation offer evidence that devotion to Mary was practiced.

200 † Composition of *The Obsequies of the Virgin*, a work written in Syria alluding to the assistance of Mary.

217 † The Church of Santa Maria in Trastevere (St. Mary across the Tiber) is founded at Rome.

250 † St. Cyprian of Carthage stresses the confidence that Christians should have in Mary and extols her virginity.

300 † The *Akathist Hymn* is introduced in the East.

350/400 † At Constantinople, Bishop Severian of Gabala issues an official public invitation for prayers to Mary.

350/390 † St. Gregory of Nyssa diffuses throughout the Middle East a Marian prayer that is a forerunner of the Hail Mary. He also chronicles the first apparition of Mary recorded — to St. Gregory the Wonderworker.

350/370 † St. Ephrem calls upon Mary's powers of mediation.

350 † St. Justina voices the earliest recorded invocation to Mary for help (reported later by St. John Chrysostom).

352/366 † St. Mary Major is founded by Pope Liberius I.

370 † Earliest known Liturgy of Mary is composed in Syria.

370 † St. Ambrose holds Mary up as a model of women and a type of the Church.

392 † Pope St. Siricus, in a letter to Bishop Anysius, upholds Mary's perpetual virginity.

394 † St. Augustine proclaims Mary free from original sin and extols her status as Virgin and Mother.

400/500 † A temple of Isis (an Egyptian nature goddess) at Soissons (France) is dedicated to the Blessed Virgin Mary.

400/500 † The Feast of the Commemoration of the Virgin is instituted in various places in Europe.

400/500 † The Feast of the Annunciation is celebrated in Byzantium.

400/500 † The Feast of the Hypapante (that is, Encounter between Christ and Simeon) is celebrated.

400 † Earliest copy of the *Transitus* of Mary is written.

431 † Mary is given the title *Theotokos* (Mother of God) by the Council of Ephesus — led by St. Cyril of Alexandria.

432 † The church of St. Mary Major in Rome is restored, enlarged, and dedicated by Pope Sixtus III.

440/461 † Mary is introduced into the texts of the Mass. In the *Leonine Sacramentary*, St. Leo the Great adds to the Canon (Eucharistic Prayer) the reference to Mary: "In communion with the venerating in the first place the glorious ever-Virgin Mary, Mother of God. . . ."

451 † The Council of Chalcedon calls Mary Mother of God.

451 † The empress Pulcheria of Byzantium sets about collecting the relics of Mary.

470 † A basilica is dedicated to Mary in Salonika.

500/600 † The Parthenon — the celebrated temple of Athena, located on the Acropolis at Athens — is dedicated to Mary.

500/600 † The church of St. Mary Antiqua in Rome is consecrated.

520/556 † The Syrian poet St. Romanos the Melodist reaches new heights in composing four greatly used Marian hymns.

534 † Pope John II, in a letter to the Senate at Constantinople, declares that Mary is "truly the Mother of God."

543 † The church of St. Mary in Jerusalem is dedicated.

550/600 † Theoteknos, Bishop of Livias, provides the earliest affirmation of belief in Mary's bodily assumption.

550 † The Feasts of the Birth of Mary, the Presentation of Jesus, and the Dormition are celebrated in Byzantium.

550 † The first completely Marian interpretation of Revelation 12 is given by the Greek philosopher Oecumenius.

553 † The Second Council of Constantinople reiterates the dogma of the Divine Motherhood and mentions Mary's perpetual virginity.

600/800 † The *Gospel of Pseudo-Matthew* appears in the West.

600/700 † The Marian antiphon *Ave Maris Stella* is composed.

600/650 † The Feast of the Purification (February 2) is celebrated at Rome (more as a Feast of Christ than as one of Mary).

600/636 † St. Isidore of Seville, last Father in the West, writes knowingly about Mary.

610 † Byzantine Emperor Heraclius has the image of Mary placed on the masts of his fleet.

649 † The (non-Ecumenical) Council of the Lateran declares the perpetual virginity of Mary.

650/675 † The Feast of the Annunciation (March 25) is celebrated at Rome (more as a feast of Christ than as one of Mary).

650 † The Feast of the Assumption (August 15) is celebrated at Rome and goes on to become the principal Marian Feast.

675/700 † The Feast of the Birth of Mary is celebrated at Rome (stemming from the dedication of the church of Mary's Nativity at Jerusalem, celebrated since the fifth century).

680/681 † The Third Council of Constantinople reaffirms Mary's divine Motherhood.

700/749 † St. John Damascene, last Father in the East, gives the clearest teaching on the Immaculate Conception up to his day.

700/740 † St. Andrew of Crete invokes Mary as "Help of Christians."

700/733 † St. Germanus of Auxerre formulates the idea that we "seek God through Mary."

705/707 † Pope John VII is called "servant of the Mother of God."

750 † The *Legend of Theophilus* is translated into Latin.

787 † The Second Council of Nicea defines the liceity of the cult rendered to images of Mary.

800/900 † The Feast of the Conception of St. Ann is instituted at Byzantium.

800/900 † The Feast of the Conception of Mary begins to be propagated in the West.

800 † The Gospel of Mary's Nativity makes its appearance.

Before 804 † The Benedictine monk Alcuin composes Masses of Our Lady on Saturday, which became part of the Missal in 875.

845/869 † St. Paschasius Radbert upholds the Virgin Birth, the Assumption (only of the soul), and a form of Mary's Immaculate Conception.

Before 851 † The *Story of the Birth of Mary* is composed, most likely by St. Paschasius Radbert.

869/870 † The Fourth Council of Constantinople renews approval of the "cult rendered to images of Mary."

876 † Charles the Bold obtains what is believed to be the dress of Mary.

900/1000 † The antiphon *Regina Coeli* is composed.

900/1000 † The *Little Office of the Blessed Virgin Mary* is introduced.

900/1000 † The *Transitus* stories about Mary's passing from this world are translated into Latin.

945 † The title "Mother of Mercy" spreads throughout the West after it is mentioned in the *Life of Odo* by John of Salerno.

975 † Saturdays are devoted to the Blessed Virgin Mary.

976 † The abbey of Montserrat is founded in Spain and goes on to become a famous Marian shrine.

1000/1100 † The Feast of Mary's Compassion is introduced.

1000/1100 † The *Hail Holy Queen* is composed and perfectly suits the attitude of medieval Christians toward Mary.

1000/1100 † The Cathedral of Notre Dame de Chartres is begun.

1000 † Hroswitha of Gandersheim, a Benedictine nun, writes versions of the *Legend of Theophilus* and the *Gospel of James* — presenting Mary as the powerful Queen of Heaven.

1050/1150 † The antiphon *Alma Redemptoris Mater* is composed, probably by Herman the Cripple.

1050/1072 † St. Peter Damian sets forth the connection between the Eucharist and Mary — and also promotes the Little Office.

1050/1093 † St. Anselm of Canterbury composes inspiring works about Mary (including three famous prayers) that go on to exert a tremendous effect on the Middle Ages.

1080/1124 † Eadmer writes *The Conception of the Blessed Virgin Mary*, the best exposition of the doctrine up to the time.

1100/1200 † The *Life of Mary* is spread to the West.

1100/1200 † The Litany of the Blessed Virgin Mary begins to take shape.

1100/1150 † The Hail Mary makes its appearance (the second part will be added only in the fifteenth century.

1100/1150 † One of the greatest Marian mosaics is placed in the Cathedral of Torcello, Italy.

1420/1447 † St. Colette of Corbie reveals her visions of Mary.

1423 † The Feast of the Sorrows of Mary is established.

1438/1445 † The Council of Florence firmly professes that the Son of God became man through Mary.

1439 † The Council of Basel defines the doctrine of the Immaculate Conception (but this has only significative value since it comes after Pope Eugene IV has repudiated this Council).

1440 † Eton College, dedicated to Mary, is established.

1457 † The *Little Office of the Blessed Virgin Mary* is printed.

1470/1471 † Martin Schongauer makes engravings of the *Life of Mary*.

1470 † Dominican Alan Rupe writes on *The Unity of Mary's Psalter* upholding the power of the Rosary with Mary.

1475 † The first Confraternity of the Rosary is established.

1492 † The *Salve Regina* is the first Christian prayer recited in the New World — by Columbus and his men on San Salvador.

1495 † The Rosary is approved by Pope Alexander VI.

1496/1501 † Michelangelo completes the world-renowned *Pietà* — a sculpture of Mary with her dead Son in her lap.

1500/1510 † Albrecht Durer produces a woodcut *Life of Christ*.

1507 † Pilgrimages to the shrine of Loreto are approved.

1518 † Titian paints his *Assumption* at Frari, Venice.

1531 † The Blessed Virgin appears to Juan Diego at Guadalupe.

1538 † The Shrine of Our Lady of Walsingham is destroyed.

1543 † Martin Luther affirms the Immaculate Conception.

1558 † The Litany of Loreto in honor of Mary is published.

1547 † The Council of Trent affirms that Mary is regarded as immune from every actual fault, even the slightest.

1550/1617 † Francisco Suarez establishes the first systematic Mariology with Volume IX of his *Opera Omnia*.

1555 † Pope Paul IV in the Constitution *Cum Quorumdam* attests to Mary's virginity before, during, and after Christ's birth.

1563 † The Council of Trent reaffirms the liceity of the cult of the images of Mary.

1563 † The Hail Mary is introduced into the Divine Office.

1567 † Pope St. Pius V affirms Mary's sinlessness.

1573 † The Feasts of the Expectation of the Virgin and of Our Lady of Victory and the Rosary are established.

1577 † St. Peter Canisius writes the *Incomparable Virgin Mary*, the first important Mariological work after the Reformation.

1600/1629 † Pierre de Bérulle, founder of the "French School of Spirituality," renews devotion to Mary.

1600/1700 † The Feast of Our Lady of Sorrows is instituted.

1601 † The Litany of the Blessed Virgin is prescribed for the Universal Church by Pope Clement VIII.

1630/1657 † Jean Jacques Olier, founder of the Sulpicians, applies mystical language to Marian concepts in a novel way.

1644 † The Feast of the Most Pure Heart of Mary is established.

1670 † *The Mystical City of God* by Maria de Agreda de Jesus is published posthumously.

1680 † St. John Eudes composes the first full-length book on the heart of Mary, *The Admirable Heart of Mary*.

1683 † The Feast of the Holy Name of Mary is extended to the Universal Church.

1690 † Pope Alexander VIII upholds Mary's perfect sinlessness.

1716 † The Feast of the Rosary is extended to the whole Church.

1716 † Alexander de Rouville publishes *The Imitation of Mary*, patterned after the *Imitation of Christ*.

1726 † The Feast of Our Lady of Mount Carmel is instituted.

1750 † St. Alphonsus Liguori publishes *The Glories of Mary*, which goes on to become a classic.

1754 † Our Lady of Guadalupe is declared Patroness of Mexico.

1815 † The invocation "Help of Christians" is added to the Litany of the Blessed Virgin.

1815 † The Feast of Mary Help of Christians is established.

1824 † Catherine Emmerich has a vision of Mary's house at Ephesus.

1830 † Our Lady appears to St. Catherine Labouré and asks for the Miraculous Medal to be struck.

1836 † Jean Claude Colin founds the Society of Mary.

1842 † St. Louis-Marie Grignon de Montfort's *True Devotion* is discovered, with its emphasis on holy slavery to Mary.

1845 † Cardinal Newman defends true devotion to Mary but deplores excesses.

1846 † The Immaculate Conception is declared Patroness of the United States.

1846 † Our Lady appears at La Salette, France.

1849 † Pope Pius IX writes the first encyclical concerning Mary, *Ubi Primum*, which stresses her Immaculate Conception.

1854 † The Dogma of the Immaculate Conception is solemnly defined by Pope Pius IX in the Bull *Ineffabilis Deus*.

1858 † Our Lady appears to St. Bernadette at Lourdes, France.

1871 † Our Lady appears at Pontmain, France.

1875 † Devotions to the Sacred Heart of Mary are forbidden.

1879 † The beginnings of the Shrine of Our Lady of the Cape in Canada are laid.

1879 † Our Lady appears on a chapel wall at Knock, Ireland.

1883/1902 † Leo XIII, "the Pope of the Rosary," issues eleven encyclicals on the Rosary of Mary, calling her Mediatrix of All Graces, Mother of the Redeemed and Guardian of the Faith, and Mediatrix with the Mediator (Christ), and advocating devotion to her as the salvation of society.

1883 † The invocation "Queen of the Most Holy Rosary" is added to the Litany of the Blessed Virgin.

1890 † St. Theresa of Lisieux expresses deep devotion to Mary.

1900 † Our Lady of Guadalupe is proclaimed Patroness of the Americas.

1904 † Pope St. Pius X in the Encyclical *Ad Diem Illud* develops the theological bases for Mary's Mediatorship of grace.

1907 † The Feast of Our Lady of Lourdes is established.

1913 † The cornerstone is laid for the National Shrine of the Immaculate Conception in Washington, D.C.

1917 † Our Lady appears to three small children at Fatima.

1918 † The invocation "Queen of Peace" is added to the Litany of the Blessed Virgin.

1918 † In the Decree *Sunt Quo*, the Congregation of the Holy Office praises the custom of calling Mary "Co-Redemptrix."

1918 † In the Apostolic Letter *Inter Sodalicia*, Pope Benedict XV sets forth the role of Mary in Christ's redeeming sacrifice.

1921 † The Legion of Mary is established in Dublin.

1923 † In the Apostolic Letter *Explorata Res*, Pope Pius XI affirms Mary's role in the Redemption wrought by Christ.

1927 † Devotions to "Mary the Priest" are forbidden.

1931 † The Feast of the Divine Motherhood is established.

1932/1933 † Our Lady appears at Beauraing, Belgium.

1933/1934 † Pope Pius XI speaks of Mary's contributions to Christ's redemptive work. He portrays her as associated with this work not only in Bethlehem as Mother of God but also at Calvary and treats all the principal Mariological themes.

1937 † Our Lady appears at Banneux, Belgium.

1941 † The practice of promising graces to those who wear a medal without any other obligation on their part is censured.

1942 † Pope Pius XII dedicates the world to the Immaculate Heart of Mary in keeping with her wish expressed at Fatima.

1943 † In the Encyclical *Mystici Corporis*, Pope Pius XII outlines the role played by Mary in human salvation and explains how she is spiritually the Mother of Christ's members.

1944 † The Feast of the Immaculate Heart of Mary is established.

1946 † Pope Pius XII writes the Encyclical *Deiparae Virginis Mariae* on the possibility of defining the Assumption.

1947 † In the Encyclical *Mediator Dei*, Pope Pius XII deals with Mary in the Liturgy.

1950 † A Marian Year is proclaimed.

1950 † The Dogma of Mary's Assumption is solemnly defined by Pope Pius XII in the Bull *Munificentissimus Deus*.

1950 † The invocation "Queen assumed into heaven" is added to the Litany of the Blessed Virgin.

1951 † Pope Pius XII writes the Encyclical *Ingruentium Malorum* on the spiritual power of Mary's Rosary.

1953 † The plaster-cast image depicting the Immaculate Heart of Mary in Syracuse, Sicily, is seen to be weeping.

1954 † In the Encyclical *Fulgens Corona*, Pope Pius XII proclaims a Marian Year to commemorate the centenary of the definition of the Immaculate Conception.

1954 † In the Encyclical *Ad Caeli Reginam*, Pope Pius XII proclaims the Queenship of Mary and establishes it as a feast.

1957 † In the Encyclical *Pelerinage de Lourdes*, Pope Pius XII commemorates the centenary of Mary's appearances at Lourdes.

1959 † In the Encyclical *Gratia Recordat*, John XXIII calls Mary "the cause of salvation for the whole human race."

1964 † The Second Vatican Council in the *Dogmatic Constitution on the Church*, Chapter eight, sets forth for the first time a conciliar synthesis of teaching concerning the position that Mary holds in the mystery of Christ and the Church.

1964 † Pope Paul VI declares Mary "Mother of the Church."

1965 † In the Encyclical *Mense Maio*, Pope Paul VI urges prayer during Mary's month of May.

1966 † In the Encyclical *Christi Matri*, Pope Paul urges prayer for peace during October.

1967 † On the fiftieth anniversary of Mary's appearance at Fatima, Pope Paul VI issues the Apostolic Exhortation *Signum Magnum*, on the meaning and purpose of devotion to Mary.

1969 † The *Roman Missal* of Paul VI is published with a revised Marian approach based on Mary's role in the mystery of Christ and the Church. Some minor feasts are eliminated, but many more prayers and readings are added for the feasts and memorials that remain.

1970 † The *Liturgy of the Hours* is published with a revised Marian approach. It makes much use of the Magnificat, Marian antiphons, hymns, and readings.

1973 † The U.S. Bishops publish the Pastoral Letter entitled *Behold Your Mother*, to proclaim the preeminent position of Mary "in the mystery of Christ and the Church" and to restore the ancient love of Christendom for Christ's Mother.

1974 † Pope Paul VI issues the Apostolic Constitution *Marialis Cultus*, which treats at length of liturgical Marian piety, popular Marian devotion, indicates the criteria for deciding which Marian practices are completely valid and for introducing new ones, and concludes with the theological and pastoral value of devotion to Mary.

1975 † The revised *Roman Missal* (2nd ed.) includes Votive Masses of "Mary Mother of the Church" and "Holy Name of Mary."

1978 † Archbishop Karol Wojtyla of Krakow is elected Pope. He takes the name John Paul II and dedicates his pontificate to Mary, taking the motto *Totus Tuus* ("All Yours").

1980 † The invocation "Mother of the Church" is added to the Litany of the Blessed Virgin.

1981 † The Congregation of Divine Worship publishes a new Marian Litany in the *Rite for Crowning an Image of Mary*.

1982 † Pope John Paul II visits Fatima and consecrates the world anew to the Immaculate Heart of Mary.

1984 † Pope John Paul sends a letter to all bishops of the world inviting them to join him on the Feast of the Annunciation in consecrating the world to the Immaculate Heart of Mary. At the Vatican the Pope prays before the "miraculous statue" brought from Fatima by the Bishop of Leira-Fatima, where God's Mother requested that devotion be established in the world to her Immaculate Heart. The Pope renews the consecration in St. Peter's, Rome, before this image of Our Lady.

✝ Notes ✝

✝ Notes ✝

✝ Notes ✝

✝ Notes ✝

✝ Notes ✝

✝ Notes ✝

† Notes †

✝ Notes ✝

Davis #CL
CEL-614-353-4517
HM-740-928-2477

† Notes †

✝ Notes ✝